ESCAPE FROM ENGLAND

FROM SACRED HEARTS TO TRIBAL ARTS

MIRANDA CRIMP

Copyright © Miranda Crimp. All rights reserved. No part of this book may be reproduced in any form without specific permission from the author.

Cover taken from an oil painting by Gary Spratt.

Edited by Linda Cashdan of the Word Process.

Published by Artepeligo Press

Book Design by *the*BookDesigners

ISBN# 978-0-578 60810-5

TO GARY SPRATT

And the players in the field who are mentioned within these pages.

CONTENTS

   1 CHAPTER 1. MEMORIES SHARED WITH A DUTCH WIFE

   7 CHAPTER 2. MADE IN ENGLAND

 39 CHAPTER 3. LIFE BEGINS AT FIFTEEN

 69 CHAPTER 4. UP IN THE AIR

 85 CHAPTER 5. UNDER THE INFLUENCE

111 CHAPTER 6. BACK TO REALITY AND BEYOND

143 CHAPTER 7. THE LAND OF OPPORTUNITY

167 CHAPTER 8. THE AROMA OF CLOVE CIGARETTES

201 CHAPTER 9. UNDER THE THUMB OF THE MONEY GOD

209 CHAPTER 10. AS FOOLS RUSH IN

235 CHAPTER 11. A BEAUTIFUL ARRIVAL - A TRAUMATIC FINALE

245 CHAPTER 12. THE MOST IMPORTANT PART OF LIFE IS DEATH

269 CHAPTER 13. BIFURCATION

281 CHAPTER 14. UNDER THE SURFACE OF SERENITY

297 CHAPTER 15. THE REAL THING

311 CHAPTER 16. THE END OF AN EPOCH

PROLOGUE

MOTHER OPINED "MEN ARE LIKE BUSES – IF YOU MISS ONE – ANOTHER ONE IS JUST AROUND THE CORNER!" IN FRANCE I LEARNED THAT "A WOMAN NEEDS THREE MEN IN HER LIFE – A HUSBAND TO LOOK AFTER HER, A GAY FRIEND TO GO SHOPPING WITH AND A BOYFRIEND FOR PERSONAL PLEASURES."

WITH THIS KNOWLEDGE FIRMLY UNDER MY BELT I SET FORTH INTO THE WORLD BEYOND THE CONFINES OF THE GRAY GLOOM THAT HANGS OVER THE BRITISH ISLES – THAT BASTION OF FISH AND CHIPS, GOD SAVE THE QUEEN AND THE CURSE OF THE CLASS SYSTEM. THERE HAD TO BE MORE TO LIFE THAN ENDLESS CUPS OF TEA, BAD WEATHER, THE PROTESTANT POINT OF VIEW AND THE POWER OF THE PITH HELMET!

CHAPTER ONE

Memories Shared with a Dutch Wife

Careening through a canopy of vivid green rising from the jungle floor, coarse fronds brush against the sides of the ancient Mercedes bus, grazing any flesh within their reach through windows stripped of glass. A torn grubby permit plastered to the windscreen decrees a maximum of sixty warm bodies onboard, indecipherable, of no consequence to the clientele haphazardly jammed on this archaic workhorse. Brown skinned, lithe, wiry mortals, draped in sarongs and assorted cloths wrapped here and there are crammed onto the hard wood slatted seats, challenging an eye to find where one starts or another ends. Here people live close together in communal societies, unsullied by the Western sensibility that one is an island surrounded by a moat, not to be waded across without prior permission. Acknowledging an invisible, respectable distance between flesh is irrelevant to this crowd, they live cheek to jowl, an extension of each other. Individuality is a foreign affair.

Encased in wicker baskets live fowl squawk their discontent at such close quarters from the overhead baggage racks. Squeaking pigs strung on poles share space with stinky spiky durians, silky purple mangosteen, breadfruit, vegetables just pulled from the soil. Strapped on top to the luggage rack, passengers hang on tight, legs dangling down the sides of the bus.

The bus lurches forward, people laugh, smoke fills the air, clouds of sweet clove fragrance from the cigarettes compete with the pungent scent of tiger balm.

Clinging to an unforgiving wood seat, cushioned by moist brown skin on all sides, a woman more attuned to the black depths of the London tube than a riotous ride through verdant switchback hills and valleys luxuriates in dreams that are now springing to life. While ensnared in the persistent grey English winter, visions of elephants, palm trees, anything alien to the drab organized boredom of the English way of so called living kept me alive until my eventual escape.

Driving at breakneck speed, the faster the better is the way to travel on this side of the globe, the tired transportation shudders under the weight of humanity, before abruptly collapsing, expiring on the rollercoaster road, in the depths of a triple tiered explosion of nature, where rich men still don the pith helmet and stalk tigers. The onboard melee decamps to the jungle's edge, laden with sweetmeats to feast off, squatting by the side of the road, not letting this interruption diminish their fun. The driver hops out too, diving under the hood to fathom which part of the engine has failed this time.

Minor delays are to be expected; it's part of the journey, liable to occur several times on a single trip. Luckily naiveté is my strong card, the thought never crossing my mind that as a woman in the middle of nowhere in unfamiliar company, there might be reason for a few fleeting qualms. Little time for such trivia. Indonesians are spontaneously social and curious, especially with such a strange individual in their midst. They view me as their entertainment, waste no time setting about inspecting me, touching with awe my white skin. Plastering me with questions—"Where is your husband?"... "How many children?"... "Your religion?"... "Where are you going and why?"—all delivered amid clouds of mirth.

Indonesians have a propensity to talk of even death and destruction while smiling, even laughing, a spectacle I initially find disturbing. When someone falls tit over arse, lying in a pool of blood, a crowd will gather around. Smiles illuminating their faces, they rather enjoying the view of a body squirming in distress. Right now the friendly interrogations are part of the deal, to be expected, somewhat similar to making polite extemporaneous conversation at a cocktail party. I'm in their world and they want to get to know me. They are top dog and I am the prey.

Waiting on the jungle's edge, my fellow travelers invite me to picnic along with them, pressing strange new delicacies my way, fleshy fruits, sticky pink and yellow sweet rice wrapped in leaves, hot tea from a thermos. My awkwardly attempting the Indonesian squat so that I can be part of the group sets them off cackling in appreciation at my less than limber efforts.

Half an hour and we are back on the bus, zipping hair-raisingly once again through the Sumatran jungle, packed as tightly together as hand rolled Indonesian clove cigarettes, skin on skin, providing no room for individuality or precious people.

The seedy port town of Medan in Northern Sumatra at last materializes through the bus window, framed partially by feet dangling from above. Fierce odors of the local cuisine and grit from the streets waft and blast through the windows, the lack of glass giving free range to these nuances. Our clothes damp and sticky from the twelve-hour internment on the bus, we spew out onto the street. The ride has given me ample opportunity to adjust to Indonesian rubber time. (It happens when it happens – God willing). The sun rises at 6 am and sets at 6 pm every day of the year; everything else is timeless, can be stretched like a rubber band. Timeframes are a window of opportunity, a rough guide to when and if.

That evening after my big day on the bus, I find myself lying on an unyielding bed with a Dutch wife as company. The latter, a colonial hangover, is a long hard bolster, meant to resemble and to be a substitute for the female comforts left back home, a consolation prize for the Dutch male who had struggled to control and rape Indonesia for over three hundred previous years.

Listening to the street life outside resonating on the high-beamed ceiling, calming myself from the effects of being a celebrity sideshow for a day, too tired to even bat away the thirsty mosquitoes emerging as the sun disappears, lusting after a blood cocktail, I ponder my past.

I was welcomed into the world as a sign of a new beginning, my birth heralding the conclusion of World War II. Father had returned from this ordained excursion, leaving many comrades behind, dead in the desert dust. On reuniting, my parents were strangers. Who knew what to expect after five years spent apart? To marry again was a way to a fresh start, a clean slate, wiping away any indiscretions that wartime might have provoked. Mother had worn black the first time around, this time she decided on a softer color, choosing a shade referred to at the time as nigger brown.

I started off as the golden girl, the product of a great reunion after years of death, destruction, bombs, blackouts and rationing of anything deemed marginally edible. I was a symbol of normality, the fruits of winning the war—unlike my brother, born just as the sabers of imminent warfare were rattling, as dark clouds descended, as Father departed to be part of the war effort, called to duty, leaving my mother with a new born babe. Brother Thomas sampled endless sleepless nights, torn from his cot, fleeing to the air raid shelter as sirens wailed and bombs exploded.

After five years of separation, father and son were estranged, never to fully resolve those years spent apart. Thomas was the first to be blamed for anything amiss. Mother, a brilliant tactician at the warfare strategy "divide and conquer" used so successfully by the British, Roman Empire and kleptocrats since the dawn of time—the art of pitting one entity against another, in order to gain and retain control—used this technique within the family to further her personal goals.

Father suffered from shell shock, even though such things were not realized or admitted to. Waking up in the middle of the night, he sat straight up in bed, choking, fantasizing that alien hands were at his throat, squeezing life from his body. He lashed out, struggling to avoid a gritty death in a foreign hellhole.

His memories of his time on the front line in the North African sand, facing the foe became more glorified as time rolled by, even to the point of extolling the virtues of Rommel and his crew, expressing the view that they had been a first-rate enemy, a brilliant team to fight. Dad had been a long-distance runner, a great rugby player. The war, at least his part of it, had been a game well played by both sides!

Twisting and turning on the hard mattress of the Dutch bed, the high pitch whine of thirsty mosquitoes attacks my ear as they seek the perfect spot for a free drink. I visualize Stamford Raffles. He had joined The British East India Company at fourteen, becoming a colonial agent, Governor of the Sumatran city of Bengkulu, the man who had challenged the Dutch for possession of these islands. Had he bedded down with a Dutch wife as the winged devils honed in on their quest?

Raffles' love of indigenous people and fauna had drawn him to uncover the Rafflesia, a flower of gigantic proportions, up to three feet in diameter, weighing in at 24 pounds with inch thick petals surrounding a cauldron that smelt of rotting flesh—a carnivorous monster, recoiling in the bowels of the jungle waiting for blow flies to land, before sucking them into its depths. He who was largely responsible for the creation of Britain's Far East Empire in the early eighteenth century, was anti-slavery and the local sport of cock fighting. Had he, too, hugged a hard pillow on a fetid night on this patch of soil?

Mildred & Reginald Crimp on their second wedding day reunited after five years apart

CHAPTER TWO

Made in England

My grandfather found himself embedded in a trench at Gallipoli in World War I. After surviving such rigors he reveled in any opportunity to recount the abhorrence of warfare. The trenches constructed by the soldiers served as bunkers for protection or graves if their primary function failed. Entombed in such pits, the men were bombarded by the enemy, the blazing sun, rain, snow and sleet. The rats running underfoot were merely a distraction, garbage disposals, feasting on the bodies struck down by the foe. Sanitation was a past privilege; dysentery and trench foot were rampant. Feet submerged in water for days became numb, fetid, and swollen, resulting in fungal infections and ultimately gangrene, if not treated. The arrival of mustard gas, a tricky new German invention, proved to be an unpleasant surprise. If the wind decided to change direction on launching such poisonous gadgets, even the instigator could be in for a nasty shock. A deadly odorless killer, with the potential, after a time lapse of twelve hours, to insidiously inflict blindness, vomiting, internal and external bleeding and leave the victim lingering in agony for four to five weeks, before actual death. Until the arrival of gas masks, the prescribed deterrent to counter the noxious fumes was a rag soaked in urine, of which luckily, there was an abundant supply.

Grandfather recalled being surrounded by the dead, the dying and the wounded. Many who survived were so shell shocked, traumatized by the horror played out at close quarters, that they were mentally and physically damaged for the rest of their days. Their conduct considered shameful, these wretched shadows of their former youth were publicly shunned when returning home, casualties sacrificed in yet another war waged by old men sitting in comfort far from the fracas.

Grandfather was awarded, by King George V of Great Britain, "The Distinguished Conduct Medal for bravery, for conspicuous gallantry to duty." As published in the London Gazette of May I, 1918, "He led his platoon forward in a most gallant manner and thanks to his coolness and energy was the means of reorganizing a platoon of another regiment." Grandfather went unscathed, one of the few to be able to regale his descendants with the gory details.

On his return, he transferred his army training to the home front, his wife and daughters replacing the troops that had been under his control. Orders were issued and to be carried out, no questions asked. The family became an extension of his time in the army. This led to my mother's early departure, she being unable to accommodate such a military setting. I on the other hand, being a grandchild, witnessed a kinder rendition of our war hero. This decorated gent never left the house without his fierce voluminous, black wavy hair meticulously *"brylcreemed"* in place, his trouser pleats perfectly pressed, white shirt sparkling, jacket and tie. His leather shoes were brilliantly polished every morning, including the undersides of the arches.

I stayed with him and Grandma Flo for several months, when Mother decided to have a hysterectomy. As she put it, "Might as well get rid of the superfluous equipment and forgo the monthly maelstrom." She actually enjoyed the hospital, being a patient, treating it as a vacation, with servants at her beck and call, to do all the dirty work, to fetch and deliver!

At my grandparents, the day commenced with a breakfast of kippers, smoked herring locally fished. This was not fast food, the kipper had to be approached gingerly, the consumer delicately attempting to release the salty flesh from the myriad of small bones. Rising early, I paced myself to have enough time to manipulate this pungent platter into providing enough protein to stabilize me until the dreaded school lunch, a noontime distraction at all British schools, as was free milk. The milk, in glass bottles, arrived at school in metal crates every morning to be placed in the wintertime by the radiators where it developed a thick, disgusting, crusty skin by the time 10 o'clock rolled around and it had to be drunk. Some kids relied on these favors, as families struggled to get back on their feet after the carnage of war, putting on a brave face during troubled times.

The school lunches, served in the cafeteria, arrived in vast steel vats presided over by women dressed in white, their hair covered by a kerchief, tied in the front, ends sticking straight up. They wielded the serving instruments, long handled aluminum scoops, with ardent intent, plunging them into the vapid offering, then deftly doling it out. Everyone received the same amount, no favors. If you didn't like the stringy beef with soggy potatoes bathing in greasy pools of lard, or the slimy rice pudding with a dollop of sticky red sweetness on top, too bad. Every morsel had to be eaten. No child was released onto the playground unless the plate was clean. Eat or forfeit your lunch hour. No deviations.

Together as night fell, Grandfather and I sat in "the snug," a room rendered impervious to the weather, immune from draughts, the snow and wind rampaging outside in wintertime. We listened to the radio. A hot favorite was the latest installment of *"The Moonstone,"* a detective novel written in the nineteenth century, set in colonial India. It was the tale of a diamond that had adorned the forehead of a sacred sculpture of the Hindu God of the Moon before being stolen by a corrupt British officer and brought to England, and with it bad luck and misfortune to all who touched it. We relived, the two of us enveloped in his special armchair, the splendors of the Indian Raj, the sweltering heat, the vibrant colors, bejeweled elephants, saris and turbans spiked with immense rubies and emeralds, the extreme wealth and filthy poverty. This dalliance into the exotic provided a superb anti oxidant to yet another freezing, drab, English night.

Grandmother was always in the background, doing her duty as seen fit by her husband. The perfect wife and grandma—warm and cuddly, tight white curls swirling above blue sweet eyes twinkling behind frameless lenses. She was always busy baking a batch of rock buns, cleaning (not a speck of dust dared to loiter in her realm), or knitting one of the hundreds of *woolly jumpers* with intricate designs which seemed to flow naturally through her fingers.

As a duo they survived two world wars. Living in a large town on the east coast of England, directly across the channel from the rest of Europe, they became a prime target, subjected to multiple bombing raids. The German fighter planes on reaching the English coast hurriedly dropped their load at the first opportunity, before hightailing it back to base. Twice bombed out of their house, they spent many years as refugees in prefab housing erected by the government.

Grandma's father, a seafaring gent, spent much time away, sporadically reappearing unannounced, at times with a monkey perched on his shoulder, or a cache of tropical fruit, prizes garnered from some far-flung adventure. He stayed around just long enough to impregnate his frazzled spouse before once again vanishing from sight for another escape on the high seas. With no mention of when he might return, he left the wife to struggle with their burgeoning

Miranda modeling a Grandma Holmes' woolly jumper

brood. These "unseemly exploits"—that was how such goings-on were viewed by the family—were occasionally alluded to but most of the time veiled in mystery, not to be thrown around for tender ears to pick up.

Grandmother spent many of her earlier years shuttling between relatives and taking care of her younger siblings. Desperate to leave home, she married at an early age, seeing it as a way out, only to realize that she had replaced one demon with another.

Flo counseled me to "never go out without wearing clean underwear, just in case the unthinkable might happen, dear." Grandma was not thinking about a sexual tryst with a handsome stranger but referring instead to the ever-present possibility of ending up in a hospitable bed, having to shed street attire and in the process exposing the unmentionables.

Brave English Holidaymakers making the best of it – At least it isn't raining.
Backrow: Grandpa Holmes, Grandma Holmes, Mum, Uncle Cecil
Front Row: Brother Thomas & Miranda

Made in England

Three girls on vacation at Gorleston on Sea. Auntie Joy, Miranda & Mother Mildred

ESCAPE FROM ENGLAND

As luck would have it, in her mid seventies while crossing the street on market day in the town center, a truck collided with poor Grandma, knocking her up in the air, the force of gravity then taking hold of her mangled body, pushed it back down, leaving it spread eagled, face down, a bloody splat on the tarmac. The driver in his early twenties, claimed in court that he had suffered a blackout and had not, as observed by bystanders, been recklessly speeding and out of control. He got off the hook but my sweet faithful Grandma was relegated to the graveyard. Her spotless undies were probably overlooked in the chaos.

Aunt Joy and Uncle Cecil, (Seashell for short) were childless, having a kid like me for the occasional vacation seemed like a deal compared to a full time liability. Their life was structured; if high tea was at 4 p.m., it happened at 4 p.m., a far cry from my mother's disjointed repertoire. In the morning I crawled into bed with them, without having to knock politely on the door first, as obliged to do when entering my parent's bedroom, my parents only letting me intrude if bearing a tray of tea and biscuits.

Simple pleasures, banned at my parent's house, were embraced here. I was free to be a child, to go ride a bike in the countryside or swim in a pool without fear of contamination from the microbes that danced in my mother's mind upon entering a public space.

When using a community W.C., including any facility out of her domain that she had not personally supervised, Mother always cautioned me to never sit down. "Stand and deliver" was the order of the day, advice I have followed ever since! In Britain it cost a penny to use a public lavatory, the coin having to be slipped in a slot before the door would open, giving rise to the term "have to spend a penny," which, to a British ear sounded more palatable than "have to pee."

Uncle Seashell a big, burly specimen was staunchly anti-royal and frequently could be heard blasting the latest antics of the British Royals. "Here they go again using our tax money so that they can live high on the hog." He was a man who always had a joke up his sleeve, to break up the mundaneness of everyday toil. He loved to shock and charm with his banter. Throwing me up on his shoulders, piggyback style, he carted me off to the speedway and motorbike racing, the smell of the methanol fuel delighting my nostrils, and to the local fairgrounds, where he commandeered front seat on the rollercoaster, as I shrieked with absolute terror as we dipped and careened up and down the wooden structure. Trips to the circus aroused my initial desire to be a performer in the ring. What child does not fantasize about such a colorful lifestyle? I hadn't quite defined what I would do in the sawdust but fell instantly in love with the elephants, the magic playing out before my eyes, knowing nothing of the tough, lowbrow lifestyle behind the glitter.

Mother viewed all of the above, as cheap, common, blue collar thrills. The very thought that her sister had married a vacuum cleaner salesman made her see red and Uncle Cecil loved to rub it into and under her skin at every opportunity. Oh, God, he was so working class, an unbearable state of affairs!

Occasionally on a Saturday morning Father took me to visit Grandmother Crimp in Streatham, London, dropping me off before plodding on to the office. Mother found it strenuous enough catering to her mother-in-laws' annual visit on Boxing Day, a grin and bear it situation, similar to what most families endure during mandatory festivities, prompting her to avoid any other contact during the rest of the year.

Grandma Crimp resided at the end of a sweeping gravel drive in a Victorian mansion, a survivor from a bygone age that had been divided up into flats, but still retained the gracious living style of the wealthy, funded by fortunes made in the nineteenth century industrial revolution. A long unkempt garden flourished at the rear, where bluebells and forget me knots fought each other for space amid the tall grass. A grand piano held center stage in the living room. Sitting on the stool with Grandma guiding me, it became clear that I had no natural musical talent. Grandma had large trunks filled with fabrics and bits and pieces from her past, together we dived in to discover treasures new to me and forgotten by her, remnants of days gone by, of past memories with stories to tell.

A trip to the pantomime at Christmas, a British theatrical treat, seemed a much better idea than going to church to view a bleeding man on a cross. At the *"panto"* men dressed up as women as in early English theatre, masquerading under wigs and frocks, the women as men, strutting around in boots and pants. The air sizzled with ribald slapstick, having immediate visual appeal to the young while the insinuated naughty language delighted the more mature.

Grandma's mansion was eventually mutilated, destroyed by the British government in the 1960's. Deemed a waste of resources, it was replaced by a concrete nightmare of state owned low cost flats, reminiscent of a communist regime. Grandmother was installed on the ninth floor. The grand piano had to be discarded, such paraphernalia from a bygone era being way too large to fit in such a tight, badly constructed space.

Although never quite the same again, she still enjoyed a tipple of ginger wine. As darkness fell over the graffiti-plastered walls of this cement monstrosity, she sipped wine from a crystal cut 18th century Georgian goblet, watching the weeds flourish in the unkempt open space below her window and the specter of the latest version of cool youth, hanging out, sprawling in leather on bikes, suspended in non action.

Grandfather Peregrine, an elusive figure, educated his sons at "public schools," a name contrived to confuse the masses. It actually meaning "private," reserved for those with money or enough brains to win a scholarship. When the sons emerged from these bastions of the stiff upper lip onto the world stage, Peregrine chose not to live with his wife. He was the director of a large drug company, May and Baker, in London. Tales were told of how during World War II, he would turn up on my mother's doorstep with a leg of lamb or side of beef under one arm, silk stockings and chocolates under the other, unheard of luxuries during the strict rationing of those times. I remember fondly the ten pound notes he always bestowed upon my brother and me when he unexpectedly appeared, a small fortune, compared to my sixpence a week pocket money.

A larger than life character, Herbert Peregrine Crimp always wore an overcoat and a trilby hat, no matter what the weather. He loved the horses, the good times and women. A Miss Vidler of Winchester in the south of England was one of the girlfriends, and when Grandma decided to drop in on this contender for Grandfather's attention, she hauled me along as a prop. The obligatory cups of tea and biscuits were dutifully provided, it was very civilized, such an English display of decorum, good manners stoically concealing any real emotions. Miss Vidler and Grandma became great pals after Grandpa's demise, spending much time in each others' company. I guess they had a lot in common, a lot of fat to chew, the ins and out of a communal, now dead, source of entertainment.

Peregrine was admitted to hospital for minor surgery around my ninth birthday. Hating to be confined and required to obey regulations, he decided to leave, walking out the front door still wearing pajamas. Unfortunately, a cold British winter was in full thrust, resulting in pneumonia for Grandpa Crimp. His funeral turned into a meeting of long lost relatives, such an event being the only time when these distant links deigned to present themselves. Friends and girlfriends also joined in the festivities, celebrating his departure, an event Peregrine would have approved of.

Growing up in England after the war, with billboards blaring the message, "Pull in your belts; make sacrifices so that we can get ahead," we kids had to improvise, come up with games to be played without the benefit of expensive *accoutrements*. Carlo the camel, one eyed and an ear already ripped off was my stuffed toy. Passed down, he had already done a tour of duty on another child's bed. We fashioned bows and arrows out of saplings with knives, to play cowboys and Indians an exciting new craze from America now showing on our cinema and television screens.

Cheyenne, a Western cowboy serial kept me glued to my seat every Saturday, the first stirring of appreciating the opposite sex rustling in my aspiring teenage body. I had never seen such a magnificent specimen of mankind. Were all American men as ravishing?

Another diversion was the fruit of the horse chestnut tree, the *conker*. These bright shiny brown nuts, once relieved of their hostile spiky outer coats were skewered and strung on a string. A game for two, one person holding his prize at arm's length, while the other took aim. The *conker* that survived the onslaught without its glossy coat suffering any cracks was declared the winner, to be fondly polished and stowed carefully in a pocket for the next duel.

I loathed the dreaded trips to visit the wealthy relatives, performances endured, because if they died, we might benefit. Dressed in my Sunday best, my manners primed to perfection, I sat in silence, longing for the polite chatter and endless tea to finish.

There was the trip to my mother's cousin, Aunt Olive, and her husband, Roy. Rumor had it that Roy, to coin an English colloquialism *"was a little peculiar."* An absolutely stellar individual most of the time, but when the moon was full he had a penchant to *"take a turn for the worse"* and disappear, later to be found walking naked in the night. Olive, a practical woman had taken on this assignment, relieving Roy's parents of their burden, while duly noting there to be no shortage of funds to fuel her romance.

Great Aunt Fan, had never married. No male tentacle had breached her pure virginal state. She arrived on her annual Boxing Day visit, dripping with jewels, her pale bony frame draped in furs. It was my duty to kiss her bewhiskered skeletal countenance. An abundance of brown moles roamed freely over her exposed skin, providing a lurid diversion from the task at hand. Before Fanny Rose and her sister, my grandmother descended, my parents stuffed anything of value under the staircase, in a cupboard, out of sight, in order not to display any visible signs of wealth that might promote the notion that we already had enough.

Sitting at the dining table on these occasions, hours passed, the leg of ham, roast potatoes and sad overcooked former greenery, apple pie and evaporated milk still lingering on the tablecloth, while the conversation dragged on. On these special days, I was not allowed to inquire whether I might "please get down from the table?" I was required to sit, speechless throughout the saga, to listen to the latest roster of aches and pains, hospital visits, the recounting of endless tales of other family members I had never met and hoped I would never have to.

I tried to appreciate my father's brother, Uncle Charles, but he was such a pompous twit, espousing the very British feeling that children were an inconvenience at best and should be avoided at all cost. He affected a highly superior, insincere accent, cultivated as a captain with the Westminster Dragoons, London's territorial army.

The wealthy members of this elite group, pleased with their place in society, strutted through life, earning the nickname "The Piccadilly Peacocks." Such an affected upper class accent, impeccably honed to impress, today would ruffle feathers. Even the Queen has modified her speech. Luckily for "the firm" as Queenie refers to the royal family, William has rid himself (and hopefully future royals) of this affliction, astutely realizing it as risky, outdated behavior. It's better to blend in, rather than stand out, if you want to continue to sit on the throne.

Uncle Charles although a rather good-looking fellow, also failed to embrace the state of wedded bliss, preferring instead the company of older women who had already suffered such joys. He horded his wealth while skimping in such minor ways as wearing under his three piece suit, a faux shirt, comprising of cuffs, a collar and a frontal strip. Surely there would be money left upon his departure. So line up we did, just in case. After he croaked, those arriving first on the scene found teapots and biscuit tins stuffed with pound notes. The rest of his estate was divided up between his latest elderly squeeze and my brother.

I abhorred these maneuvers, circling like carrion crows waiting for leftovers. I would make my own dough, not pander to, or seek favors from, those heading towards the grave. Which was just as well, as obviously I was not good at playing this game.

In the morning, Father rose early, as Mother still languished between the sheets. He started his day with a glass of hot water while hovering over the stove tending to the eggs and bacon sizzling in pig's lard, along with white bread soaking up the grease. He prepared the much vaunted English breakfast, the perfect solution to keep the body warm on a frosty morning.

After dutifully feeding his offspring, he shaved, lathering up with a brush and applying the blade. When every whisker had been vanquished, he donned a white shirt, the only color available, attaching a stiff white collar with studs at the neck, tied the tie in a Windsor knot, climbed into the three piece suit, and topped it all off with a bowler hat. Placing a furled black umbrella on his arm (in England rain is always possible), he was ready to set off, sporting the uniform of the white collar slave of that time. After hustling us out the door to school, he strode briskly to the train station, always on time. He was never late.

Later, living in London, I marveled at the waves of men emerging from the Victoria Train Station at a morning rush hour, a stampede of buffalo charging to the edge of a steep cliff, or at least to the edge of their seats at office desks, all equipped with the suit, bowler and *brolly*, a newspaper tucked under their arm, a necessity when commuting. The latest news in print provided a particularly English way of evading eye contact, when sitting in a carriage with five other lookalike individuals. It averted the chance of getting involved in an annoying conversation. The only permitted noise in the train carriage was the rustling of paper when turning a page. Each page was folded and refolded to just the right proportions, to avoid entering the airspace of the adjoining passengers. Carriages of white collar drones, all carbon copies, were on their way to another tedious day in the office.

Father, attempting to alleviate the boredom, before clocking in, would stroll through the early morning antique markets of Bermondsey and Portobello, seeking a distraction in the shape of an irresistible piece of art, a prize that he could gloat over while strapped to his desk for the remainder of the day. If he had been successful in his foraging, the acquisition would be furtively, discreetly dragged back to the house, in an attempt to avoid my mother's frenetic gaze.

If these finds initially went unnoticed they would later reappear as if they had always been part of the furnishings, my mother muttering, on acknowledging their presence, "another thing to dust."

We shared our house with portraits of other peoples' ancestors, grandfather clocks that told time but not the actual time. My father spent long hours tinkering with the insides of these behemoths, adjusting their weights and pendulums, trying to make them tick on schedule. In spite of this continuous attention, their chimes continued to peal at inappropriate moments. Art was everywhere. We had much of everything we didn't require, a surplus of stuff, but to find a plate without a crack, a knife and fork that matched or functioned could be a challenge. I vowed to be a minimalist.

In the front garden of every house my parents owned a white marble statue of a naked, radiant young female was prominently displayed, an unexpected mirage in a middleclass neighborhood. As a pubescent female in the throes of exploding hormones I became the recipient of many a snide comment by my peers. Accordingly I loathed this exhibition of womanly glory.

Banking was Father's domain, a respectable occupation in those days but his greatest thrill was time spent alone with his manual Underwood typewriter, transferring his memories of the front line in World War II to paper. Other times he could be found communing with his rose bushes, feeding them a steady diet of horse manure, freshly delivered by the race horses that pranced past our house on their way to the Epsom Downs. The smell, the fleeting beauty of these beauties that he had nursed into bloom, warmed his shrapnel scarred soul.

My mother thought that one of the worst things in life was to be bored. She was my initial inspiration, a fountain of fun, always managing to turn an ordinary situation into an exciting event. Stories flew spontaneously out of her imagination to amuse me as a child—the gingerbread man a pastry chef had just removed from the oven, the newly baked dough boy taking off, straight out of the pan, flitting through an open window, out into the wide unknown, landing on a dog's nose, barely escaping with his edible self intact from the crashing canine jaws, then prancing off to discover a gingerbread girl taking shelter under a leaf in a rainstorm, only to be swept off her feet by our hero and whisked away to tango in Buenos Aires.

In her company, even grocery shopping and mundane people became fascinating, as Mother converted them with her great choice of words and wit. Luxuriant red hair sprouted abundantly from her scalp framing blue eyes fringed with golden lashes, encased in white skin. She would remind me that my own locks were inferior in color and pure quality to her own, but balanced the bombshell by admitting she adored my dark eyebrows and hazel eyes, these features being a rarity in East Anglia, an azure eyed enclave on the East Coast of England where she sprang to life.

She never ventured onto a public street unless suitably attired, always clad in hose, heels and lipstick, the face powdered, gloves and, of course, a hat to match her outfit. So equipped, she was ready to deploy and attack the world. The hat became a part of her ("A woman isn't complete without one"). Even when presiding over a pan of *bubble and squeak* the hat was often still perched in place. She found the advent of blue jeans absolutely appalling. She dressed for dinner, throwing on something glamorous to greet my father on his return from the office, along with a kiss and a cuddle. As a child, I considered this normal married behavior. After such a resounding reception, if I was already in bed my father would climb the stairs to wish and kiss me goodnight and, in winter, tuck the heavy blankets in so tight that I could hardly move. After which I lay motionless, freezing in the dark, clutching my hot water bottle, just about warming up by the time daylight peered through the frost glistening on the inside of the window panes.

Mother had Father totally wrapped around her little finger and he enjoyed it. She dominated the dinner table or any table with her sparkling anecdotes, even managing to make the milkman's daily delivery a humorous happening. Money was a foreign realm, she could never quite grasp how quickly it disappeared when in her possession, even though she bought the best of everything, often purchasing several of the same thing, just in case.

Her passion was to paint in oils on canvas. She had attended the Chelsea Arts College in London in her youth, before the burdens of married life and war interrupted. Colors, the emotions they evoked, the effect they had, how they reacted to each other were important and relevant. She became obsessed with the brush, dipping it into the medium, relocating it onto the cloth, spending more and more time creating a current masterpiece in her studio and less and less time in the kitchen.

My first nine years, I translated the world through her eyes, what I encountered on her terms. This has stayed with me, even though as a teenager, I longed to escape from her controlling clutches. She ruled her husband and their life and would have loved to add me to her entourage. I had other plans. I had been under her powers long enough, peeling piles of potatoes, darning my father's and brother's socks, shopping and cooking the Sunday lunch, always at her beck and call, while she supplied the entertainment. During a grueling session with the spuds, she might burst into song, a rendition of a World War 11 chestnut, "Bye Bye Birdie," a soulful ballad of parting and not knowing whether a loved one would return, thereby reducing me to tears, or, on a more jovial front, she might launch into "Knees up Mother Brown," accompanied by lively illustrations, a raucous romp usually embarked upon after a few drinks at a party in order to disperse the British reserve. Other times, leaving the worn socks, we would break into a *"valeta,"* twirling around the kitchen as if dancing at a royal ball.

The Sunday lunch was a British institution, consumed around mid afternoon. A heavy meal of roast beef and potatoes, Yorkshire pudding and the mandatory two variations of vegetables, followed by a lemon meringue or apple pie, all dutifully prepared and delivered by me in my budding teenage years masquerading as the female serf. Brother got off with mowing the lawn and drying the dishes. How I longed, if nothing else, to either be alone in my room, my fingers stroking the pages of a library book, or roaming the soggy English countryside with my dog as company.

As time ticked slowly by, I dreamt of my eventual escape. A thunderstorm was the only event that turned mother into jelly, the exploding noise and crackling lightshows brought back all the horrors of the war, sending her fleeing to the cupboard under the stairs, dragging me along to hold her hand. This was the moment to extract from my quivering mother a request or favor. With the storm prevailing, her equilibrium in tatters, she would promise me anything, more pocket money, an extra hour in front of the T.V.

My parents moved frequently, Mother finding the same old scenery tiresome. Acquiring a four story Victorian house just outside of Guildford, way too big for a family of now three, they rented out the top floor to the local registrar, a man who recorded births, deaths and performed civil marriage ceremonies. Stanley loved the opera, and arias floated down from his loft. On sporadic weekends, a male friend would visit, staying over. Mum and Stanley conversed for hours on the staircase separating his quarters from ours. She informed me in a loud stage whisper that "Stanley prefers boys." This was at a time when gays were firmly sequestered in the closet. She adored anything different and I followed suit, just happy to be made aware of another interesting facet of life.

Shopping, strolling along the local High Street, as we crossed the street holding hands, I felt her squeeze mine, a signal that something of great interest was happening that could not be put into words. Looking avidly around to encounter this possible highlight of our day, I spotted my first black man, a rare and intriguing sight in an English country town in 1956. His skin was an amazingly shiny blue black, his long lean frame elegantly attired, a riveting apparition in a land inhabited by pasty, flabby, white people.

Waves of immigrants from the Caribbean had been arriving on British shores since World War I, invited by the British government. Many more descended on the British Isles to work in the underground and on the London buses after World War II, due to the lack of interest by the indigenous workforce in taking such bottom-feeding jobs.

Can you imagine leaving the splendors of sand, sea and palms, to toil under and above the grimy streets of this capital? At the height of British colonialism, was any consideration ever given to the thought that the very people in the countries which were so blithely taken over, might respond at a later date with a fervent desire to come roost in the nest of their colonizers? Citizens from the formerly pink parts of the world (colonies of Great Britain as portrayed on maps of that era) might throng and tightly squeeze themselves and abundant relatives into the miniscule British Isles? This state of affairs is to this day a thorn in the British backside. Would my father have risked his life for his country had he known what triumph and winning the war would actually achieve? Father having helped save and build up his country, now saw the middle class lifestyle that he had strained and struggled to maintain being diluted by a government handing out subsidized housing and free health care to not only low class Brits, who could now afford bigger T.V's and cars than their middle class compatriots, but also to any other group who dropped in from afar. A bone of contention he gnawed at until his dying day.

As a team Mother and I visited stately homes, trips to witness the wealth and glamour of those who possessed both class and influence. A jaunt to *"The Royal Pavilion"* at Brighton, yielded the fantasy of a former Prince of Wales who later became George IV. The pavilion had been transformed from a gentleman's farmhouse into the Pleasure Prince's idea of Xanadu. Reconstruction started in 1787, continuing until 1822, performed by a host of architects, at the British tax payer's expense. It was, and still is, an amazing sight, rising up in oriental splendor from this placid English town.

Extravagant opulence is an understatement when describing this gorgeous mirage of exotic architecture, the interior resplendent in *Chinoiserie*. The prince escaped here from his royal father who abhorred him, to a life of mistresses and decadence. Happily, I noted, there was more to life than bangers and mash, grey skies and God Save the Queen.

Mother loved clothes, dressing fashionably. This was not considered necessary for me. I had my Sunday best, clothes only to be worn on high days and holidays, my mandatory school uniform and the exquisitely patterned Fair Isle sweaters that had spewed from my grandmother's mind and hands. Early on, when I could do no wrong, Mother had handcrafted adorable dresses for her darling daughter. The soft yellow seersucker outfit, the Oxford and Cambridge, a light blue and dark blue frock, named after two major towns and colleges in England who sported those colors. The gathered satin bathing suit and net tutus, for my flight into the world of ballet, my dear Mother having been inspired by *"The Red Shoes,"* a film with Moira Shearer portraying a ballerina. I was to be the next Margot Fonteyn.

Accordingly at the age of three I was enrolled into the world of ballet, which persisted for six tortuous years. I pirouetted on my toes, did the *"pas de deux,"* executed my *"plies, arabesques* and *chasses"* in order to please, but my heart failed to comply. It was eventually acknowledged that I was better at high jump than the *"grand jete."* As I came to the end of my first decade such dreams and frills evaporated.

Then came the all important test, the eleven plus exam that determined whether a kid sank or swam, whether she went to a grammar school (a good thing) or a secondary modern school (might as well give up). I succeeded in failing this strategic hurdle twice, consequently reducing my parents to a state of paranoia. In addition they were gently informed by one of my teachers that I had a wild streak, which needed to be diffused.

I had failed in spite of my father's determination to make me proficient at reading by age four, and the fact that I had my head continuously stuck in a book since that time, although that was partly to escape from reality and partly due to the nature of the English weather that excluded enjoying a lot of exterior activities. My family had staggered home every week from the library under a mountain of books. When I finished reading my selection, usually tales of boarding school adventures, which fueled my desires to leave home, I would dive into my Mother's D.H Lawrence, Collette, Somerset Maugham and the satirical cartoons and ravings of Ronald Searle, my brother's favorite. Father's preference for the dry tomes of Proust and the likes of Thomas Hardy never appealed.

I had failed, perhaps because a year before this life changing exam which would chart my future course, Mother had succumbed to one of her numerous stays in a hospital bed and I was shunted off to stay with my grandparents for a few months in Great Yarmouth on the East coast.

The local school, having no space in the appropriate class, placed me at a higher level. Sitting at the wooden desk, the well worn seat slippery under my woolly skirt, I understood little of what was being taught. I showed up midterm, and cliques had already formed. Every girl already knew where she fit in, already had a niche in the hierarchy. I was a new face, an unknown quantity, an alien intruder, younger, more vulnerable, and smaller than they, a perfect target to taunt with their superior knowledge. I dreaded the classroom breaks, opportunities for my persecutors to gang up on me, to drag me off into the lavatory, to strip me of my numerous layers of garments, to search for signs of emerging puberty. Was I sprouting signs of change? They crowed with satisfaction at their superior strength, holding me down to inspect any progress made. My grief was their entertainment, a break from the boredom of the blackboard.

My new classmates seemed to know all about procreation. I had been briefed by Mother, already informed that certain parts of the body were kept private, safely under wraps until married. To yield to such things before a state of wedded bliss could result in terrible diseases. Her imagination soared with descriptions of sores bursting and blistering inside, instantly catching my attention. The only cure was an umbrella type vehicle inserted into that space between the thighs, thrust deep into the body, then opened and slowly pulled out, scraping off the pus-filled pustules as it emerged from the dark moist cave. This somehow stuck in my mind. To become pregnant, Mother informed me, would result in immediate rejection by and ejection from the family. Such dishonor was unthinkable and would not be tolerated. The actual how one might arrive at achieving any of these dreadful circumstances was not forthcoming.

My new classmates talked endlessly about sex, delighting in my ignorance, as they saw it, and teasing me relentlessly regarding my peculiar southern pronunciation.

I arrived back home with a broad East Anglican accent and a big gap in my education, only to encounter the test of my life or so it was decreed at the time, a multiple choice. Failing to realize that I perceived the world differently than most, I was beginning to understand that I hated performing for the powers that dictated who I should be and having to conform to their theories of round pegs in round holes. I later concluded after resisting the system that it was easier to see where these types were coming from and cut my cloth to suit their pattern, if it was in my interest.

Since I had ruined my smooth passage into an appropriate education, my parents saw no other option than to secure a private scholastic path for me—a convent, the Convent of the Sacred Hearts to be precise.

Before I could tread on this vaunted soil, I had to be baptized. Having not already been subjected to this ritual, the Catholic Church saw me as a heathen, unfit to enter their world. Accordingly, at twelve years of age, along with a host of newborn babies I found myself in a house of God, in order to be purified of original sin.

A special trip by train to London was required to procure, at great expense, the school summer and winter uniforms. This repertoire included saintly cream dresses for summer with black string ties. Mother had just informed me of the glories of the menstrual cycle, which could arrive *chez moi* at any given moment. When wearing this pristine pastel frock, I spent much time furtively inspecting the rear, checking for any evidence that this female affliction had made an appearance. The dress was worn with the school blazer and a Panama straw hat, both emblazoned with the school colors and badges. For winter we switched to heavy blue tunics and a reefer coat, all purchased on the large size almost reaching my ankles in length, ensuring that they were big enough, that I wouldn't grow out of them too soon. Felt hats, white shirts and the school tie, big blue bloomers, hockey shorts, scarves and gloves rounded out the required wardrobe. My name had to be sewn into every article. No makeup, hose or jewelry was to be worn with this ensemble, the only exception a small crucifix. Christianity, the popish version was after all the raison d'etre on this turf.

The bane of my life to be worn with the uniform, were the Startright footwear. Dark, turgid brown lace up shoes, that tightly enclosed the foot, right up to the ankle. These abominations were declared by my mother to give the foot a great beginning in life. They were more than I as a budding teenager attempting to be cool could abide. On leaving the house, safely out of maternal and paternal eyesight, I unlaced and discarded these brutish monsters, stowing them in the thick hedge that surrounded our residence, replacing them with slip-ons that I had surreptitiously stowed in my satchel.

When out of the confines of scholastic endeavor, I resorted to a pair of baggy jeans which I wore with a leather belt, the aluminum buckle displaying an eagle standing on top of a swastika, surrounded by the motto "got mit uns," a piece of finery my father had removed from a dead German on the front. Probably rather an insensitive choice but we made do with what we had, I at the time thinking that it was pretty hip. I finished off the look with an ancient hand knitted sweater purchased at a jumble sale and a pair of bright neon lime or shocking pink nylon socks, a fashion straight out of Elvis Presley's America. They were all the rage.

It took me half an hour to walk to my new school, no matter what the English climate was dishing up. I was a "day girl." Some of my peers were "boarders," confined to the convent, no escape for them after the last bell. It was a beautiful campus surrounded by extensive gardens and sports facilities. Pupils and staff gathered each morning in the assembly hall to start the day with hymns and prayers. Before each class we recited a *"Hail Mary"* and at twelve noon, the *'Los Angeles'* prayer, a mandatory necessity day in and out, just a bunch of words that had to be uttered. Visits to the school chapel were encouraged. Every pupil had to enjoy or endure an hour a day of religious instruction, just another subject to remember and then forget.

Most of the teachers were nuns encapsulated in cream flowing robes, a flaming, bleeding sacred heart plastered on their bosoms. Whenever our paths crossed or the reverend mother put in an appearance, we had to curtsy and utter "Good morning, reverend mother," or "Good afternoon, sister".

Mrs. Twilly the math teacher was terrifying. She dressed in grey blue Harris tweed suits, sensible shoes, her head a mass of calculated tight grey curls, her countenance bereft of enhancement. With a ruler in hand, she strode through the aisles, cracking the knuckles of any daydreamer like me who was attempting to mentally escape out into the garden beyond. She drilled and drove her class, determined to make us mathematically viable. With me she succeeded. I became so attentive, I achieved the giddy heights of top of her class.

The other extreme, the history teacher, Miss O'Leary, read us the past straight from the book, paying no attention to the chaos exploding around her, babbling straight through the havoc, seemingly unaware of her total loss of control, Strangely, we never studied Henry VIII the man who single-handedly saved England from the pope!

I blossomed on this terrain, captained both the hockey and netball (a tepid version of American basketball) teams, played tennis and garnered a silver trophy with my name engraved on the surface when awarded first place in class.

I was still glowing from my recent triumph, basking in the new sensation of achievement, when my parents informed me that we were moving. Mother was bored, needed a change of venue, a more fancy piece of real estate to hold forth in. The dutiful husband went along with the scheme coerced into the situation, knowing he would get no peace if he didn't conform. Saying goodbye to my brief encounter with scholastic success I had no choice but to go with the flow, I was just a player without a point of view.

Another convent loomed on my horizon, this one a mere hour and a half journey by train and foot from our new house. Yet again an appropriate space was unavailable and yet again I was dumped into a class a year ahead of my abilities, another blow beneath the belt.

The Marist nuns at my new detention center had none of the flashy, wealthy disposition of their Sacred Heart sisters. Strict, terse and sullen, they taught every class and performed every menial chore.

Presiding over a temple of tubes and Bunsen burners, Sister Cecilia, enshrined in blue with the bleeding dripping heart beating above her own seemed to find holy redemption inspiring gaggles of teenage girls with hands-on science. Slapping a dead mouse on a board in front of each of her charges, she instructed, "Nail it to the board as Jesus was nailed to the cross. Hack through the rib cage from neck to rectum and pull out the innards." That left us to prod through the slime and blood to identify the parts, as she hovered behind us, peering over our shoulders, obviously enjoying our initial horror while helping identify the stinky entrails.

Another day a plate with a cow's eye swimming in the bottom would appear. Slicing through the tough, fleshy exterior, a jelly like substance jumped out as the lens peered back from the mass of translucent liquid, the rear of the retina a kaleidoscope of iridescent blue green and yellow, all quite fascinating after the initial distaste. But despite such thorough inspection of the animal species, the study of human reproduction was not considered appropriate material and confined to the activities of stamens and pistils, the birds and the bees.

When the reigning pope kicked the bucket, the whole school was sequestered in the nun's quarters, forsaking algorithms and past participles to watch the spectacle of the remaining religious Roman Catholic elders withdrawing from reality, their only contact with the outside world sent by smoke signals via a chimney. With them safely ensconced behind closed doors, who knew what might be happening? These men of the cloth, princes of the blood, were probably slurping down piles of plated pasta, the garlicky tomato sauce mingling with their scrawny whiskers and dripping down to stain their beautiful red outfits, or sucking up truckloads of creamy gelato and zabilone, no doubt all washed down their clerical throats with liberal amounts of fine wines. Satisfying their stomachs, munching and quaffing, were they taking note of the attractive boys waiting table, eyeing them as a digestif?

In the meantime the world, or at least the Catholic part of it, glued to their television sets waited for these grey hairs to motion by means of a signal, the result of their quest, a replacement head of their mob.

Mirrors, were a no-no in the convent; nuns did not preen in front of such. Whenever a man was spotted, which was a rarity and usually a priest or a plumber, the nuns were all a twitter, smiling and blushing. God forbid! Most of them carried a rather sour demeanor throughout life, crabby, always bickering, a result of their decidedly peevish dispositions. Being married to their God was obviously as difficult as most arrangements.

Convent schoolgirls were a wild variety. Maybe it was the total lack of testosterone on campus that fueled their desires. Boys were a mysterious, unknown quantity, and of course, that made them much more interesting than the actuality. We were saddled with the school uniform, to be worn proudly, to portray shining examples of the perfect dutiful schoolgirl. The uniform advertised and upheld the reputation of our school. Sporting the school colors did, indeed, make it more difficult to pull off the requisite shoplifting excursions and boy baiting adventures to be performed after the last bell. Having busted out of captivity, we needed some blood sport before wrestling with the persistently ordained homework. Clothed in our garb made us instantly recognizable, meaning we would be promptly reported by stalwart members of the community if spotted reveling in unsavory pursuits. This indeed was an added challenge, that increased the risks, but made the rewards only more delicious.

Waiting for my train to and from this latest excuse to chain me to a stake, I took in some of the local splendor. The "Teddy Boys," the latest version of uncouth youth, were on display, resplendently lounging and leaning in black "drainies,"—drain pipes, or skinny trousers. Separating the bottoms of such crotch suffocaters from the concrete platform were a pair of winklepickers, sharply elongated, pointy boots. A long tight jacket discreetly covered the rear end. Greasy hair was slicked back in a duck's arse, to reveal white spotty teenage faces. This species could often be found snogging (necking) with their "birds" (the female part of the duo), who teetered on stilettos, their chassis' clad in short tight skirts, slit up the back and clinging sweaters. This splendid rendition of the female form was accompanied by stringently back combed, dyed straw-like hair piled high on top picturesquely, and aptly named a beehive.

Homeward bound one day, I spied in a first class compartment, General Field Marshal Montgomery. My father had served under him in the Eighth Army in North Africa during World War ll. Like any child, even a teenager, I was always trying to impress my father, mine not being an easy target.

I decided to approach this important piece of British history, thinking that he was lucky someone my age would even recognize him, let alone appreciate his existence. I hoped to procure his autograph, proof to my father that I had actually encountered one of his heroes. The general did not feel the same way and when I popped my head into his presence, he firmly, but politely asked me to leave. Somewhat crestfallen, I did as I was commanded by the great man and withdrew.

On recounting this episode to my father, he sided with the general. A young girl approaching an older man in an otherwise empty compartment, what was I thinking? Totally out of the question! My father preferred children to be seen and not heard. Young ladies in particular were to be taught how to read and write, but in his eyes, not to be too clever. They should possess a genteel sense of humor but not be too witty. Prospective husbands would not appreciate the competition or enjoy a personality that might outshine their own skills. I did not inform my father that the idea of a man further managing my life, to whom I was to kowtow and obey as he looked after me was not on my agenda. I would be a person who did not have to rely on such outdated Victorian ideals, a woman appreciated for her worth, whatever that might be, an equal partner or not at all.

At the age of fourteen, one summer staying with my favorite aunt and uncle, I wandered down to the Gorleston coast, the stretch of freezing North Sea, where I had learned to swim, and made sand castles with my bucket and spade, and where my family, dressed in street clothes, maybe taking off their shoes and socks to let their toes penetrate the warmth of the golden sand, had slumped in deck chairs behind wind breakers attempting to enjoy the pallid sun.

I sauntered into the swimming pool arena overlooking the churning ocean constantly whipped by the ever-present whirling wind, the beach where brave English holidaymakers were making the best of it. At least it wasn't raining. I was on the cusp of conversing with my first foreigner. He sidled up to me with a blue Gauloise cigarette between his fingers, olive skinned, brown hair and eyes in a combination I found somewhat appealing. But it was his stance that exuded confidence, his air of insinuating what might be fun, dangerous—maybe both—that separated him from the native species and marked him as decidedly French. He was here to study English and the English and I considered myself fortunate to be on the curriculum.

We spent a few exploratory days poolside, stealing kisses. What was a French kiss? Could only a Frenchman deliver such a thing? My interest was aroused. This was my first real contact with boys. I had previously spent much time avoiding them. Walking to school, I would trek an extra half a mile rather than be confronted by this abominable tribe whose main reason for living seemed to be to denigrate, chastise and crush their female peers, with slurs, threats, obscenities, and gestures.

My mother had a fascination with anything French, the accent, the body language, the heavy romantic sexual innuendo, which made Englishmen look as if they had just emerged from the cave, complete non starters in the Casanova Olympics. If she could see me now!

Aunt Joy somehow caught wind of my secret liaison and was absolutely horrified, suspecting the worst scenario—her niece, under her care, impregnated and disgraced. I was shipped hurriedly back from whence I came, back to my parents, thus shattering my first steps into my newly found attraction for the opposite sex.

I had primarily been consumed by the adventure, the opportunity to fathom this yet unknown territory, to sample what previously had only been whispered about and veiled in intrigue. Jean Marc Mollinghoff had been my vehicle of exploration in this initial foray, I knew my boundaries and they had not been infiltrated, I had only just begun, Jean Marc had served as a pleasant stepping stone.

My school life came to a screeching halt the moment I turned fifteen, which in England, was the legal age for opting out. I'd had enough, I told my parents. Their response showed their relief. They must have been tired of looking after a second pimply adolescent, probably embracing the opportunity to get on with their lives and succumb to the joys of just being together after having been submerged in wars, children and the war recovery effort for the past twenty years.

CHAPTER THREE

Life Begins at Fifteen

My education terminated and lacking any credentials I land a job in the local department store; model gowns are my future. Miss Steiner is the buyer, a large woman with a large nose who rules with an iron fist, managing her department like a small fiefdom. She knows every one of her customers personally, buying exclusively for their consumption, their every whim seriously observed and catered to. Two super sales assistants patrol the showroom, Miss Todd and Poppy Palmer are poles apart but get along famously. Miss Todd, having lost her fiancée in the war, now devotes her life to living with and looking after her ailing mother. Toddy is tall, elegant and attractive in a masculine, classic way, her grey hair neatly secured in a bun, a smudge of color hovering on her lips. Poppy, in contrast, exists under drifts of white face powder, an overdose of mascara, lashings of green eye shadow and ample use of red lipstick that has a tendency to dissolve and run in rivulets at the corners of her mouth. Having been endowed with a magnificent bosom and an equally ample behind, she appears to be on the verge of bursting out of her mandatory black clothes, which are always a little too tight. This diverting landscape is precariously supported on skinny legs that splay out, bringing forth images of a chicken attempting to do the splits. Soft pinkish blonde curls jiggle behind soaring diamante spectacles.

Miss Todd is by the book, upright, straight as a die. Poppy the romantic, seems to have lived a lustful life at breakneck speed and is just coming to grips with the results. We spend many an hour reliving their lives, standing (no sitting is allowed) on the thick pile Chinese carpets, surrounded by gilded furniture and racks of perfectly arranged model gowns, waiting and ready for action when a live customer materializes.

As the girl Friday I cater to their demands, unpacking, repacking, ironing and keeping the gowns perfectly primed on the racks, one inch between each outfit at all times. Miss Todd and Poppy have their own special clients, each of these wealthy women expecting undivided attention when they show up and take up residence in a dressing room for several hours. Costumes deemed flattering for their particular body type and image are presented and if approved by the client, deft hands help her undress then pour her into each outfit, a chiffon scarf is draped over the head to avoid makeup blemishing the precious piece. I hover and help the aging dynamic sales lady as the client is showered with attention, advice and entertainment. It's show time and we put on a great production. We know that "the customer is always right."

Personal service is in full swing at a time before name brand stores will fester around the globe, supplying the same merchandise everywhere, the same lack of quality in every store. We cater to discerning individuals who expect the best and pay the price.

The lingerie department next door, featuring exquisite French lace personal items, is presided over by Miss Clinker, a bright, snappy, virile, older gem. It's a place to be fitted for exactly the right uplifting vehicle, to swaddle, encase and uphold those two vaunted female projections, a garment to exactly suit your intimate needs, in a secure female environment. This is a store for women with time, taste and money.

As I'm acclimatizing into the world of model gowns, early one morning before leaving for another interesting day on the deep, luxurious pile of the Oriental rugs, a knock on the front door makes me pause. Standing, gracing the doorstep is Jean Marc Mollinghoff, as nonchalant as ever and looking rather pleased with himself. With a classic Gallic flourish, garnished adequately with foreign charm, he announces his arrival. "Bonjour, Madame & Miranda. Je suis si content de vous voir," uttered as if he is just dropping by for a casual visit. Mother, swooning in the doorway, is overwhelmed by this handsome apparition, immediately falling for his undiluted romantic swagger, but I'm somewhat annoyed. Having participated in a spontaneous summer fling, I had not particularly wanted a follow up. Maybe a letter, but there he is on the doorstep, without even an invitation. Mother who had never before encouraged any of my friends to visit ushers him in. A Frenchman, after all, is an entirely different cup of tea! Following the initial formalities I'm happy to escape to my new occupation, leaving my dear mother in charge. She, hardly noticing my departure, is totally preoccupied with the new foreign distraction. For her it's like discovering rich creamy camembert after having been restricted to a diet of hard English cheddar.

Jean Marc starts his day by consuming a bowl of cornflakes with a shot of whisky on the side. With my father absent at the office, he and mother sit and drink endless cups of char and chat. Already an expert at using the French accent to every possible advantage, Jean Marc soon has my Mother palpitating with delight at every mispronunciation. Spending her life buried in the depths of the beautiful but monotonous English countryside, this visitation is a gift from the gods, providing someone to flirt with, to remind her that she still has what it takes. Jean Marc is a willing purveyor of sexual innuendo and harbors a natural ability to make any woman feel good.

Mother is breeding longhaired dachshunds and a new litter has just arrived in the basement. Jean Marc, showing that he is not just a handsome face, helps with the feeding and cleanup. He and my intrepid mother take long walks to the nearby town of Godalming, where she can show him off. She has a young Frenchman with an attitude to escort her around. What a catch!

Even Father enjoys the dinners with this new emphasis on La France, grabbing the opportunity to practice his French. Aware that mother has a diversion, he seizes the opportunity to disappear and pound his typewriter or dive into a book, escaping into blissful solitude, far from her chatter. He has already endlessly listened to her stories and has perfected the ability to interject a "mm" at the appropriate moment on cue, a habit accrued after many years spent together, to indicate that he's listening even though his soul is far away, foraging the pages of some ancient tome.

Two weeks into this French farce, a telegram arrives from the Frenchman's mother with an urgent recall notice: "Come back to France immediately." He apparently has run away from home, hearth, and school, and his mother is not amused.

He writes from Paris, inviting me to stay, but Mother decides this to be out of the question, even before I have time to vocalize my lack of enthusiasm for such a scheme. My intuition tells me that she is jealous; she's the one who wants to be invited! I know that I will make it under my own steam at a later date and not on account of Monsieur Mollinghoff.

Needing a change of pace, bored with being everybody's lackey in the rigid world of haute culture and in spite of my two old accomplices, I switch to a swivel stool in front of a switchboard at the Telephone Exchange. Faced by a three foot wide expanse of sockets and plugs on cords at my finger tips, I'm introduced to the art of whipping these plugs out of their sockets to pick up a live call, of the correct way to ask the number the caller wants, then how to flip the cord, whirling it up in the air and to plunge it into the appropriate outgoing socket before dialing the number.

Listening to private conversations is one of the perks, another, the possibility of verbally encountering an attractive male voice that might be interested in more than just placing a call. A chance to squirm on the stool while fantasizing, conjuring up visions of a gorgeous stranger without ever having to meet or see him, as well as practice a little repartee. Men had yet to be admitted to the rarified atmosphere of the telephone exchange.

Seeking a little exercise after being stool bound for long hours, after dinner with the parents I often hop on a bus into town to dance the night away. One night after the last "twist" has been executed, I realize that I've missed the last ride back. A trudge through the deep snow looms in my immediate future, but my dance partner offers to walk with me. Three miles later, my house at last visible, he hugs me goodnight and starts back.

On entering, my father comes hurtling down the stairs demanding, "What the hell do you think you are doing, resurfacing at this late hour. Your Mother is sick with worry!" Never having sampled this sudden change of demeanor before—Dad was usually studious, caught up in his own daydreams, reliving his time spent browning his knees in the desert, which increasingly was the most exciting part of his life—I'm taken aback. Father rarely got roiled. Now I felt like a member of the opposition in a rugby game, not knowing that my brother had frequently seen such action. Mortified that my father does not trust me to act responsibly hurts me more than the skirmish. Crushed that he has so little faith in me, I decide to take complete responsibility for my actions and move out of my parent's house.

A bedsitter on Nightingale Road in Guildford provides a roof. It's one of many rooms rented out by the owners, where the lodgers sleep, cook on minimal equipment and use the facilities down the hall. My new domain is roughly ten by ten feet but it's all mine. I can do as I wish, except have the opposite sex stay overnight. I guess a daytime encounter would not qualify as the real thing? I'm the only one in my small group of female cohorts to have a place of her own, a secluded oasis, where we gather and discuss the important issues of the day, boyfriends, and sex. Together we form an inseparable clique and become involved with a local rock n roll band. We religiously follow the guys on the road to gigs at village halls, dancing together as they rage and roar on stage. *The Twist* is the dance and *Love Potion Number Nine* the top of the pops. Still, being virgins, at least in theory, the hot topic of the day or night when sequestered in the safety of my four walls is, "How far did you go?"—a state of affairs that seems excruciatingly important, we pounce on any insight in our quest to understand and conduct business with the opposite sex.

A policeman named Simon lives upstairs. He performs the night beat, roaming the streets with his truncheon, a sentimental soul completely unsuited to this task. He slips poems under my door and invites me to sleep in his bed while he's patrolling the streets, just to keep it warm. I rather enjoy encountering these poetic offerings after a hard day on my stool. He says he wants me to run away to the Isle of Wight with him. I become less interested, the more he presses.

At seventeen I'm ready, ready to escape the gloomy starchiness of living in the United Kingdom, even though this is being seriously challenged by four vocal Liverpudlians, riding on a tidal wave of rock n roll, striving to overcome the rigors of the stiff upper lip. Taking the train from Waterloo to Dover on the South coast, where a ferry is waiting to carry me off, I see the white cliffs recede in a blanket of fog, a redeeming sight. A French train whisks me to the Gare du Nord in Paris where I realize, cast adrift in this busy crossroads, that in spite of studying French at school for years, these people don't understand me or I they.

The trip evolves into a twenty four hour odyssey, the last leg from Paris to Nice departing at night, to arrive on the south coast just as the sun rises up out of the Mediterranean. No mention had been made when purchasing the ticket of the need to reserve a couchette (sleeping accommodation) and after locating the train south to the Cote D'Azur I find myself standing in the corridor with no place to park my backside. To the rescue comes a Frenchman. "Mademoiselle, there is a vacant couchette in my compartment. There is no need for you to spend the night out there. Please come in and make yourself comfortable."

Apparently there are no hang ups about different sexes sharing the same sleeping quarters in La France, complete strangers, without benefit of a curtain, snore into the night three aside, one on top of the other, six to each cabin with barely enough room to sit up in bed. Relieved I hoist my gear and body onto the available top bunk, the prospect of standing up in the corridor all night fading into the distance.

Just as I feel myself drifting off into oblivion, I realize that I am not alone, something is stirring between my newly acquired sheets. Flipping the switch above my head to shed light on the rat infiltrating my space, I recognize the decidedly unattractive countenance of my latest French friend, in the very act of revving up, getting into position to discharge his weapon and accomplish his mission! His bunk, just beneath mine had made for easy access, enabling him to scale the ladder without attracting the attention of the four other sleeping beauties. Having squeezed his bulk into my space, he no doubt believed his irresistible presence a gift to a maiden in distress.

I scream, lights illuminate and our fellow travelers lurch awake, angrily uttering, "Mon Dieu, What the hell is happening?" My former friend apologizing profusely, alludes to the idea that he had mistakenly lost his way, taken a wrong turn as he slinks back to his quarters.

Chalking it up as just an experience along the tracks of life, I escape back to the corridor, just as the sun starts to illuminate the brilliant Cote D'Azur, a glorious sight to eyes escaping from an emerging English winter. Pink and white villas dance on the horizon, the soil is a radiant red, the Mediterranean a brilliant blue reflecting the immense sky above. The train pulls into the station at the end of the line.

I've signed up to be an au pair. The job description seems to be just what I'm looking for. "A young lady who voyages to a foreign land to learn the language, to perform light household duties, to look after children and is to be treated like a member of the family." I had arranged through an agency a position with a family that they had vetted and recommended. They had sent to my prospective employer a photo so they could see what they were expecting on arrival.

Nobody rushes to greet me. Soon I seem to be the only one left standing on a now deserted platform. A few hours pass. I'm just happy to be here and sitting on a bench, I absorb life as it strolls by before deciding to try the French telephone system to contact my future employers. There's no one there, no reply from the family who had requested my services.

Locating the agency on the map, I make my way on foot to their office. I travel lightly, having few possessions to my name. The pavement is hot beneath my feet, the streets sun drenched, full of people dressed to be seen, adding glamour to life as it elegantly unfolds.

Sitting in the waiting room, more time ticks by. Eventually, a woman turns up to claim me, a Madame Shultz. No excuses or salutations are offered as she brusquely motions me towards her car, before driving out of the city I'm falling in love with, to St. Laurent du Var. On the way Madame makes it known that the family's previous English au pair had been so wonderful that on parting they had given her a gold watch.

My job, Madame informs me, is to organize the three children, get them ready in the mornings and to school, at lunchtime when they reappear, and after school to provide snacks and supervision. Baths and bedtime are included in my duties. Cooking, washing, drying the dishes and waiting table while the family has dinner are also on the agenda. Last but not least is the thrill of making breakfast for Madame and delivering it to her in bed, while not forgetting that in between there is housework to be done. But the finale, at the conclusion of the endless list of performing tasks strikes me as particularly profound: after I have served the evening meal and cleaned up I will be allowed to sit in the kitchen and eat the leftovers. This is not quite as I had envisioned the job description.

The only joy is the food! Growing up in England, eating seemed more like a chore consisting of meat roasted until it was tough, stringy vegetables stewed to the color khaki and desserts heavy and filling enough to anchor a Brit to the English way of life forever.

By comparison food in France is deliriously delicious—the sweet crispy bread baguettes filled with dark cooking chocolate that I give to the kids for snacks, the wild array of exotic cheeses, a welcome change from "pass the cheddar please." The multitude of fruits, cantaloupes, peaches, exquisite globular fresh figs make the canned gooseberries which so often graced the English table a distant memory. Not to mention *La Patisserie* shops filled with the most exquisite pastries, an entrancing sight for eyes used to rock cakes and currant buns. Standing looking in the window at these divine creations, I know I'm far from life in England and gain fifteen pounds in three weeks.

Moored to a broom handle aimlessly sweeping, the third week into serfdom *chez* the Shultz family, a family friend appears at the door. He and his wife had been over for dinner the week before. My patrons are out, but he seems pleased to see me. "Well, what do you think of my beautiful city?" To date I hadn't even had enough time to dip a toe in the inviting sea witnessed from the train window when arriving. Horrified by my lack of awareness of the beauty all around he mutters "Quel dommage—what a waste" and whisks me into his waiting car, I jumping at the opportunity to explore a world beyond the household chores. We drive along the seashore. The Mediterranean sparkles. The Promenade Des Anglais, one of the most gorgeous stretches for sophisticated strolling, glistens. The palm trees sway, and the Negresco Hotel, a long time resident on this vaunted strip basks in its glory. We meander up through the old town, past villas and bougainvillea.

How thoughtful of this friend to escort me around, to show me the sights. Dusk falls as we climb the ridge of mountains overlooking

Life Begins at Fifteen

this enchanted city, an incredible view of the whole bay glimmering at our feet, the moon a skinny banana in a cobalt sky. On reaching the summit he pulls over to relish the manmade display of lights glittering below and the ocean shimmering beyond as he mentions that he is a mobiliere, a real estate agent to you and me and has a property for sale in the neighborhood and as we are here he might as well check on it.

I follow my tour guide on his reconnaissance mission. While he inspects the house, which is furnished but vacant, making sure nothing is amiss, I enjoy the view, relaxing after three tortuous ball crushing weeks of medieval survival, only to be abruptly brought back to reality.

The family friend unexpectedly swivels around and without even a whiff of notice flings me on a couch. He's now on top of me, pressing his masculinity into my groin, breathing hard and close, hot stale breath scorching my face.

Shrieking a string of expletives I had read but never before uttered, I attempt to extricate myself from under him, squirming, my long fingernails now a weapon. He becoming more frenzied the more I lash out. Realizing that I'm not such an easy target, he stuffs a wad of franc notes down my now exposed bra to show me that he is willing to pay for what he wants.

The obnoxious conditions I have endured for the past three weeks, crowned by this sudden assault reduce me to a typhoon of tears that throw him off course. He recoils, the look of a defiled demon coursing through his sagging Gallic facial flesh. Running out of the house, clutching my now disheveled clothing, I ready myself to walk back to my current life of bondage.

He's right on my heels, catching up, a torrent of French pouring from the bewhiskered lips that minutes before had forcibly tried to assault me, "Je suis desole, Je regrette," etcetera. Even though my schoolgirl French had not encompassed such situations, I gather that he's attempting to convey that he's beside himself with grief and solemnly promising to drive me back. I slither into my clothes and into the car, not relishing trying to find my way back alone despite my angst. Two unwanted sexual encounters in one month on French soil. What else is out there to claim my somewhat intact innocence?

Stopping at the large central square in the busy shopping district of Nice, we sit outside sipping cafés as life swirls around us. He carries on as if nothing has occurred.

A few nights after this fumbling futile bombardment on my personal property, this saboteur and his wife dine again at my patron's house. I sallying forth from the kitchen laden with platters, ignore past incidents. But when I am asked to sweep the crumbs from under the table, from under his chair while the festivities are in full swing, the final straw looks me straight in the eye. It never occurred to me to mention the incident to Madame, the struggle above the shimmering lights of Nice, not wanting to embarrass anyone, knowing that she would take her friend's side, and that consequently I would be cast out onto the pavement. But even though I'm an optimist, I decide not to hang around for the gold watch. The down payments seem to be far too grisly for my digestive tract.

In the waiting room of the au pair agency I encounter Amanda, an English girl, the beginning of a great friendship and a new start to my French adventure. Amanda is working as an au pair for a family who live in a large two-story villa, occupying the top floor. The family ensconced beneath, recognizing the benefits and freedom provided by installing an au pair are on the lookout for one too. I pack my bag and leave the Shultzs', not even demanding the monthly stipend that is my due, having secured a new roof over my head thanks to Amanda.

Isabelle is Parisienne. Marcel had grown up in North Africa before returning to France. They welcome me warmly into their home. They have three children, Luke, Evelyn, and Muriel, eleven, thirteen, and nine respectively. I'm desperate and thrilled to even share a room with the two girls, to be treated like a human, rather than a slave sold into servitude. Isabelle, bright and bubbly excels in the kitchen. She's on a diet and invites me to join her. My newly acquired bulk evaporates as fast as it had appeared. I vow never to linger in front of a patisserie again.

Chez Isabelle, red wine is always served at lunch and dinner. This is not my first encounter with alcohol; my mother had included me in her sorties to the King's Head, a local pub, when I was thirteen. After one of her numerous operations, the doctor had prescribed a *Guinness* a day as part of the recovery effort and she hauled me along for company. I would have a Babycham, a light champagne beverage, while Mother downed her medicine, no one raising an eyebrow at my presence.

At my new domain I work in the mornings, then Amanda and I take off into the sun for afternoons at Cagnes Sur Mer, a stretch of endless smooth grey pebbles with a few shuttered cottages on the edge. After roasting our pallid English skin under the fierce Mediterranean rays, we return to our digs for dinner with our respective families.

One of my duties is to supervise Luke's bath. Luke has already been classified as the bad boy. The sisters delight in telling tales on him. Accordingly he is often sullen, preferring to be on his own. Always ready to side with an underdog, I like him instantly, but he hates being bathed by a girl, so we broker a pact, I will look the other way if he washes himself. His face lights up as he realizes he has found a friend.

After dinner and bath time, Amanda and I slide into Nice to sample the scene. She has a natural ability with languages, her French is fluent and she picks up others with equal ease. Even though I realize that practice makes perfect, I often let her take the lead.

When I was leaving England, the Beatles were blasting the toffs out of the water and the Rolling Stones were stampeding through the barriers of good manners, but in France we find the air is still dominated by romantic ballads. Charles Aznavour and Jacques Brel hold sway. People dance, bodies pressing against each other. Rock'n'roll, it seems, has not yet arrived. The clubs start late, winding down just in time for the satiated crowd to drift out to sample the dawn, as the early morning markets start to stir, the coffee machines ramp up for yet another day of operation. We sit in an outdoor café on the square fortifying our depleted bodies with lattes while puffing on a *Disc Bleu* cigarette as the street sweepers wash and clean before the start of the day and the streets became alive.

We explore the coast from St. Tropez to Monaco and northern Italy, soaking up the sun, trying to cultivate the bronzed goddess look essential for any player on the Riviera, chatting up the local talent along the way, improving our French and knowledge of this interesting new species, in spite of my recent history!

My French family decide it's time to visit the relatives in Paris, Isabelle's extensive family. They take me along for the ride, but it's vacation time for me too. The nieces and nephews show me the sights, from a Russian orthodox church with an enchanting lack of pews, the faithful standing throughout the elaborate proceedings, with much ado about smoking vessels and priestly robes swinging, to jazz clubs on the Left Bank secreted away in dark dank basements. They all fight for the honor of showing me their favorite corner of their city. I put out a few smoldering fires with less than family oriented thoughts but these people are my age so the playing field is level, a two way street.

As a family, we explore Saint Tropez, suffocating all together in a small tent, sweltering in the heat while providing a banquet for aggressive sand fleas, an adventure that would put me off any pleasure trips involving the art of camping in the future. We pitch our tent, unaware that in future times, massive yachts, waves of celebrities and the paparazzi will take over. Brigitte Bardot the ultimate femme fatale of the sixties wearing her trademark gingham dress can be seen tripping through the cobbled streets, basket in hand, on her way to purchase the fruits of the sea at the open air fish market.

Marcel and Isabel in true French fashion decide that it's time for a romantic revival, a holiday for them alone far from the realm of children, they need to reinvest in their love for each other. The French have a different set of priorities, honoring above all marital relationships; the children come in second. The children understand this order, displaying respect for their parents, but with anyone else, like a teenage au pair, it's open season.

After sweetly bidding their parents "Bonnes vacances," they transform into juvenile delinquents and try their best to break my spirit. They tease my broken French, flouting their superior knowledge, emulate my pronunciation while roaring with laughter at their efforts. I achieve some form of order, and with my new role as commander in chief, my knowledge of the language, out of necessity, improves rapidly especially with words not found in the dictionary which the kids delight in teaching me, hoping that I will make a fool of myself by using them in the wrong situation!

Luke appears, his skin a mosaic of red lurid gashes, but seems cheerful enough despite the tragic appearance. After my initial horror I deduce the inner artist in him has raided his mother's makeup box and made ample use of the red lipstick. I march him straight into the tub for a thorough scrubbing. Surprised at my audacity, he even forgets to complain about being woman handled. Using a stiff brush I scrub him down until he glows like a ripe strawberry. That shuts him up, but the girls continue to trip me up whenever they can, tittering at my inadequacies, doling out that special brand of torture that shrill young girls are so good at.

My time in St. Laurent du Var expires. Placing an ad in the United Servicemen's Organization in downtown Nice I receive an invitation to an interview. A nondescript woman of about thirty with a baby in tow and her divorced mother, who had left Paris to retire, are looking for help.

Madame Deluze lives in old Nice, a warren of cobbled streets, just wide enough for a small car to transverse. The walls of the houses are thick. They stand close together to keep them warm in the winter and cool in the summer. An intricate maze of activity thrives all around. Washing hangs out the windows to dry and just two minutes away is the Promenade des Anglais and the Mediterranean. I have my own room with shutters on the window that I can close at night and fling open in the morning to drink in the glorious blue and the life throbbing on the streets below.

The daughter is married to an American newspaper man who never physically materializes. It seems that she suffered as an au pair in England and now appears to want to extract revenge. The first few weeks are filled with housecleaning and mountains of ironing, sheets, napkins, underpants, not a piece of cloth is left with a hint of a crease in it. Then all of a sudden without a word, she disappears and it's just Madame and I.

Madame speaks only French with the clean perfection of a true Parisienne, providing me with no alternative but to practice the native tongue. Under her tutelage and tender care I now even dream in French, which I take as a sign that I'm merging with my surroundings.

Life Begins at Fifteen

Every morning at Madame's request, basket in hand I head for the outdoor market just around the corner from our second floor apartment. It's an opportunity for loud, off the cuff bantering with the merchants, their rough use of the language far removed from pristine pronunciation, and a place to be surrounded by piles of smooth purple aubergines, gorgeous green tapering courgettes, plump ruby

Madame Deluze - the epitome of a true Parisienne

ESCAPE FROM ENGLAND

The old section of Nice circa 1965

An off duty moment in the life of an Au-pair

red tomatoes, glowing peaches, and air filled with the smell of crusty, freshly baked baguettes. The necessities of life for the French are so far removed from the cabbage, potatoes and sliced white bread that satisfies the English appetite.

The odiferous splendors of the cheese emporium seep out the door of the cheese monger's cavern, where enormous wheels of the pressed curds of the milk of the goat, sheep and cow are stacked from floor to ceiling. Flotillas of forms and textures line the antique counter cases, the atmosphere rife with aromas from the more vocal varieties of Roquefort, Munster and the oozing presence of Napoleons' favorite, Epoisses, explicit rarified bouquets that might stop even a gastronome in his tracks. Hauling the catch back from the fray, Madame and I juliene and blanch, saute and deglaze, creating dishes worthy of Julia Child.

Afternoons are spent perfecting the art of nursing a café au lait for hours at a sidewalk café. Amanda and I, taking our cue from the French, adopt their national pastime of critiquing the constant parade of passersby, sharpening our vision and wit at the expense of the continuous stream of fashion parading before our eyes. Such cheap fun! Or we head down to the beach to bare our bones on the stretch of large uncomfortable stones that unfurl at the base of La Promenade des Anglais.

The French, like most southern Europeans prefer to enjoy life, an ability not shared by their northern cousins, embracing the Club Med attitude as opposed to enduring a nine to five routine. Eating is an important ritual, not just an occasion to fuel the furnace, it's an enjoyable interlude to be taken seriously. Madame, the newly arrived Parisienne is still finding her feet in this unfamiliar territory and often invites me along to share her leisure and passion for food. Small bistros serving up Mediterranean cuisine are all around us. Sitting in dimly lit stone caverns surrounded by great barrels of locally grown salt packed olives and anchovies plucked from the Mediterranean, Madame in her crisp clear beautifully formed French gives me the skinny of her life in Paris. I drink up her elegant use of the tongue that is now becoming second nature. The educated French love their language and have great respect for the way they use it.

In Antibes I have my second spontaneous encounter with a native son, a medical student on vacation from Grenoble. Waiting at my second floor window, the shutters thrown ajar, I listen for the tap of his clogs on the cobbled streets below. Together in the twilight, caught up in the throes of teenage lust we dance on the sands of Juan Les Pins, wrapped tight together, our hormones throbbing to the sounds of the waves crashing, the strains of *The Great Pretender* blaring through the night. Strolling along the ocean front in Nice, a trend made popular by Queen Victoria of England in the nineteenth century, the warm night air strokes our skin, as the Promenade des Anglais majestically glitters for our benefit alone. We glide along, hands entwined, full of anticipation, surely this is forever, not just a brief holiday dalliance. But he has a métier to pursue and a sweet heart back home already lining up for wedding bells. Our dreams are allowed to be just that without the hindrance of actuality.

Slender, bronzed and so much more sophisticated, I return to the motherland. My mother is impressed, my father somewhat amazed that I have picked up some French! It's October and the English damp is oozing out of the earth, attacking from all sides. The bright lights of London look more appetizing. Amanda is in Hampstead Heath in London, staying with her brother. This seems like a better plan than the dark, dank English countryside. Using her pad as a base I find employment as a telephonist/receptionist and acquire a bedsitter in Earls Court, sharing the meager facilities with a friend, Barbara, one of my old cohorts from the Guildford days. The new crash pad, a room in a converted Victorian house has just the basics. Rooms are furnished, making it easier for a landlord to extract a tenant if necessary. The bathroom is down the hall, hot water forthcoming only if the meter is fed, a coin inserted. The bath and lavatory as well as the pay phone are to be shared with a host of other inmates. Bright orange curtains adorn the tall windows shielding us from the continuous flow of traffic and throngs of people stampeding past outside. They cast a vivid burst of warmth over the tired décor and deceptively mask the constant grey skies that continually hover above.

Earls Court is awash with Australians and Kiwis. London is a stopover on their global trek, their islands being so far flung they feel the need to visit the rest of the universe before settling down back home to daily toil. At social gatherings and waterholes the male variety of this species, drinks Foster's beer and gets blasted together, not so much as even offering up a "no worries" or "shrimp on the barbie quip" to any of the females in the room. As an afterthought, they might chat up a *"Sheila"* the colloquial term for the Australian version of the softer sex on their way out the door expecting to get lucky or maybe it's a move to prove that they are not of other persuasions? Reconnecting with a male friend I'd met at a party before my French excursion I find the former fling still has a zing about it. Historically we had taken naked midnight strolls on the moors in the sticks south of London. With him I made the important discovery that semen is almost impossible to remove from a dress. I'm sure I'm not the first to make such a diagnosis, and I know I won't be the last! We saw each other infrequently, keeping in touch by letter. He respected my teetering resolve to abstain from the final act, despite the fact he was training for inclusion in Great Britain's swimming team for the forthcoming Olympics and had been informed by his coach to exercise all muscles to ensure maximum performance, including the so called "love muscle." Being regarded as a medicinal aid for his greater glory cut no shrift with me. During summer vacations from college he often drives a mini bus overland through Europe, Asia Minor and beyond, acting as a tour guide to the uninitiated. He now invites me on a trip to Morocco. What a great way to really get to know another human.

It's Easter weekend and he's in London taking a break from his studies in Wales. Being a humanitarian, a god does not feature in his personal inventory. In fact Drew had been responsible for successfully purging from my soul any ideas of that nature that had lingered on from my Convent days. It's Easter but as religion is not on our agenda we go to see the annual Easter Bonnet Parade in Battersea Park. A parade of floral headgear bravely worn, bright and hopeful, which contrasts strikingly against the backdrop of a winter that still endures, The trees are still leafless, as they wait patiently for the sun to bring forth their springtime finery.

My roommate is out of town. Heeding the advice given by the nuns in school to "never put off until tomorrow what you can do today," we take full advantage of this opportunity. I drop my guard and knickers to experience a visit to a higher realm and become for the first time, at one with the universe. He's in love and my pleasure is his passion. Life seems more vivid after this foray. Nature takes on a stronger, more intense hue. I have picked a sensitive man well equipped for the job at hand! Besides, if we are to travel ensemble this will be inevitable.

It's refreshing that he doesn't mind, *"taking coals to Newcastle."* Newcastle is a large coal producing region in England and used to demonstrate the stupidity of hauling stuff on trips that's readily available anywhere.

My employer, who had been gracious enough to put me through secretarial night school is outraged by the idea that an employee should get three maybe four weeks off. "Out of the question" is the response when I state my case, "Two weeks maximum vacation is all you get." I quit, pack my straw shopping bag and, with thirty pounds sterling in hand, jump on the tube to the airport and board a student flight to Barcelona.

Hitch hiking in Spain is a brave new idea. Cars are sparse on the roads. The industrial revolution has not yet reached these shores. The rich and the poor are miles apart, this disparity resulting in rides that are all pioneered by wealthy patrons, amused at our presence. We are treated with great hospitality, sometimes even fed and housed on our trek south. We steam through Spain in Mercedes and Citroens, after sometimes waiting days for this honor. We sleep in furrowed fields, stand beside roads, thumbs in the air, under amazing trees with giant seed pods reminiscent of part of the male anatomy, enjoying just being together, keeping the flag flying. Undaunted, never knowing literally what might careen around the corner, to carry us away from the dust of a small village in the middle of nowhere.

We dine deliciously on paella in Valencia and find it's possible to get totally legless on alcohol for pennies. Unfortunately in this elevated state we manage to lose the key to our room and on returning to our bed for the night, discover that our landlord is fast asleep. He's already suspicious of us. We seem to be having far too much fun to be married and now we have to wake him up, using a tangled mess of Spanglish to wangle a substitute. Spain is still firmly under Franco and the thumb of the Catholic Church, making it impossible to spend a night in a hotel room as an unwed man and woman. Luckily I had bought a fake gold band to wear on the nuptial finger to dispel any doubts as to our relationship. In Southern Spain people are still living in caves and this is 1966!

The Alhambra in Granada is within our sights. The Arabic edifice built by Moorish conquerors originally as a small fortress in 889, was allowed to fall into disarray, but now it stands transformed into a monument of Islamic architecture. The delicate interior stone carvings and calligraphy give us a whiff of what we are about to encounter and goad us on to fulfill our mission to reach the Sahara. Taking the ferry from Malaga at the tip of Spain, we reach the shores of Gibraltar, to find ourselves back in the land of fish'n chips, Watney's brown ale, and all the familiar institutions of a colonial English outpost. Climbing the namesake rock we visit the monkeys, a symbol of British rule. If they disappear, some say, so will the British.

Next stop Tangiers! On disembarking, a man in a flowing robe is already poised to greet us. The turban swirling around his head and the turned up toes of his sandals are straight out of Ali Babar and the Forty Thieves. City streets flow right down to the water, stopping at a sidewalk café we celebrate with tall glasses of hot mint tea, the beverage of choice in these parts. Mint leaves float on the top as we inhale and sip the perfect antidote to the blasting heat, apparently perspiring cools the body down.

Vendors squat in the street under the blazing sun, behind a few bundles of produce as they wait for a sale. Inured to their place on the ladder of life, the hopelessness of their task, they appear to have lost even the energy to fend off the constant and overly familiar flies landing on their skin and in their eyes. People with nowhere to go and nothing to lose, a dangerous combination, scraping the edges of society for a crumb to survive another day, many afflicted by a disease where the pupil of the eye and the whites blend into one, a grey blur.

In the cool night air we stroll on the beach, a treat after the heat of the day. We are not alone, a man brandishing a knife emerges from the crowd veering in our direction, a man who seems to have an agenda. Drew pushes me out of his path, disorienting the attacker who lunges off on a different course as we flee back to the safety of the YMCA, where we're shacking up for the night. It's cheap and the place to encounter other souls pursuing similar travels, a place to pick up information, where to go, where to stay or not, travel guides to every corner of the planet have not yet arrived.

That night, prone in a basic single cot, happy to still be with the living, a deep all encompassing voice booms down from above, penetrating every particle of the sweltering dormitory, allowing no escape from the droning that seems to emanate from the skies as it sucks all the air out of the room. Is it the voice of a god I had failed to acknowledge and my comeuppance is imminent? I lie there fascinated, trembling, not recognizing the call to early morning prayer. This is my first brush with Islam.

Getting an early start is not a problem when bunking at the "Y." Most residents rise when the first sunbeam filters through the naked windows. After a night of fitful rest on a hard pallet, permeated by loud snores and people talking, all seem ready to discard their berths and dive into new adventures, to leave the safe but noisy rest haven far behind.

Cobbled streets wind between solid ramparts. French style sidewalk cafes sprawl. A few well heeled Europeans toy with a morning café. Hosts of shrouded women flock past. Men in the fez hat and baggy pants jockey for space trying to coax a few shekels from our pockets. Thankful to be walking and not lying in an African morgue we take the bus to Tetouan, a vast stretch of sand on the Mediterranean, a wide swath of virgin grit without a trace of humanity scarring it's immaculate surface. Pitching a small tent (oh no, not again!), we bury the camera, our only valuable possession, stowed in a plastic bag in the sand, hoping it won't be ripped off while we enjoy the surf. Rinsing the wear and dirt of our latest exploits off in the waves, we realize we have nothing to eat for dinner. Drew suggests going to a cluster of huts down the trail to see

The Souk Tetouan Morocco circa 1967

what they have to offer, while I stay at base camp to watch over our scant belongings.

Wandering the beach, thrilled by this undefiled piece of paradise, I gaze up and spot on the horizon a group of women advancing. Continuing to roam, admiring and collecting a few seashells, my solitude is broken by a stone landing nearby. The women are now quite close, their rugged faces, worn by the elements, poke out from shrouds, their hands are in the air. Through the sound of the waves

Life Begins at Fifteen

I hear them screaming, stones are whizzing through the air. I seem to be the target! Turning tail I skedaddle back to the frail confines of the tent, hoping that having lost sight of my bikini clad body they will pass on by.

Dinner is waiting, a loaf of bread and a few eggs. My compatriot assures me, as he breaks the loaf in two, scooping out some of the dough and cracking the eggs, their slimy liquid gliding into the chasm, that we need the protein. As dusk falls, with nowhere else in sight to park our backsides, we spend the night stifling under the canvas. As the sun rises, gathering our gear we head out, forgetting in our rush to retrieve the camera containing a roll of film with the memories of our trip so far, buried in the sand for safe keeping.

After scoring a bus out of Tetouan, we are unceremoniously dumped by the roadside in the middle of nowhere, leaving us no choice but to march over the Rift Mountains. Small, bare bones villages appear. Kids follow us, curious, laughing. We are the freak show, the carnival, the talk of these desperately poor enclaves. The children in tattered remnants skip and play. We feel like the Pied Piper leading a flock to a promised land. A few hours, and buckets of sweat later, a crate of a bus stuffed with locals and livestock rolls out of the void, clambering aboard we abandon our growing troupe of ruffians. We wave as they fade into the dust. The gates of Fez, a magnificent walled city, are on the horizon but we press on through Meknes, Rabat and eventually Casablanca. The latter of course is a disappointment after the movie buildup. Finally we make it to Marrakesh on the edge of the Sahara.

The smell of rancid meat cooking over hot coals greets us. This seems like an excellent place to lose weight. We have met a few other Western types along the way, most of them have been

ESCAPE FROM ENGLAND

holed up in caves for months, flying high on drugs, Morocco being on the map for these thrills. They are now penniless and ragged on the streets asking for cash to get back to their country. Every foreigner appears to have one thing in common, diarrhea. We have survived pretty much intact in this dimension, until settling into the Hotel Cecil on the square in Marrakesh. Hotel Cecil a blight on the dilapidated landscape, it's only attraction is location. Our room gives us four walls, a bed and a sheet along with a more than adequate supply of native filth, fleas and other things that creep and crawl.

As night falls, the square, a vast expanse, becomes alive with the sounds and odors of Morocco. Throngs arriving from every corner of the land, dressed in their native splendor, have come to sell their wares, food, spices, leather goods, jewels and cloth. Story tellers squat surrounded by spellbound audiences, entranced by their hypnotic spiel. Drummers pound, dancers writhe as they entertain the multi colored milieu milling through the acrid stench and desert dust blowing in from afar. Men charm snakes out of baskets as the dentist equipped with pliers and a camel, places a string tightly around a doomed fang, attaching the other end to the beast. A quick tap on the camel's rear instigates the required jolt meant to extract the putrid culprit. Well that's the desired outcome. The crush of humanity, seethes, twirls and manipulates in the heavy thick Saharan night.

My partner succumbs to internal strife. He's chained to the nearest hole in the ground for several days. Meandering through the Kasbah, I return with black hot tea and canned soft drinks for my collapsed comrade, to fend off dehydration. The smell of rotting food is enough to make even a seasoned traveler puke. Something dry and basic like bread seems the best choice to put between the lips to ease and solidify the frequent eruptions pouring out of the rear end as well as to pacify the churning stomach.

The dromedaries in the desert, hiss and spit when we pay them a visit, the constant haranguing by merchants in the Kasbah is getting a little stale and the main distraction in town, the night market a little old hat. We consider our trek to the African sands to be complete. It's been a rugged assignment, mere survival definitely being cause for celebration and in spite of the less than idyllic circumstances, we're still talking to each other. Packing our stuff, we head back, a bus and a hitch at a time, to the London tube. The journey, after all, is the fun part, not the destination!

It takes about a week to shed the friendly fleas that have found refuge on my body and blend back into the circuit. Jobs are easy to let go and pick up. Without much effort I become a secretary at a commercial real estate firm just off Grosvenor Square, biding my time until I'm twenty one and can fly, my latest plan to escape the nine to five life of an office drone and the predictable English lifestyle.

I share an office with the big cheese's secretary, the epitome of her chosen field, London bred and always impeccably turned out. Her short red hair is sprayed stiff and flawlessly coiffed. Spectacles perch on the nose, lips are perfectly painted, the eyeliner fastidiously applied. Pale powdered skin completes this vision of office efficiency. She favors the knee length pencil skirt, slit up the rear that enables the wearer to walk on stiletto heels while encased in a tube. The sheerest flesh colored stockings grace her slightly plump legs. She finishes off the look with a subtly clinging sweater. Her long finger nails with which she amazingly pounds her manual typewriter are obsessively, perfectly polished.

When called, we strut into our respective bosses' office, pad and pencil to the ready, to sit with our legs appropriately crossed, to take a letter. Dutifully waiting for the thoughts and words to flow, we take them down in shorthand before returning to our den to deliver them to paper.

We sit facing each other, with the typewriters in between. She's in her thirties, living with her mum and possessing under this smart secretarial veneer a tarty streak intertwined with a ribald sense of humor. She loves her job but I have a feeling there is more to it than plays out during office hours. She stays behind long after I have fled my desk. In between the fingers flying over the keyboards, mine not as swiftly or eagerly as hers, we laugh and groan.

Whenever I have a chance, an idle moment rears its head, I write to international airlines, all around the world and cruise ship lines, they being a second choice for the great escape.

My day arrives, I receive the letter in the mail and with sweaty palms tear it open, there in print is my acceptance to a brand new dimension, the world of airplanes, travel and exploration, the life I have dreamed of! Shedding my secretarial seat, I receive a traveling alarm clock, a departing gift from my boss, to carry with me on my travels.

CHAPTER FOUR

Up In The Air

Sixteen scrubbed, buffed and perfectly poised, hopeful air hostesses listen attentively to "how the perfect stewardess always anticipates a passenger's needs, even before the passenger knows what he wants." As nubile ears tentatively absorb this fascinating view of female subservience, a violent explosion rattles the room, drowning out the well modulated voice of the instructress. Elegantly dressed in the navy blue uniform of those lucky enough to have graduated from out of these four walls, she falters, the color in her perfectly powdered cheeks evaporating, but in true stewardess style, she carries on in spite of the probable turmoil throbbing in her skull. We, oblivious to the relevance of these earth shattering sounds (maybe this is just life as usual at London Airport), continue in our posturing as ideal ladies of flight.

The airline fails to inform us of the actual realities, but the newspapers are full of fiery photos and details. A British Overseas Airways plane had crashed just two and a half minutes after takeoff, one of the Rolls Royce engines, suffering, it was later found out, from metal fatigue, had broken free and fallen to earth, narrowly missing children playing. The plane having gained an altitude of 3000 feet was travelling at a speed of 417 miles per hour, the left wing subsequently catching on fire. A flight controller in the control tower viewing the spectacle, managed to clear the nearest runway, enabling the craft to be brought down.

The cabin staff, even before the pilot had given the O.K., as the cabin windows melted and the undercarriage exploded, had sprung into action, opening the doors and activating the emergency slides housed in the door frames, before hustling the passengers off the stricken bird. Five people died, four passengers and one stewardess, from asphyxiation, the billowing thick, acrid smoke the culprit. The young hostess, braving these foreboding elements, had positioned herself by a door, to push those who hesitated into the slide, before going back into the cabin to pry the remaining four of her flock out of their seats and off the doomed, burning airship. She was posthumously awarded "The George Cross."

It's considered a privilege to be chosen and accepted into this field, a one in a hundred chance. Requirements are strict, a prospective hostess has to be single. Just the idea of female availability is balm to the male ego strapped into an airborne seat with time to daydream. It's mandatory to conform to height (neither being too tall or short) and weight restrictions and to have the correct British accent, the Oxford accent, the only accent allowed on the airwaves or to come out of the T.V. set, the only one to have if you want to get anywhere!

Luckily my Mother has made sure that my pronunciation fits this format and although my upbringing had been less than perfect,

I had drilled into me all the signs of so called good breeding. With that, my ability to converse in French and a little stretching of my scholastic achievements, I am seen as fit to serve!

In order to arrive promptly, I have to jump out of the sack as 6 a.m., to tube, bus and walk my way to the training center at Heathrow Airport, a one and a half hour trip each way. Five days a week for six long weeks, I have to be on time and perfectly turned out.

The emphasis in the training is on personal service, very little time is spent rehearsing for the inevitability of an emergency. It's the wealthy who take to the air, men with class and distinction. The airplane seat provides ample leg room. The flights are never full! Each passenger is individually greeted, his luggage, at the most a small briefcase, is placed in the overhead bin, the attending hostess relieving him of his outer garments, folding the coat, placing it in the rack with the hat on top.

When conversing with a seated passenger a hostess must squat, keeping of course her knees firmly together, adopting a position to project a personal approach, to make the client feel pampered and special. But most importantly we must never forget that as a B.O.A.C. hostess we are carrying the flag representing Great Britain around the world and at all times it is our responsibility to look and act the part and to be on best behavior!

Needing to break free at the weekends after digesting so much etiquette, the London party scene beckons. A fashionably skinny man freshly arrived from South America catches my attention, an Englishman who has spent time in San Francisco and traveled south when the prospect of a trip to Vietnam sponsored by the U.S. government seemed unavoidable. I vow to resist these distractions or any other that might lure me from my chosen path, graduating from the flight academy. I'm ready to soar!

A female crew member when reporting for duty, before being allowed anywhere near an airplane, has to be checked out. In the supervisor's office she pirouettes as the eagle eye checks the hair, to be worn either short or up, preferably in a French pleat, every strand in place, it must never touch the collar of the uniform! The hat must sit at precisely the right angle. The face should be enhanced with carefully applied makeup but never too much and the hands are required to be fastidiously clean, the nails manicured and polished. The uniform fresh from the dry cleaners should not cling tightly to the vibrant female form that pants from within but rather saunter discreetly in a becoming fashion. The hose must be the right shade of pale with shoes of classic cut and color to match the uniform. Dyed hair is not permitted or jewelry, with the exception of a pair of negligible gold or pearl studs. Before every flight a stewardess is weighed in and if the scale reflects a rise in size, she is placed on a diet, with the possibility of being taken off flight status and ultimately fired if this problem is not addressed. Having passed such scrutiny or successfully reworked the look to suit this unswerving dress code, it's possible to proceed to the departure lounge.

My first flight is to Montreal. Palpitating, I arrive at headquarters to be checked in and hopefully out. I pass the inspection and am released into the lifestyle I dream of.

The hostesses work the aisles and the passengers. The stewards control the galleys, guardians of the food and booze. For the boys this is a lifetime occupation, the girls are expected to last a few years, before being whisked away by a white knight to the altar, which we have been informed is cause for immediate resignation or dismissal.

The chief steward who had weathered many a flight and witnessed countless brand new stewardesses, noticing my awkwardness hands me a glass of fine French Champagne, "just to get over the initial terror dear". By the end of this inaugural outing and lubricated by a few more glasses, I'm flying higher than the plane.

After each flight, our tired bodies having been deposited in the hotel, it's mandatory to participate in the crew party, we need to decompress from time zones and passenger overdose and this I am told is the way to do it. Whether five in the afternoon or five in the morning, it's a required ritual, the first class cabin donating the necessary food and liquor to oil the occasion. It does provide an opportunity to see the social sides of the men up front as well as those working the rest of the plane and to witness their amazing capacity for booze.

Following the bingeing, the rest of the layover is spent sleeping it off, rising from the bed just in time to fly home. I soon discover that most flight crew consider flying a job not an adventure, consequently my sightseeing expeditions at foreign ports are mostly a solo experience.

On my first trip I try, as I have been taught in the mockup cabin while training, to perfectly place the meal tray in front of the passenger with all the implements and offerings organized by the book—the handle of the cup in the five o'clock position, the act accomplished with confidence, style and, of course, a smile. I soon get the message, as part of a flight team in the back of the bus, that the priorities are slightly different. Get the food out as quickly as possible and concentrate on selling the more important alcoholic beverages, the miniature bottles of liquor. I'm instructed to unscrew the cap and pour the drink, before returning the empties to the galley for the steward to clandestinely replenish from a large bottle of the same booze, which he had previously purchased at a duty free source! This system of rotation provides a little extra income for the boys in the galley, The women working the aisles, it seems, are just unpaid accomplices! I just want to plant my flag around the world!

This first tray is one of many thousands I will place in front of a passenger, who always seems eager to indulge in the vapid cuisine. It's challenging to comprehend that seemingly rational individuals can flounder on the cusp of despondency if their choice of entrée has expired. Looming in the future there will materialize the pissy passenger who will inquire whether the beef or chicken is fresh or frozen, farm raised or wild and which one of these delicacies would I recommend? Initially I service their request with polite recommendations but as flights roll by, I offer up in retaliation, "They are both equally unappetizing but don't worry about which is best. They look different but taste the same"!

On a flight out of Asia, three people are sitting in the front row, in my territory, a British couple severely impeded by protocol and their

Reporting for a trip B.O.A.C. Primed for inspection

Up In The Air

Back home—time to decompress

birthright and by the window with feet curled close to the crotch and knees fanned outward, dressed in flowing cloths, which cover the necessary parts but reveal much sun kissed flesh is a Ghandi-esque figure. I can feel the discomfort emanating from the starched, inflexible pair, but I rather enjoy the view of this incongruous trio sharing such close proximity. Dinner is served. My window passenger, ignoring the utensils happily uses familiar fingers instead. Gnawing the chicken down to the bone, he abandons the residue, launching it mid air, scattering the accompanying rice underfoot. Fuming as this exhibition unfolds, our intrepid Brits, frothing at the gills at having to put up with such a performance demand to be moved. They are discreetly rearranged in first class, as my remaining client, thrilled to have the whole row to himself, proceeds to curl up and sleep, a whole row of seats now at his disposal!

ESCAPE FROM ENGLAND

I fly the long haul flights, longer but fewer flights to more fascinating destinations. 747 airplanes are looming on the horizon, the enormous growth in air traffic is around the corner. Rampant construction and development around the world has not yet started, countries are still insular, people still live in their countries of origin. Tourism is on the verge of materializing as an instrument of the masses, but not quite yet. In far flung destinations people are still existing much as they had done for hundreds of years.

The last golden moments of visiting the Royal Palaces of Bangkok, to be the only person there except for a few resident monks, is still possible. Sitting, consuming a beer on Bugis Street in Singapore, open sewers gaily coursing down each side of the road, watching the transvestites strut their stuff, picking up foreign sailors on shore leave, is still a tasty layover thrill. The Johns, off the boat and full of booze, are way beyond recognizing any aberrations in genitalia and provide easy willing targets, no doubt waking up the morning after their ride on the wild side, alone and without a wallet. All the above naughty exploits are still thriving, Singapore is not yet sanitized. Jaywalking, spitting, chewing gum, and littering are not yet reasons to be arrested.

Geckos climb the walls, run upside down on the ceiling of the hotel room, antics made possible by their specialized toe pads that adhere and stick to surfaces, the fan whirs overhead.

Visiting Bangkok, every stewardess purchases Thai silk to take to Singapore for a Chinese tailor to custom make into an outfit. It's a tried and tested path that every full-blooded hostess has trod through the ages and considered acceptable behavior, a *stewardesses* rite to be observed! I'm drawn into the "what you are meant to do mindset," only to come up against the rice curtain, a point of view more attuned to covering up the female assets than exhibiting them. I decide as I am not getting my vision across to the Chinese tailor to go for a cheongsam style pant suit. But the ravishing length of glistening lime and pink hand loomed silk, although beautifully stitched, never feels right, is never worn and ends up at Goodwill.

We fly into Bahrain a dusty crumbling oven, staying and drinking at the Gulf Aviation Rest House, the lone distraction in town. The only passengers in and out of this desolate stretch are the reigning sheik, his multiple wives and entourage. Is the British government trying to ingratiate itself with the Bahraini powers by boosting local prestige and glamour? The airline is obviously not making money out of this godforsaken destination. The foresight of the power of oil!

The local sheik loves to invite the female crew members to parties where food and liquor flow, despite the fact that Islam is the way of life in this realm. Men in thopes (the long flowing white robe worn by men in Arabia) seem to be just as available as any other kind of man if a stewardess feels inclined to hustle in the dust. One particular blue-eyed blond hostess, a member of our merry band of entrepreneurs is actually awarded a pink E Type Jaguar. No doubt her special qualities had found their way into the right camel skin tent!

The sheiks' many modes of transport are lined up, gracing the sand dunes, a fleet of expensive metal Rolls Royces, Ferraris and a brand new Cadillac, a sedan, all flashy chrome and shiny chassis, the seats covered in fur. The Tribal Chief can be seen being driven in the caddie, the American monster, in circles on his sorely limited road system, the air conditioning blasting on overdrive. These people were riding around on camels a few years before! But unlike their predecessors who could survive eating grit, these expensive metallic new beasts of burden, succumb quickly to the swirling desert sand storms and are abandoned after a short life, left to expire in the changing landscape, replaced by later models.

We tread in the tracks left by Winston Churchill and Karen von Blixen staying at the original Norfolk Hotel in Nairobi, Kenya, bungalows set in a garden oasis. We walk downtown over mud roads to the market to bargain for enormous ostrich egg shaped avocados, pineapples and tropical delights to take back home to impress and share with our fellow natives shivering in the depths of a typical bleak English winter. Airport customs officials have not yet invented rules about transporting such stuff in and out of countries.

The game parks in Nairobi are just around the corner, a mere jaunt to experience the magnificent Maasai in beads and cloth tending their herds, to catch an incredible display of high jumping warrior dancing and schmooze with the giraffe and wildebeest, the gorgeous low slung trees afire with flaming orange blossoms under skies so close the idea of reaching up to touch the fluffy contours of the clouds seems feasible.

As flight crews fresh in town loaded with news from the motherland, we are invited to the Nairobi expat parties, wild, raucous affairs. The Brits, far from home and need for decorum, let down their hair, get blitzed, with erotic dancing and wife swapping playing out in the coarse tropical grass, far from prying stuffy English eyes. A middle aged woman of portly construction performs a sensuous strip routine, slithering out of layers of black feather boas and the requisite articles of her trade, physically caressing every note of the accompanying music, artfully, slowly revealing with flourish her voluptuous natural offerings, setting the tone for further debauchery as stars peer down through the warm dark air and houseboys mix libations and proffer food, while no doubt thinking that this must be some sacred religious foreign ceremony.

Next stop Johannesburg, South Africa, where the immense material wealth sparkles ferociously up from beneath us, a strident advertisement as to the might and powers of the Boers. The local white males avidly await the arrival of a fresh young female flight crew to entertain and try their luck with, lounging in the hotel lobby as we check in, they wait for an appropriate time to pounce. Invitations to poolside parties, cocktails and dinners flow. Any visitor, celebrity or other suitable alien presence is of interest in this isolated tip of Africa, a welcome change from the usual roll call of known available regulars.

Apartheid is in full swing, endless human labor mixes and serves the drinks, delivers mountains of canapés, giant steaks that drool over the sides of the plates as the white mistress stands guard, wielding an invisible whip, mentally thrashing the local color into shape, treating them as slaves if they are fortunate and stray dogs if they aren't. The white ruling class consider this their right, just business as usual, the beauty of the setting diminishing with such vulgar behavior.

A trip to the diamond mines is a chance to further witness the black man incarcerated into a feudal system, sent down dubious shafts to the bowels of the earth, to claustrophobically claw for prized rocks to satisfy his white master, in shameful conditions far from family and comfort. The reward for such drudgery, a paltry wage and a lifetime of hazardous, agonizing manual labor, so that a future western bride might enjoy a radiant sparkle on her nuptial finger, while the diamond mine bigwigs suck up the enormous differences between obtaining and selling the goods.

I had a chance to be on the wrong side of the equation when a payload of white supremacists boarded the aircraft, throwing around their illusion of superiority, demanding service and responding to our less than willing subservience with a cocktail of insults and slurs.

In another time on another continent another monstrous flight materializes, a trip that's hard to forget or forgive, a charter out of Newark, New Jersey, every seat taken on a ride to Montego Bay, Jamaica. Nothing can appease this crowd, sandwiched in seats too close for comfort, their demands continuous, everyone fighting for attention, climaxing in riots breaking out in the aisles when the flight crew can't service their demands soon enough. We try drowning them in free liquor but that only further ignites the squabbling. As a last resort we call upon the guy up front to manufacture a little spine-chilling turbulence in an attempt to restore some semblance of order in the cabin, to shake up these clowns with a subtle reminder of their vulnerability, hanging in the sky in a manmade metal tube at the mercy of the elements and now the flight crew. Crewmembers take to the restrooms, locking themselves in as the plane erratically rocks n rolls 'til landing.

Putting up with the foibles of mankind, surviving attempts at being demoralized by such bottom feeders is all part of the curriculum, but after landing, shedding the uniform and accommodating attitude, at least there's the chance to replace the hazards of in-flight bad behavior with some earthly delights. There is the thrill of water skiing in Trinidad, guided by a handsome black tutor as to how to settle into the skis and rise successfully out of the waves, hurtling behind the boat as it ploughs through the surf, the joy after a marathon crossing of the Atlantic to let everything subside, to totally abandon strife in the company of steel drums in Antigua, imbibing rum and coke with Nelson's dockyard on the horizon, cycling around Bermuda, in tune with the twenty mile an hour speed limit, rolling in the startling white sand and bathing in the turquoise oceans surrounding the soft green hills dotted with pink and white perfect villas. Licking our wounds and hanging out in deluxe hotels way beyond the budget of most plebeians also acts as a placebo.

Beirut, the Paris of the east, the fashions and shopping on a par with any western metropolis, situated on the Mediterranean, is a playground for the attractive, animated natives, a smorgasbord ranging from fair complexioned with blue green eyes to the hairiest olive skinned specimens. Taking in the local color at the neighborhood watering holes, invitations open doors to the local scene, to gatherings, eastern Mediterranean cuisine and often the Lebanese elite. The local bazaars are stuffed with gold, gems and leather goods. The nights provide an excuse for exotic dancing, gaming Monte Carlo style, all frenetically set against the magnificent Beirut backdrop, blissfully unaware of troubles ahead.

B.O.A.C. incorporates on its flights, a stewardess culled from our destination, arrayed in national costume, for a little taste of the beauty of the region, before actually putting a foot down on the terra firma, to get one in the mood before arriving on scene. On a trip to Pakistan, a beautiful girl from Karachi clad in a sari is onboard to help with the flight duties and assist in communicating with any Pakistani traveler. With much time to spend on the back jump seat together as the passengers snore seat bound in the cabin, a brief friendship transpires.

It's February in Pakistan. The air is crisp, the sun vibrant, springtime is exploding. Downtown in the bazaar, blasts of curry greet the nostrils. Stunning lengths of hand painted fabric to be folded and draped on the body flap in the breeze. Banter and bartering fill the air. Women haggle over pots and pans, the chaos, the hot reality of daily life throbs, the pulse of any Asian city. On a whim, caught up in the moment, I purchase a glorious black and gold sari. On arriving back home, it slumbers in a trunk for twenty years, the chance to flaunt it never arising.

Invited to dine with my new friend's family, curry of course is on the menu. Curry houses dot the English landscape, serving up diluted renditions of the real thing, contrived to suit the placid British palate not attuned to drama, dishes a resident of Pakistan would barely recognize. Here in the land of spice I come face to face with a steaming pile of mutton glistening through a glowing sauce. Salivating with expectation, I dive in, only to be engulfed by flames, which the accompanying glass of chai fails to extinguish. My calm disposition takes a severe hit as I try to cover up the discomfort, not wanting to perturb my hosts who are clearly unaccustomed to western ways.

When the Pakistani bombshell has a London layover I'm out of town but I loan her my current beau who is more than pleased to take this exotic package on tour in his sports car. I never find out whether she was presented with an insipid English curry!

Most of the trips are the more bread and butter variety, a reliable cash flow for the airline, the transatlantic crossings London, to New York, Chicago, and Montreal, leaving in the morning and arriving at night, with just enough time on the ground for the mandatory social intercourse, then to sleep off the effects and then to jump back on the plane the following night and fly back to London, arriving when the nine to fivers are just starting their day.

I often excuse myself from the party scene in order to rise early and explore the new soil beneath my feet, all the usual tourist stuff—in New York, climbing the Statue of Liberty inside to the top, riding the elevator up to the highest point of the Chrysler Building, taking the tour by boat around Manhattan and sitting in on a session of the United Nations, to hear all the members congratulating themselves and seemingly getting nothing accomplished. The trip to the

Metropolitan Museum to view an exhibition of Tribal art is my first encounter with this medium. The catalog I buy will later prove to be instrumental in my life.

Most of the B.O.A.C. destinations are either colonies or ex colonies, countries deemed relevant to the wellbeing of the United Kingdom, having current or past ties. Always intrigued by globes and maps, the perfect tools for a day dreamer, at school I had been made aware that the pink parts of the world, those parts that were colored pink on the globe were either colonies or ex colonies, having steel clad ties to the British flag. The color pink seemed to dominate at least a third of the world and we kids tied to our school desks were duly impressed by the propaganda. Rule Britannia and God Save the Queen was drilled into our souls accompanied by a heavy dose of Christianity.

CHAPTER FIVE

Under The Influence

In 1969 as a stewardess if you marry, you have to resign. The stewards can be married and secure in their positions for a lifetime but women are to be discarded if encumbered by a husband. Youth and feminine freshness are of paramount importance in this line of business, a stewardess is an available attractive female. Grey hair and a thickening waistline are not considered appropriate for a hostess working the aisles of an aircraft.

Even friends and family make sure young women know they have an expiration date stamped on their foreheads and that to be left on the shelf to become a spinster is an unimaginably awful fate, to be avoided at all cost!

As a woman wanting to fly, the idea of applying for the job of pilot never even crosses my mind. A woman in the left seat, sitting behind a joystick on a commercial flight? What a ludicrous idea! What poverty of thought, what lack of imagination of what should and could be.

ESCAPE FROM ENGLAND

The rumblings in the cockpit—so aptly named, referring to the only gender to be found within its confines—rises to a crescendo as the advent of women even being considered to be allowed to tread upon their sacred turf starts to be a possibility. Surely a female cannot perform as adequately the duties that have for years been male only territory. They, the pit, would have to clean up their act for starters. No more talk about "LBFM's" an abbreviation for "little brown fuck machines," used by the boys up front when referring to their off duty pleasures in certain parts of the world. No more swearing and farting up there. How they hate even the thought of admitting women into their ranks!

While in training for my hard won place at the flight academy, I encounter a freshly arrived piece of talent, a man just flown in from the Americas, bristling with endless stories of adventure and not bad looking either. At evening's end he deposits me on my doorstep, by way of a ride in his 1956 MGTF. But I have no intention of getting involved with a mere man and jeopardizing what I have been striving for so long. Besides, I already had more fun than I could handle.

He calls again requesting to talk to "Rose," the name I had used so I would recognize who it was at the other end of the line, caller I.D. and answering machines having not yet been invented. Pretending to be a roommate I let him know that "Rose is "out of town, unavailable, otherwise engaged."

After holding out for two weeks, I teeter, give in and partake of a Chinese meal with this interloper. An avalanche of invitations follow, an outing to Ascot to the horse races south of London, where the upper crust can be seen dressed to kill balancing large hats on aristocratic heads while parading down the paddock to peruse the live, prancing, four legged entertainment before the race, trendy restaurants, trips to the country, to Dublin to drink Guinness, to dance at quaint village shindigs and mingle with the gypsies, drinking tea in caravans. My new admirer has a way of inviting himself into other lives, I find that I am no exception to this charm.

In Paris staying next to the Vietnamese Embassy, students are rioting in the streets and a Northern Vietnamese delegation is trying to negotiate with the Americans. It's the merry month of May, 1969. We observe the magnificence of Versailles, the Bois de Boulogne and wander through the Louvre but spend more time lounging in The Deux Maggots Café on Boulevard Saint Germain, taking in the scene as it passes by.

The apartment is furnished with Napoleonic day beds. It's a spot where many rendezvous and parties erupt spontaneously. In true Parisienne style, at one event, our host places a table and chair in the center of the jostling throng, calmly demolishing a boiled egg with toast, ignoring the surrounding insanity. The Marche Aux Puces is still a real flea market, disheveled, chaotic, with real people offering real stuff with no hint of the sterilized chandelier and rococo style fakery of later times. May in Paris, what can I say, even better than April, a little warmer.

The MGTF is a great lure to attract the opposite sex. A man with a sports car, even a Midget MG is considered a worthwhile diversion. The MGTF "CHF 124," it's official name and number plate can be relied upon to break down consistently, having to be ditched frequently in some far flung environment, this is part of the adventure. Even a short trip around London can result in CHF 124 spluttering to a halt, requiring a warm body armed with a crank to restart the beast.

I learn to drive in CHF124, the bucket seats are slung so low, the backs of my fashionable footwear scrape against the floor. I master the need to double declutch when shifting gear. This is the first of a few temperamental English sports cars I make the acquaintance of. In Tehran on a layover I purchase a goat hair coat, which provides the necessary insulation when riding in this steed. As we zap along at the maximum fifty five miles an hour, the convertible roof and side screens flap and shudder, proving absolutely futile at blocking out any wind. Heating of course is for lesser folks, not part of the equipment.

It's a club, waves are mandatory whenever a similar vehicle approaches and sails by. Crowds gather around the parked vehicle, drooling in admiration and needing to know all the relevant minutiae regarding this rare animal.

I offer to drive my friend Virginia from London to Brighton. It's spring, bright green leaves, fresh and sweet let us know that winter is behind us. We glide down country roads, happy to have left the city, a Jaguar with two cops inside follows our progress. The MG starts to slow down, putting a foot down on the gas pedal yields no response and the car finally lists to a halt. The men in blue who have been tailing us seem happy to find us stranded. Looking under the bonnet they discover that the oil tank top had been loose and fallen off. They are thrilled to be able to show off their superior mechanical knowledge, and we are thrilled to be the recipients of it. So much for my beau's reassurance that he had checked the oil! One might say in hindsight "a red flag."

Peter, the beau in question, the owner of this difficult piece of metal now informs me that he's planning to return to the States with or without me. The pressure is on, over a candle-lit dinner a proposal takes me off guard! Will I or won't I marry him? It's now or never!

As you probably know and I become aware of, one acts insanely when under the influence of romance.

August 23rd 1969 after a champagne breakfast in our studio flat high in the trees above Gloucester Square, I don a short white lace sleeveless dress and matching white lace knee high boots, my hair piled high on the top of my head. A tan from a recent trip to Nairobi, a definite status symbol during a pallid English summer, contrasts admirably with the conservatively white attire. We arrive at the Chelsea Register Office on the King's Road in CHF 124 after a slight detour to the tailor to pick up a cream linen three-piece suit for the groom. It's a low profile affair, the long honeymoon we have planned around the world on a ten percent fare, my departing gift from the airline, is more to my taste.

My two best friends are present, my brother and an assortment of relatives. Peter has insisted on my parents' presence. Buoyed by the bubbly at breakfast we sail through the short ceremony, before heading down to the Fox and Hounds a pub on Holbein Street just off Sloane Square, the size of a small dining room, just large enough to fit everyone in. A few drinks enables a more friendly atmosphere to permeate this gathering of strangers. On to the top floor of the Cadogan Hotel on Sloane Street, we dine off steak and wine as London pulsates at our feet on the streets below.

My mother is elated, having the time of her life, as ever attempting to focus the spotlight on her while taking full advantage of the flowing wine. She glows and preens as mother of the bride. My father takes a back seat, preferring instead to tuck into the feast, avoiding too much verbal interaction, observation is his strong card.

A piece of paper now declares my union to the man I love, which of course I believe to be a permanent state of pleasure. A few guests have arrived bearing gifts, six steak knives and a set of wood salad bowls. The giving of gifts is not a strong English proclivity. I'm neither surprised nor disappointed.

Taking the bus to London Airport, we embark on the more important part of this occasion, the honeymoon. After dropping

ESCAPE FROM ENGLAND

the B.O.A.C. uniform stuffed in a brown paper grocery bag at Flight Operations, we take off for Rome. As the plane soars through the night sky, pangs of *What have you done?* flit through my mind, along with a nagging persistence that perhaps to seek marital bliss at this time is a crazy idea.

Peter's an avid sightseer, I'm happy to recover horizontally, but the Coliseum, the Roman Steps and the Via Veneto where the cream of Roman society parade their bountiful wares for all to admire and visually gorge on awaits us. Sex is in the air, wafting around every corner. The art of coffee drinking is a beautifully acquired talent and posturing in fine clothing a serious pastime. To flirt and gaze with molten eyes and urgent intent is part of the drama playing out, executed by both sexes in order to set aflame and stoke the libidos of these people who fully understand that to play is much more fun than commitment.

Having nothing to cover my head with, entrance into the Vatican is denied. The Pope, anyway, is probably nowhere to be seen possibly carousing, gorging and having fun of many descriptions far from public view behind closed doors. Peter delights in modern architecture, and as the Italians are masters of this craft, there is much to see.

This is just an interlude, a brief beginning, the initial escape from the sound of wedding bells as we strive to put more distance between us and England.

Athens and the Acropolis greet us, moussaka and retsina are on the menu. In the Plaka plates are thrown and smashed in our honor when the waiter learns of our recent merger. Retsina the local wine tastes like paraffin, the wine vessels having been sealed with local pine resin to keep the contents air free and in the process infusing the wine with that special taste and aroma.

We need some sun, beach time. The inter island ferry is at our disposal. Hoping to avoid the usual destinations crammed full of packaged tourists, we jump ship at Kos only to find a dusty outpost. Sailing on to Rhodes we pause momentarily to scale the impressive stone walled fortress and take in the medieval town before heading south to Lindos, farther along the coast. Lindos is tourist free except for buses that arrive at ten in the morning in the town square and spew out their load for an hour, before carting them off again to the next distraction on their agenda. No hotels deface the whitewashed dwellings gathered on this rocky outcrop, steps link the houses and travel by foot is the only way to negotiate the terrain.

Contrasting against the stark white and vivid blue skies, ancient crones with bronzed skin go about their daily grind, swathed in black, grey hairs, beautiful faces creased by myriads of lines offer smiles as we pass them on the steps. Men are scarce and the young have fled, falling victim to the bright lights of Athens.

Resting in the square, refueling our minds and bodies, an American writer engages us in the art of English conversation. We are the only other strangers in town and this poor boy hasn't seen a viable female since he arrived. I now have two men vying for my attention. We're invited to stay at the house he has rented for as long as it takes him to pen his latest tome. It's a barnlike structure, with high ceilings, blanched wood beams and whitewashed like everything else, it's the roof over our heads for the next week. We wake to the freshness of alabaster, it seems the only color paint to be had, cerulean sky visible through windows not marred by glass, straw covers the floor.

The remnants of an acropolis stand poised above the village on a rocky promontory, way below is a perfect crescent of golden sand. An informal gathering of tables and chairs on the square serve as the local dining room. People gather at night. It's the place to gossip, to gorge on moussakas, the perfect peach, the real meaning of yoghurt and of course our old friend, retsina, always graces the table.

ESCAPE FROM ENGLAND

Lolling on the perfect beach soon loses its allure. This trip, after all, is meant to be a world tour not just a quick dash to paradise and back.

The plane embraces the tarmac in Tehran, Iran. The last Shah is still securely seated on his throne. The lavish crown jewels, the first stop on our program, provide an exuberantly overt display of rubies, emeralds and diamonds set in lashings of gold which the Shah and his second wife Farah Diba still parade in on ceremonial occasions. They make the Queen of England's baubles look insipid by comparison.

The feel on the street is heavy. Men surreptitiously attempt to touch a piece of this foreign female, they brush close by or cop a feel after passing, in spite of the fact that my brand new spouse is by my side. Even this does not deter their stealthy fingers! Alien women are sparse and up for grabs, this unsavory onslaught jaundicing my whole view of Iran. After consuming an Iranian dinner, Peter ends up in the bathtub submerged in cold water, sick as a dog, hot and heaving. Being English he wants to get over this in solitude. I oblige, happy to stretch out naked and alone after a day of being manhandled and undressed by Persian eyes.

Recovering from the ravages of diarrhea and the foraging attacks by the locals, we decide to forgo the trip to the ancient and holy cities of Qom and Isfahan to avoid any further contact with this crowd. Buying and wearing a shador to blend in is an alternative, but we're here to have fun, not to go undercover and are in no mood to press our luck. Besides which, many Iranian women are walking around in western regalia not covered tip to toe in voluminous black. Maybe they are immune to these encounters or more likely the men wouldn't dream of trying their luck on their own kind.

Delhi in August, the hottest time of the year. This is my first time in India except for a transit stop in Calcutta. Tsunamis of Indian and

Pakistani immigrants have already arrived on British shores, so we feel somewhat familiar with this country, besides Queen Victoria had considered India the jewel in her crown, Britain having previously ruled this vast expanse for roughly 200 years. Accordingly most people speak English, the major religion is Hindu and to top all that off, curry, the locale cuisine, has already replaced fish and chips as the national dish in England.

The pounding heat sends rivulets of sweat down our backs, as the crush of the crowd dressed in magnificent colors numbs our senses. The filth and pungent aromas of strange and familiar types invade our nostrils as the beggars push their palms in the face of any stranger passing by. Begging is a profession in this land where children are maimed to make them objects of pity to jump start their career, their mangled bodies meant to induce more money from the onlooker.

Having seen too many Peter Sellers films, with Sellers masquerading as an Indian gentleman, my husband has acquired perfectly the Indian accent. He tries it out when attempting to bargain for a ride in a sidecar attached to a motorbike, a turban wearing sikh in the saddle the recipient of this performance. The sikh doesn't appear to enjoy his accent echoing back from a white face or the burgeoning, robust, bargaining skills of my mate and a lot of shouting ensues. A crowd forms around us, joining in the fray. Somehow we manage to extricate ourselves from the fuming throng and escape into a side street teaming with people and a few sacred beautiful white Hindu cows.

Wherever we go we have to find a bank to withdraw money on our credit card to fund the trip. A law in Britain circa 1966 decrees a person can only take fifty pounds sterling out of the country at a time, we of course did not let this stop us but much time is spent getting around this obstacle. I'm sure the Queen has no such problems on her royal tours. It's just another law to encumber and encase the worker bee while the government which has devalued the currency tries to balance the books.

We find that guest houses institutionalized by the British during their stay here, offer inexpensive but clean conditions. Bacon, eggs and toast are on the breakfast menu, with tunic attired, turban clad attendants on duty, hovering over our every move and hungrily eyeing the food on our plates.

Rising at four in the morning en route to The Taj Mahal, in the hope of catching the sun as it rises over this monolith, we have to step over sleeping bodies that litter the streets on the way to the train station. The trains, and accompanying bureaucratic system of buying tickets are a remnant, yet another memento of British Victorian rule. As our budget dictates we settle for third class, third being not quite as gruesome as fourth, which involves standing up all trip, in third one gets to sit on solid wood slats. Hailing from England we are totally cognizant of the class system but amazed by the audacity of the multiple tiers in the Indian example. Here they even have a class of people doomed to clean lavatories their whole lives.

Sitting in such close quarters with our fellow passengers, I'm happy that I've brought a sheet from our hotel bed with me to wrap around my head and body in an effort to avoid and deflect the incessant stares aimed at penetrating my personal effects. The train rolls slowly past endless fields where people toil inefficiently under the now broiling sun, without tools to be productive. An air of complete hopelessness reigns.

We arrive at the Taj Mahal with deep grooves imprinted on our rear ends from the merciless, rigid wood strips of the seats. I'd been somewhat blasé about the expedition. We'd been living the high life in swinging London and for the last two years I'd been winging around the globe visiting countless other edifices erected for the greater glory of gods and men, but the splendor and perfection of The Taj Mahal is breathtaking. The white marble shimmers as if a mirage as we approach. We and countless Indian pilgrims find ourselves pulled irresistibly towards this monument to love, constructed in the 17th century by Shah Jahan to commemorate the death of his favorite wife, who had died struggling to deliver their fourteenth child. I marvel that mere men created this superb masterpiece.

On entering, we take a cue from our fellow travelers and lie down on the cool white marble, which is salvation after the blasting heat and relentless sun. In the presence of greatness we are transported to a higher level, a rare moment to be at peace and one with the universe, when the world for once seems to make sense.

A trip to the Red Fort is mandatory. My new husband seems to have a passion for battle grounds, canons and everything pertaining to historical warfare.

At Delhi airport, hot and sticky from the lack of air conditioning, we realize that although the British colonized and ruled this land for centuries, they had failed to impart the basic knowledge of how to correctly form a queue. Passengers push and shove in front of the ticket counter. Following the "When in Rome, do as the Romans do" tack, we join in the melee, much to the surprise of the native sons.

Touching down in Thailand we find the gracefulness of the Thais salve to our senses after the brashness of India. Of the ten days in India, seven were spent trying to come to terms, not to be repulsed by, the carnage of poverty and extreme heat in a land where the degrading circumstances of many of the world's citizens, scraping and grasping at the least shred of existence to survive, was everywhere to be seen. The odors, the stench of mankind and the flaming vivid colors of gorgeous saris and tunics displayed on moist brown skin are permanently imprinted on our minds. The aristocratic aquiline features portrayed on even the most humble face. Nothing can prepare you for India.

A friend I later encountered in Bali had spent time and met his wife in an ashram in Poona. He had initially been intrigued by how Indians could wander through life, through the squalor of their surroundings and seemingly attain nirvana. He played the part in search of enlightenment, sporting cloth wrapped around his crotch and head, in an effort to unravel their secret, before finally realizing that in India, the trick of appearing to rise above the festering hulk of humanity is just a survival technique, not spiritual ascension. He caught a glimpse of his rotund form, the cloth through his legs resembling a diaper and the one perched on his flowing locks, the uniform of supposedly higher beings, and discarded it. But he had encountered the love of his life and collected a lot of material for future cocktail conversations.

The outrageously festooned gold Buddhist temples, royal palaces and playgrounds of the Thai nobility are decaying and deserted when we stumble upon them, we seem to be the only people in the world who want to admire and visit. A few saffron draped monks wander amongst the remnants of past power and glory, one of them obliges when we request he pose for a photo but doesn't seem too happy with the assignment. Many religious sites later, uniformed police arrive on scene, their hands gesture in the direction of my dress or lack of it, I'm wearing a mini dress, the latest London has to offer. We gather through sign language that something is amiss as we are promptly escorted off the premises.

The day has not yet arrived when a visitor will be equipped with suitable attire before entering the Palace grounds, to jostle with the masses experiencing these monuments to past glory resurrected, once more bright and shiny.

Peter, never one to miss a thrill insists that we check out all the nightlife. The United States involvement in Vietnam is in full swing and Bangkok is the rest and recuperation center for American servicemen. This sudden influx of boys in uniform spawns a particularly seedy district, Patpong Street, an area which services all the needs of men let loose for a short time before and after facing death and destruction on a daily basis.

We sample the topless bars featuring small, delicate Thai females and discover that for the price of a glass of very expensive colored water it's possible to chat with any of these working girls and for a higher price it's easy to access more in depth knowledge of their slight bodies. The foreigners and service men frequenting these dives are big and burly, the thought of such encounters makes me shudder. We visit the rooms upstairs where women perform all sorts of tricks with their genitalia, inserting ping pong balls, coke bottles, name your request. We witness the vagina consuming the object, then it being ejected with a flourish! We take in the simulated sex acts between male female, female and animal, which are also on the menu. Not exactly usual honeymoon fare but - why would I complain? I have declared myself to be a liberal. The crowd laughs and hoots as these young women defile their bodies in the name of money, innocents plucked from the sticks at a tender age to provide entertainment for jaded eyes.

The new husband proceeds to check out every avenue for so called illicit sex in town. The clubs for Japanese men only are also on the agenda and my charismatic companion manages to talk his way into the front lobby. Because of his insistence we are treated to a view of a bevy of girls in their early teens sitting in a glass enclosure with numbers hanging around their necks, waiting to be picked out by a client. From there on out it's strictly Japanese men only. Is this because these males do not have as much to offer as other species, or as an island race their distaste for other than their own is rampant? The Arabs have their dens of vice too, but don't seem to mind anyone else sampling the wares.

Aids has yet to appear but a veil of cheap sex is already starting to hang over Bangkok, a city destined to turn into a hellhole of oppressive traffic and jumbled architecture. When to cross the street is Russian roulette, five lanes of aluminum careening towards anyone insane enough to try his luck. When the sight of older foreign men escorting young pubescent girls to tawdry hotels will just be business as usual. But in between the jungle of haphazardly erected cesspools of the sex industry, golden temples will still rise to cleanse the mind and eyes.

The floating markets provide a change of pace. Armadas of long skinny canoes ply the waterways. Women paddle vessels stacked high and overflowing with fruit, vegetables and flowers, their coarse voices shrieking the wares they have for barter or sale. We see brown, wrinkled skin under straw Asian hats, toothless smiles, continual motion.

We visit the sleeping Buddha enshrined in its own temple. An enormous deity 49 feet tall and 141 feet long, the body encased in shining gold leaf. He lounges in a tightly enclosed atmosphere of dripping golden finery, which offers only a narrow path around the perimeter and an opportunity to gaze upon his glittering body, an intimate view of the outstretched form, the right arm supporting a head framed in tight golden curls. The massive 10' x 15' feet are inlaid with mother of pearl and display auspicious symbols on the soles.

Fired up by this magnificent apparition, we visit art shops and find walls lined with sacred religious artifacts torn from temples.

Thousands of Buddha's smile and glare at us as they stand, sit or lie, looking outward and inward, all seemingly very pleased with themselves. Twenty five English pounds secures a Buddha cross legged with eyes closed, contentedly holding a betel nut, while sitting on top of a heap of indecipherable sanskrit. Brought up under the guise of Christianity this is a beautiful relief. We find the contemplative features and composure of the Buddha a gratifying sight compared to that of a dying Christ on a cross.

Taking the train up country, we reach Chiang Mai, a small market town. The seafood is divine, and it's a great place to become acquainted with an elephant. The mahout, the master, sits up front, just behind the ears. The guests climb into a cage attached around the girth. We have a bunch of bananas to snack on and offer our friendly pachyderm one. With a knowing smile and gentle poise he swipes the whole bunch out of our grasp with his trunk, depositing them smugly into his mouth and in a matter of seconds peel and all disappear. This beast has obviously stumbled across many stupid examples of humanity in his time.

Japanese men are packed onboard the flight out of Bangkok, having raided the sex clubs and the duty free store at the airport when leaving. On the flight back home these Asian gentlemen spend their time consuming copious amounts of Johnny Walker scotch whisky, their beverage of choice. Now after disembarking they are stumbling and puking all over the arrival lounge where people are industriously bowing many times at differing heights, greeting, meeting and saying farewell, clothed in kimonos and suits. The customs agent inspects our bags wearing immaculate white gloves.

The two single beds at the Japanese style hotel are back to back, the room is long and thin, making the idea of rearranging the furniture for a more intimate setting out of the question. The bathing facilities are on another level, separate from the room, different bath houses for men and women. As we explore this intriguing new slant on the quest to refresh our jetlagged flesh with soap and water, we encounter big wooden tubs busy with natives conducting intimate cleansing rituals, soaking and scrubbing in communal water. I decide after my initial plunge into a tub filled with chatty, well fed, Japanese women, all well past their prime, that in future I will proceed in French courtesan style, living with and enjoying my own particular aroma and forsake the joys of feeling clean, until the surroundings prove more auspicious.

Running out of prophylactics, we need to find a pharmacy to replenish our stash. English is definitely a foreign tongue on this soil, but leave it to Greenwood, my stalwart companion, now husband, to explain in great length and accompanying gestures as to why we are here in the drug store. The astonished clerk pays great attention, trying to understand the requirements of this wild, long-haired stranger whose sign language and mime performance fail to translate our request. As we are not making any headway, the clerk provides us with a pencil and paper to depict how this product looks and is used. At last recognizing our need, with a discreet smile, he comes up with the desired package.

Using the subway system, we are intrigued by the painted lines on the platform, which we discover correspond to the doors on the train when it arrives at the station. We learn to our discomfort that during rush hours passengers stand in these sections and when the train arrives and the doors open, it's surge time, station attendants get behind the throngs and push them, packing them tightly into the carriages. We resolve to travel off peak in future

Japan is still rebounding from their defeat in World War II; the big climb into electronics is still in its infancy. On the crowded streets, we tower above the people scuttling here and there. Eating might have been a mysterious experience but luckily the restaurants all display in the front windows plastic replicas of the dishes served. It's only necessary to point and an edible replica is delivered.

The trip to a department store is a cultural revelation, the basement a sea of culinary delights. Chefs dressed for the task, artfully craft appetizing miracles that are given away as tasty lures. Who knows what we are eating. Who cares? The store escalators are manned top and bottom by two uniformed young ladies sporting more pairs of white gloves. They welcome each and every venerated client to every level. On visiting the kimono floor I'm amazed at the cost of some of these magnificent gowns. In the department displaying business attire for construction workers I find a pair of black cotton boots with a separate socket for the big toe, ribbed flexible rubber soles and a row of metal fasteners up the inside of the leg. They are meant to be great for balancing on scaffolding. How can I resist?

We always have our destination and where we are staying written on a piece of paper in Japanese. Whenever we get lost, which is frequently, we accost one of the locals to point us in the right direction. These residents of the land of the tea ceremony and samurai go to great lengths to help, even taking us to where we want to go. They seem to be genuinely interested in our wellbeing, but we find it's the custom to treat all strangers, even those regarded as intruders, with great respect. It's seen as a Japanese duty to uphold the flag in the presence of barbaric invaders. We are most grateful for this superficial extreme politeness.

Kai Tak airport in Hong Kong is a handy, quick drive to downtown Kowloon, the landing strip is one of the most challenging in the world, a narrow corridor between towers of apartment buildings. Washing hangs on bamboo poles out the windows to dry, no doubt absorbing airplane vapors along with the sun. The airplane wingtips almost seem to graze the low cost housing on the final approach. We are close enough to look into the bedrooms of the residents, living in close proximity to neighbors is one thing but this is incestuous.

We check into the YMCA, adjacent to the Ferry Building and right next door to the prestigious Peninsular Hotel. We're back in the colonies; people can understand our mother tongue. Bacon and eggs instead of raw fish are on the breakfast menu. Our room is small with cheesy furniture but the location is the best in town and the view magnificent, especially from the roof garden. We drift into the Peninsular Hotel, to see how the rich and famous are getting by. The doors are swung open by a regiment of smartly uniformed staff. In the spirit of old England, which we are happy to embrace, we partake of afternoon tea in the cream and gilded lobby of this magnificent structure, reveling in a time when there was time for tea.

This is a duty free port. Electronics, cameras and Swiss watches can be bought at prices well below the usual retail figure. Crafts from China, silk Chinese style blouses intrinsically embroidered, cloisonné, kung fu slippers, silk paintings, all carefully produced in mainland China are available in the Chinese government store.

The streets are teaming, so crowded that the people walking behind tread on the backs of your shoes. When buying anything we encounter a humorless countenance, a bored attitude. The art of bargaining is a difficult, unfriendly process but a way of life in these territories. To pay full price is the mark of a fool. The British are still running the joint and are perceived as the villains, and we are no doubt viewed as part of the problem.

The ferry to Hong Kong Island, a ten-minute ride away, is fast, efficient, and twenty five cents, a continuous service between these two points. The water is jammed with sea going vessels. Working ships with cargos and junks ply the scene. For some the junk is their house, where they live, several generations in tight quarters. On board they cook and wash, sleep and play.

Taking the cable car to the highest point of this rocky promontory, we see that every piece of land has been used. The buildings are thick on the ground reaching high into the sky. We note with awe the way bamboo is used as scaffolding when constructing these vertical towers that shoot through the clouds and wander out of sight, far above the squirming masses hustling below. An ancient bus propels us around the island. At last we encounter green fields, peasants working the soil and fishing the ocean for sustenance and livelihood.

It's my turn to be laid low by our continual parade through international cuisine. A lethal dose of crab foo yong has me bent over for twenty four hours with agonizing stomach somersaults. As my dear husband explains, "What a bad choice; probably day old crab, past its prime, disguised and masquerading in a dish which only a foreigner would order!"

On arrival in Singapore my sidekick is informed that his hair is too long. "Not allowed in Singapore," we are informed by the clean cut immigration officer who illustrates the law by showing us pictures of acceptable styles welcome in this increasingly tight little corner of the world. My accomplice is yanked from the line and directed to an area to obtain a haircut. Determined not to let this derail our expedition and also resolutely refusing to shed the beautiful black curls so keenly cultivated, Peter backs off. After an interlude he emerges from a restroom wearing a hat concealing his offensive crowning glory and sails unimpeded through a different customs line.

Singapore is another colonial outpost, having recently attained independence but still wallowing in and under British influence, its

British pubs and restaurants surviving and flourishing. The Raffles Hotel hasn't changed since the days of Somerset Maugham and Graham Greene, the rooms they stayed in still bearing their names. The bar where they quaffed down gin slings still offers the updated version, now the Singapore sling. It was invented right here at the long bar, a wicked concoction of lots of gin, the so called mother's ruin, along with a myriad of digestifs and fresh fruit juice, and let's not forget the angostura bitters. The wicker furniture continues to stand in place as fans whirl overhead. Of course we stay - why not? – it's only a matter of time before it will be destroyed and revamped into efficiency. To have the chance to amble with all those memories and history, what luck!

The open sewers still flow through Chinatown, servicing the rickety Chinese dwellings. We tour the magnificent downtown Emporium offering all manner of stuff from Asia and Europe,

Singapore circa 1968, before purification by Mr. Lee Kuan Yew

Under The Influence

Committing a sin in Thailand

including Chairman Mao's little red book. We're just in time before the demise of old Singapore, before Mr. Lee, the cleanser and purifier sanitizes this tiny strip.

Australian customs are rigorous. I'm carrying a bag of peanuts just in case we are stranded without any other edible options. Who knows? With changing time zones it's always wise to have something to nibble. The nuts are discovered and I am relieved of their presence. I'm told that they are contraband and could contaminate the whole Australian continent. The customs officials are hell bent on protecting their territory from any intruders, be it immigrants, especially those not conforming to their all white agenda, or a bag of nuts.

Winter is starting to happen, a season we hadn't packed for. We wear all our clothes in layers to ward off the drastic change in temperature, our last stop having been hot-as-hell Asia.

The Sydney Opera House is under construction. People are up in arms, the streets are rife with demonstrators, protesting that such a monstrosity could vilify their landscape, unaware that at a future date it will be lauded as a landmark, a magnificent and much loved institution. People are slow on the uptake, most minds are small and resistant to change, even for the betterment of mankind.

The Victorian houses stacked on hills side by side are so much like those I will find in San Francisco. In fact, in many ways climate, the physical feeling of being close to the water and views in every direction, as well as an abundance of gay men, makes the similarities even more profound.

We have friends in Sydney, people we knew in England. Having escaped the dictated doldrums of the stiff upper lip and been born again as Australians, they delight in escorting us around their new quarters, proud of the different life style. The double decker buses and driving on the left side of the road remind us once again of where we come from. The attitude is decidedly macho and the women appear to be almost as tough as the men. Men-only serious drinking establishments are an interesting feature. It's standing room only, tiled like a lavatory, a place for real men to congregate, bringing back memories of my time spent in Earls Court!

My spouse has tailored this trip to include as many destinations as possible that have connections to the United Kingdom. The stopovers not fitting this category have been included to make this Union Jack, British flag waving world tour a possibility. Not relishing the sudden climate change we search for warmer weather, knowing that a frigid English winter is on our horizon.

A buff, bronzed male with an afro swaying on his head, a pole of freshly caught fish hanging over one shoulder, strides by, his deep resounding voice brings us back to reality. "Bula," he shouts. Luckily

Under The Influence

he seems to be happy to see us. "Bula," we find out, means hello in Fijian. We find that this magnificent apparition speaks English. He invites us home, back to his village on Man Friday beach. What a treat, our only sin had been trying to catch sunbeams.

Greeted by the big chief, we're invited into his hut, a tattered portrait of Queen Elizabeth 11 dominates the room. Fiji is still the color pink on the map. Two chairs appear for us to sit on. Our new friends sit cross-legged at our feet, much to our dismay, but we are honored guests and have to go along with the show.

It's mandatory to visit every hut to admire personal shell collections. I've always had a weakness for sea shells. Just as well. Every clan member wants a piece of us, but that seems like a good deal in exchange for the hospitality offered in return.

After a dinner of fish and taro, we bed down in the chief's hut in a carved wooden four-poster, draped in heavy, lacy mosquito nets. The chief and his wife snore loudly and blissfully in the bed next to us, we lie awake listening to the sea thrashing on the beach, the wildlife calling in search of a mate, relishing this moment in time, resisting any honeymoon escapades.

The young studs invite us to go fishing, to catch dinner while their female counterparts, who are just as big but not quite as handsome, organize the open-air kitchen, where enormous cauldrons splutter over open coals, ready for our return. Our shipmates show us how it's done. They dive off the boat and sit on the seabed and wait for the next meal to pass by. When it does, they grab it. It's a hands-on job and requires an amazing capacity to hold breath under water. Squid, lobster and many brightly colored tropical fish slither on the bottom of the boat as we head back to shore.

That night we reap the rewards of the day spent at sea. A ceremony follows to celebrate our arrival. In spite of not fitting the gender requirements, it's a men-only affair, I'm invited to join in the ritual. Sitting on rattan mats under the stars, waves crash on the sands as bowls of kava are passed around and around. The potion served in half coconut shells has a grey and slimy look. It's my turn to take a gulp. It's one of those situations that pop up in foreign parts when a polite, "No thanks; I'll pass" is not an option. It would be offensive to my hosts.

Kava has the texture of a minced slug, thick, slippery and gritty, it oozes slowly into my mouth, a medicinal aspirin like flavor. It's obviously an acquired taste, something akin to limburger cheese. Made from the roots of a plant of the same name, it's an anti energy drink meant to promote a cheerful comatose ambiance. When totally tanked, our Fijian friends reel off to their respective huts.

One of the clan steps on a stone fish, a creature that lies on the bottom of the ocean, disguised as its namesake, whose venom can fatally poison a human if not treated right away. In our rental car we cart the victim off to hospital and save him from an early exit from planet earth. We're instant heroes. Our new comrades now want us to move in, to be part of their life. When we tear ourselves away, the whole village turns out to wave and wish us well.

We read in a newspaper at a later date that Man Friday Beach had been hit by a cyclone, villages swept away, people drowning in the eye of a storm that had decimated lives and any infrastructure in its path.

In Nandi, the capital, huge Fijian police patrol the streets, clothed in white "sulus"—sarongs with a deeply serrated hem. We meet an older Fijian woman, previously married to an English sea captain before his demise and stay at her house. She's happy to rent out a room and have some company. We're happy to stay, as the hotels are expensive and cater only to the crowd who can afford the price tag. People with a less fluid cash flow are not encouraged to visit this particular paradise.

Our landlady fills us in on the local racial tensions between the original Fijians and the growing Indian population, brought to the island by the British to administer their affairs. The East Indians, the British had discovered, were even better at bureaucratic red tape than their colonial masters. The Brits have ruled Fiji for about a century and are just on the cusp of handing it back to the rightful owners, the original Fijians of Melanesian descent who have resided in these splendid tropical surroundings for over 3500 years, but the Indians also now regard this as their homeland. Even amongst Fijians, our hostess confides, discrimination abounds depending on the hue of the skin.

Dining at a local café we strike up a conversation with the Fijian waiter who lets us know that his ambition is to go to England "to enjoy the opportunity of a free house, medical care and unemployment benefits." Good news travels fast. Colonizing probably seemed like a great idea at the time but can come back to bite you at a later date.

A boat takes us to an island where the practice of fire dancing still survives. Long troughs filled with white-hot coals afford the locals in grass skirts the opportunity to display their ancestral skills. Palms wave overhead and warm sand squishes between our toes. Long green banana leaves are presented to celebrate our arrival, filled with offerings of starchy roots and sweet stringy steaks culled from the local vegetation and fauna. The meat has an unfamiliar taste and we realize that it probably once spent time swinging high, from tree to tree in the local jungle. We're eating the flesh of our near relative – the monkey.

ESCAPE FROM ENGLAND

Back on the bus to the real world we suffer a wakeup call transiting Frankfurt. Winter is already in full swing. People trudge morosely in heavy coats. Dour faces prevail. What a change in pace from our recent escapade.

"Catch of the day" Male magnificence Fiji

CHAPTER SIX

Back to Reality and Beyond

A frigid October wind and grey drizzle greet us at London Airport. The start of another leafless winter is already descending on the British Isles.

We settle into a one-room pad on Upper Cheyne Row in Chelsea. Mick and Bianca live around the corner. Their pea green Rolls Royce is part of the local scenery along with a statue of Sir Thomas More, a former friend and advisor to Henry VIII before losing favor and his head when he chose to stick to his principles and Catholic faith, refusing to recognize Henry's second wife and the brand New Church of England.

The streets are alive with bell bottoms, long hair and platform shoes. Competition is rife to be best in show, to be noticed sporting the look of the moment or a streetwise alternative. In England it has always been a challenge to garner attention. The soggy weather makes people scurry to their destinations rather than linger and look at the action on the sidewalk, and with so much history under their British belts, the preference is to live and let live. To gawk and stare is considered a mode of behavior performed by more drama imbued types like the Italians. Even a naked Lady Godiva on horseback failed to draw much scrutiny!

A tide of youth has risen out of the carnage of WWII. Growing up in the post war years of constantly making do, they are now hell bent on ignoring the stiff upper lip and on course to smash through the pent up class barriers in place for centuries, ready to challenge the values and views set in stone and refined by the so called elite echelon since they grabbed power. It's a crusade to crush and exterminate the confines of the proper accent, to toss aside the "Sloane Rangers," the debutantes so confident of their superiority, their money and position in society. Dressed in twinsets, pearls and designer silk scarves, they are stuck in their upper crust rut, seeking a male equivalent to keep them in their accustomed arid aristocratic style.

The new scene is constantly unfurling, set to conquer the world or at least make a dent in it, the only wealth required, an imagination and the zest to create change. Similar resentments had bubbled in the blood of our ancestors. They too had challenged the inequalities of the system when the snotty, self-appointed upper class became unbearable.

In the sixties these ideals re-immerge subconsciously, giving us the gall to question the status quo. As any new generation we have to distance ourselves from our parents, the wonderful humans who had slogged and strained through hard times, fought a war so that we might surface and in the process of procreation had extended their bloodlines. The dark ages of war and conforming to social status seem on the verge of expiring or at least dwindling. Life is cheap, jobs abound and the birth control pill has just arrived, so much to celebrate!

Even the food is changing, although "greasy spoons" and tedious purveyors of solid, survival grub still have a stranglehold on much of the British palate. The British Pub, a stellar purveyor of Shepherd's pie and Bangers and Mash is abandoning the love affair with warm beer in favor of foreign cold lagers and wine. The Pub is an institution that defies reproduction on any other part of the planet, a unique formula, akin to a French baguette, the secrets of which don't travel well, eluding duplication in foreign quarters. But in spite of these classic British bastions, East Indian and Chinese interpretations of cuisine are making inroads onto the restaurant scene, challenging the former inbred favorites. Even in the boonies you can stumble across a dish of Chop Suey. Bistros and wine bars are popping up with offerings from around the globe, introducing the tired English taste buds to delightful new adventures, leaving the Joe Lyon's Corner House Café and The Golden Egg, chains serving up oily food and endless cups of neutered tea or an excuse for coffee, heading towards extinction.

The Baghdad House on the Fulham Road is a favorite with rock stars and Lord Harlech one of the more fluid members of the British aristocracy, a place to sprawl on cushions, inhale the Middle Eastern atmosphere, to smoke the hookah and down couscous and kebabs. The Chelsea Kitchen on the Kings Road is a great place to fill up your food tank on a budget, a spot to feed the inner man after raiding the boutiques to clothe the outer one.

The Portobello Road is the venue to be seen of a Saturday morning, to satiate the mania for clothing and trinkets from bygone timeframes. It's there we first hear rumors of people with flowers in their hair in San Francisco, embracing free love.

To aid and assist us in our need to dress, the iconic clothes store, Biba, opens its doors. The second edition on Kensington Church Street has black glass windows with the logo in gold art deco letters. This, the only image visible from the street is enough to lure in the eager throng. Inside the lights, subdued by Victorian fringed velvet lampshades, cast a dull glow. Potted palms somehow manage to survive, their fronds wafting in the cigarette smoke. Stuffed couches provide a place for the boyfriend to park his rump while taking in some of the best looking female flesh in circulation.

The clothes, different styles every week in great fabrics, designed and priced right, hang on antique wood coat stands, floating on raised platforms. Music engulfs the extensive cave-like interior. One large communal dressing room services all the girls who want, of course, to try on any or all of the great offerings, all female shapes and sizes suiting up and flaunting the wares together in the pursuit of a 'have to have' new look. An honor system still survives. The necessity for plastic numbers, signs advising that shoplifters will be prosecuted have not yet arrived. Identification is not needed when passing a check. The Chelsea Cobbler handcrafts python boots for any pair of feet that have $150 dollars to splurge.

The mail arrives through the letterbox twice a day. An invitation to a 'Vicars and Tarts 'party tumbles onto the door mat, a veiled solicitation to serve God in the company of the world's oldest profession. Strolling in our costumes to the local pub for a pre-event cocktail, Peter's in full papal attire. Diana, a fellow "stew," her hair blown up into a bouffant beehive, a skirt barely covering her curvaceous rump but providing a splendid view of her mile high legs, is masquerading as a cheap sixties tart. I'm a platinum blonde buried in mascara and lipstick, a whip wielding dominatrix. Fishnet stockings cover the flanks and black leather boots climb up my thighs.

The blokes and birds downing their nightly tonics at the local take one look and declare "drinks on the house." Peter is kept busy fending off an avalanche of male interest in his accomplices.

Having imbibed of the holy water we wander through the streets of Chelsea to the hallowed heathen event to find men of the cloth and women of the street engaged in the rites of celestial dancing. Whirling multi colored lights swirl above as passion vibrates off and within the walls. Another party, another Saturday night adequately spent.

Life is inexpensive in Britain. We had grown up eating meat and dairy products from Australia and New Zealand, our trading partners. We ate seasonally, fruits and salads only in summer, vegetables in winter produced on British soil, the fallback position being canned goods. The advent of Birdseye frozen peas was a moment of pure joy for my mother. A banana was an exotic and exciting experience, coming all the way from South Africa by boat. But times are changing. Avocados, melons, and asparagus are on the shelves of the local supermarket, vying for attention next to the homegrown cabbages and parsnips.

Life suddenly becomes expensive overnight with the formation of the European Union. The currency, the government informs us, has to be changed, to embrace the decimalized system, the politicians assuring us it is a necessary step so that we might fit in with our future trading partners. This foray into decimalization is a mammoth undertaking, machines that accept money having to be converted to the new coin of the realm. The London underground system is a disaster scene. Many fail to notice in the ensuing mess that prices have doubled overnight. Older people will never really recover from yet another burden to their aging brains and withering pocket books. In the aftermath of this seismic shift to align us with our future partners, Britain decides not to adopt the Euro!

Leaving our former trading partners in the lurch, they quickly pick up the slack, finding new allies in Asia. We, instead, have to deal with the likes of France and Spain, paying exorbitant prices for their expensive produce and creating in the process a middle class from former peasants in these places.

Having resigned rapidly and with some regrets from my former employment, I try a different tack. I've always loved clothes, spent much time pouring over glossy fashion magazines absorbing the latest fashions, so I decide to sign up with a modeling agency, "The Lucy Clayton School of Modeling," on Bond Street, London W.1.

Jean Shrimpton and many other supermodels of the sixties have passed through these doors. We learn how to prance up and down a catwalk, hips thrust forward, books piled on the head. False eyelashes and eyeliner surround the eyes in a raccoon lookalike mode set against a backdrop of a white skin and pale pouty lips. We're instructed in the correct ways to present ourselves, all of which my mother had previously pounded into my skull. Six weeks later I hit the road clasping my photo portfolio under a wing, attempting to sell my new found talent, only to find what I should have known all along—that I'm not that special, different, elongated or required in this rarified zone.

The swinging sixties are screeching to a watered down version of their former selves. The glitterati are less glistening and the infiltration of outsiders gawking is proving to be irritating. Many friends and middle class members of my generation with bankable credentials are leaving England, seeking higher pay in Canada, America, Australia and New Zealand. This exodus, namely "the brain drain," is a sad day for the British Empire, although never acknowledged, a period when a wide swath of this country's most viable, educated

Back to Reality and Beyond

young citizens, the future wealth of the formerly Great Britain, decide to move to more lucrative pastures and opportunities not available to them on their own soil.

My husband already has a green card, the alien's entrance to live in America. He is a desired commodity, an engineer. The U.S.A. is a place to go and make more at least in terms of material wealth. Applying, I receive a green card on the strength of being married to an alien, not qualifying on my own attributes to be part of the brain drain.

We buy an E type convertible Jaguar with a primrose yellow chassis and a black leather interior, picking it up from the factory in Birmingham then racing it back to London on the freshly

Advertising "The Mini" in the Daily Mirror, a British rag December 1969

'Just looking' Kings Road Chelsea

ESCAPE FROM ENGLAND

Miranda & Henry Moore

Married bliss a vicar & a tart

Back to Reality and Beyond

Parting shot before boarding "The Alexander Pushkin" destination America

constructed M1, the first freeway in England. The idea is to take this British beast to America, drive it across country and sell it when we reach California and buy somewhere to live. That's the plan.

My green card set to expire if I don't enter the U.S. by a certain date precludes any further dallying on my part this side of the pond. Accordingly a passage on the Alexander Pushkin, a Russian vessel positioning from Southampton on the South coast of England to New York to perform charter trips to the Caribbean, provides an appealing mode of exit. The Pushkin is taking on paying passengers for the relocating voyage to New York.

My cabin is a bed and a porthole with an ocean view. I'm in heaven. Saying goodbye to the husband who needs to finish and conclude affairs in London, I'm free to revel for seven wonderful days and nights in my space, on my time. A young crowd cheaply positioning themselves on the American continent for the summer are sailing with me. The lure of starlight nights, dancing under the glorious mid-Atlantic heavens proves a fermenting ground for inviting romantic excursions, but under duress I spurn any advances.

The Statue of Liberty holding court on the waterfront greets us. Not that I want to arrive, to spend the rest of my existence circling the world at sea, far from contact with reality seems much more inviting.

Once again on firm terrain, I board the Greyhound bus for Lexington Massachusetts. My seat companion, a young stag about my age is hot to talk, inviting me home to meet his family, an invitation I decline. I'm staying with friends of Peter, a newspaper heiress married to an English Yale graduate who's currently engaged in sorting out the signage on the Aga Khan's resort on Corsica. They live in a beautiful house with two sons five and seven years of age, brothers who fight continuously. After a few weeks and showing me the ropes, all four take off on vacation leaving me to tend the estate. An old Volvo is at my disposal. It's an automatic, a breed I have not yet encountered, a rarity in Britain. "It's easy," I'm told. "Just don't get any tickets!"

Having never actually driven on a freeway and only once having sampled such a highway as a passenger didn't bother me. After a few false starts, with the new-to-me automatic gear, instead of the stick shift I had learnt to drive with, I take off for parts unknown. I manage amazingly to enter freeways the wrong way and survive. The road signs are strange new features. I eventually succeed in getting on the freeway in the right direction but find myself continuously going way beyond my planned destinations, not being able to translate the signs fast enough. It's all an adventure and worth the jeers, embarrassment and strange hand signals proffered in my direction.

A temporary job as a secretary at a stockbroker's office keeps the cash flowing until Peter arrives and we move into a flat above an Italian restaurant on Beacon Hill. The guys downstairs are friendly, often inviting us after hours to share the leftovers from the dining room. We notice black limousines constantly arriving and departing nocturnally below our windows. Shots are fired, followed by the sounds of glass shattering. The building, we find out, is owned by the Mafia.

Hating the monotony of the nine to five syndrome, I decide to explore a quintessential part of American culture, a job as a Playboy Bunny.

Arriving for my interview I'm zipped into a bunny suit to be eyeballed by the powers that pick the specimens for this sought after position. This apparently is a great honor bestowed upon a select few. According to the Bunny Manual, only forty out of five hundred girls succeed in attaining this vaunted vocation! To have the right to dive into a life of male dominance and female subservience is indeed a triumph. I'm accepted into the fold! For me it's a journey into another zone, somewhat like visiting a different country or planet.

The bunny uniform, another uniform to add to my repertoire, resembles a one piece bathing costume with fierce whalebone ribs like a corset. The girls are poured into this straight jacket for the duration of their shift. They hold their breath as the wardrobe mistress zips them up. It's designed to give emphasis to the waistline and is meant to squeeze the female attributes of the upper torso upwards to create a more stunning vista. If not adequately endowed, a few stockings stuffed under a less than spectacular pair of bosoms, achieves the same effect. We also learn, later on the floor, to augment the size of our mammary glands by stuffing covert tips between the globes, bolstering our boobs and our wallets at the same time. Black hose, Bunny ears, a white collar and cuffs, cuff links, a black bow tie, high heels, a fluffy white tail and a nametag complete the outfit.

A two-week training course ensues. The prospective Bunny is presented with two pink manuals, which reveal every aspect of future employment to be diligently adhered to if successfully completing the course.

We learn by heart, forty-nine popular mixed drinks—the pink squirrel, the banshee, the Senor Playboy, to name a few—each to be

Lexington, Massachusetts

Back to Reality and Beyond

Exploring American culture

served in the proper (one of thirteen) glasses or mugs. Each beverage has to be accompanied by the specifically required garnish, stirrer or cocktail straw.

We're informed of the rule regarding mingling. "Mingling by any female employee with any patron or guest is not allowed and shall be cause for immediate dismissal. Bunnies may, however, converse with patrons, provided that conversation is limited to a polite exchange of pleasantries and information about the Playboy Clubs. A Bunny may never, under any circumstances, divulge personal information about herself or any other Bunny. A Bunny may, at some clubs, have a picture taken or dance with a patron, provided there is no physical contact whatsoever. Again, any violation of this rule will be grounds for immediate dismissal."

Continuing to listen as if our lives would teeter on extinction if these commands were not heeded, we grasp that repeated costume offences such as bunny ears not worn in the center of the head or bent incorrectly, bikini panties showing or not worn, or having an unkempt, unclean or fluffless tail, all accrue demerits. A long list of other offences makes us quake in our nasty pastel colored stiletto heels. Enough demerits, and you guessed it, is grounds for immediate dismissal.

We are advised that, "Good grooming starts with a daily bath and a good deodorant," to always remember that the General Manager is, in bunny speak 'the head man of your hutch,' that 'Bunnies should address male supervisory personnel as Mr....., and accept instructions in a cheerful, cooperative manner,' that 'Bunnies on arrival will report to the Bunny Mother for appearance inspection."

We aspiring Bunnies have to master the "Bunny dip", the "Bunny stance" and the "Bunny perch". The Bunny dip is used when a Bunny sets napkins or drinks on the far end of a table, she does not awkwardly reach across the table—she does the Bunny dip. This keeps her tray away from the patrons and enables her to give graceful, stylized service. The Bunny dip is performed by arching the back as much as possible, then bending the knees to whatever degree is necessary. Raise the left heel as you bend the knees. (Attempting this while wearing stilettos with a tray full of drinks is not to be scoffed at!)

Bunnies have time cards to be signed in and out by the floor manager, on arrival, departure and for breaks, which have to be authorized. A Bunny receives a demerit for every minute taken over the ordained break time.

There are even rules for Bunny off the job. "Although we do not in any way try to control your behavior away from the club, you must always conduct yourself in a manner that can only bring credit to your job and the other Bunnies with whom you work." I like two of the helpful hints for these glorified waitresses. "Hose should be rinsed in cold water and refrigerated before wearing for extra service, and to relieve tired feet try rolling them over an empty coke bottle."

We're all young. I don't think Bunnies are allowed to grow old. Several of the women I encounter while squeezing our assets into the required outfit in the dressing room, are here for reasons similar to mine, just masquerading at night to support themselves through school or other causes. One, a Polish girl is striving to become an opera singer and lives with a piano in a magnificent old apartment, devoid of any other ornament. Another student attending law school, poses somewhat naked for a calendar to boost funds and gets the Playboy axe for bad behavior.

These fresh young things are dismissed as temporary contenders by the hardcore career Bunnies, who take the job seriously, sometimes augmenting their goodies to suit the occupation. Plastic surgery is just emerging, often resulting in breasts that resemble the shape and look of baseballs, hard and strangely round. The professional Bunny seems drawn to some of the more notorious low profile card members, frequently turning up for work bruised and raw, only to be sent back home until an undefiled, pure appearance can be presented.

The mob gather in the basement, soft drinks are their style. They practice overt charm and leave big tips. One might be rough and ready in real time, but one always has to be a hero to someone sometime! The cops enter by the basement back door, getting their dues, burgers and drinks on the house. It's a friendly no man's land where all peoples can congregate to enjoy the view.

ESCAPE FROM ENGLAND

We are beholden to the Playboy key holder, the key, a plastic or metal card is required for entrance to any club, a passport to enjoy the uptight "to see— but don't even think of fingering the goods" synthetic atmosphere. A member is welcomed at the entrance by the door Bunny. Covering this position, wearing my blonde afro wig, my accent still pretty much just off the boat, just doing my job, espousing the happy to see you but don't touch required approach, a woman obviously distraught to be accompanying her husband to this den of vice comes through the portals. I greet this unfortunate pair and request to see his key. She takes one look at me before delivering a slap to my face! Taken aback but laughing, I almost say, "Lady, this is about the safest place on the planet. We only want your money. It looks like it's about sex, but it's just a façade, a Disneyland for men who want to play but wouldn't know how to if they tried."

Solo middle-aged men, either single or escaping from another evening of domestic bliss often find comfort within these confines. A Bunny is always ready to bend an ear, even if not as discreetly as requested by management, to listen to their patter. I have a couple of these gents who ask to sit at one of my tables. One is an immaculately turned out, refined guy from the Caribbean who enjoys mingling with my accent and attitude, the old colonial touch. The other is a nerdy looking specimen with no evident natural splendor but a wicked sense of humor, a quality I have always found irresistible. One evening he tells me the reason his last wife quit. At the breakfast table she had inquired what he would like to eat. He replied, "Two eggs, one boiled and one fried." That, he divulges, was the strategic last straw before she walked out.

I get off work late at night, and walk home across the common to Beacon Hill. Mentioning this to the girls, they reel in disbelief, amazed that I'm still around to tell the tale. Used to walking around most parts of London during any of the twenty-four hours without anxiety, I vow to curtail this apparently perilous excursion and take a taxi instead.

Arriving stateside with my modeling portfolio intact, I successfully snag some catwalk work, making a few appearances on T.V. in the process. This would be something to talk about in England, there being only three channels servicing the whole country, but in America it's not a big deal.

We furnish the flat above the restaurant with stuff found on the sidewalk, abandoned by university students when leaving town. We possess nothing of real value and are consequently flummoxed when this magpie's nest is broken into, our assailants only finding and making off with a wad of greenbacks, tips from the club and a ruby ring set in gold, a gift from a playboy patron, which in spite of much resistance on my part, had been pushed into my palm as a tip! It's a strange feeling to know that an intruder had been rifling through our meager offerings. We need to know who and why? It turns out that the landlord's son had been in the building that day, keys to all the apartments in his pocket.

A call to the landlord results in an invitation to his office to sort things out. Following through that afternoon, we arrive in a raunchy part of town, a burly guy manning the entrance to our destination wants to know our business before we are ushered in to wait for the boss. Blinking from the brightness of the day outside and the sudden darkness inside, we become aware of girls in pasties climbing poles, cavorting on platforms above men hovering over drinks. This is not how I had planned my afternoon off. The boss, exuding an oily charm, listens patiently to our tale, inviting us up to his house in the country to iron things out. Peter, always ready for a change of scenery, agrees, much to my chagrin. This doesn't sound like something I want to pursue. I've already seen enough. What other pleasures await us?

On the shores of the Atlantic Ocean an expensive piece of real estate looms through the windshield. Venturing through the portals, feeling rather queasy at this assignation, life sized porcelain leopards stationed each side of the entrance leer in our direction as we are sucked into a twilight zone of gold leather button tufted sofas and walls hung with gilded flock wallpaper. Velvet drapes collide with elaborate, heavy rococo, gold painted furniture. Underfoot, thick carpets ooze, overhead chandeliers sparkle, illuminating a temple of tasteless tackiness. Arranging ourselves on the sofas we are plied with drinks and platitudes, a smarmy, overbearing attitude wafting dangerously around the pleasantries as sensations of foreboding wash over us.

Even Peter gets the message: get out. Forget this ill-advised investigation. Write it off. Surely a close brush with the belly of the snake is enough. Let's exit with skins intact! Chalking it up as an excursion into new territory, an experience to avoid in future, we retreat behind our best accents, turn on the full British charm and plaster the old geezer with an overdose of compliments and now refer to the heist as obviously a mistake, a case of mistaken identity. Our host glowing with vindication offers us another glass. But we have to excuse ourselves, showtime at the Bunny club is drawing nigh. He ushers us out delighted with the outcome, while we acknowledge when out of earshot that a few greenbacks and a ruby ring are not that important.

The Jag arrives by boat, heralding a new segment in our adventures. A trip to San Francisco, our final destination, dances provocatively on the horizon and demands attention. A short six day excursion taking a direct route would be far too simple. We plan to linger and loiter, to gain knowledge of this immense land. We have the time, the transport and each other, two sleeping bags, a camera and the will to wander.

Everything fits into the trunk of the car. It has to, the Jag is sleekly glamorous but lacks a luggage rack or other space to stuff & store belongings. This particular mode of transportation has black leather seats and is not equipped with air conditioning, disadvantages we will find out when clocking up the miles in Florida and Texas in the blazing summer heat. The first lap will be north to Quebec. Driving a primrose yellow E type convertible we find is not for shy retiring types or those seeking a low profile existence, especially when it's still wearing British number plates.

Pulled over by the Canadian customs officials when attempting to sail across the border slows down our escape. Peter dressed in pink bell bottoms, flowing black curls cascading down to his shoulders and that damn British accent is definitely not their cup of tea: guilty until proven otherwise. These gents are unaware that my husband, after suffering a near fatal motorbike accident at twenty one resulting in his being sedated by drugs for six months while on the road to recovery, never touched them again. He might be persuaded to partake of a small beer or glass of wine under peer pressure but he doesn't need the buzz. He's high enough already, but what a perfect decoy at our expense!

We are commanded to vacate our steed and wait. The border agents take their time removing and inspecting carefully every tightly packed article from the vehicle, turning the car inside out. They are so sure they will find something. We look the part, presumed guilty before the fact! Finding nothing, disappointed, they leave the stuff sitting on the sidewalk. We take our time repacking before revving up the engines, making sure a blast of fumes and dust lands in their unfulfilled faces as we soar into their territory. Welcome to Canada!

Quebecois admit to speaking French with what they term is the old accent. To an ear that is acclimatized to the Parisian version, their lingo is almost unintelligible. After so much time spent arriving we are exhausted and seek out somewhere to recover and try the YMCA in an effort to stay within our budget. The "Y' turns out to be a large gymnasium with cots and planks to collapse on. As we decompress, we realize that we have checked into an insane asylum. An ambiance of chaos and discord prevails, altercations and fights erupting all around us. Using our sleeping bags to soften the experience, we feign slumber clinging tightly to our funds stashed under our clothes and leave hurriedly in the morning to hit the sights of Quebec City.

On the streets a decidedly anti-British atmosphere is in full force, restaurants refuse to serve us, nightclubs deny admittance. We're hip to the fact that the inhabitants of this zone are known to have anti-British tantrums periodically, we find out that we've arrived just in time to experience such an event. Adopting the stiff upper lip and after sampling our first taste of discrimination on this continent and the less than pleasant conditions at the YMCA, we decide to spend the next night safely in the expensive Chateau Frontenac, a hotel dating from the nineteenth century which had previously sheltered the likes of George 1V of England, Alfred Hitchcock and Montgomery Clift. Forgetting the bad sentiments throbbing outside of these walls, we succumb to the luxury that only money can buy.

After a night enjoying to the fullest extent the wonders of crisp clean sheets and fluffy pillows we leave for Prince Edward Island, named after the fourth son of George III of England, father of Queen Victoria. It became a fashionable retreat for the British nobility in the 19th century and is now inhabited by people of Scottish, English and Irish descent. Parking the car we ferry across the water, a pony and trap with a Dickensian character wielding a whip, a top hat perched on his head, deposits us at a Victorian enclave far from the madding crowds fomenting on the streets of Quebec City. Far from the French point of view, we can take in the pastoral beauty of a place still planted in past times.

Back on the mainland deciding to avoid further friction we head west. Endless wheat fields later we arrive in Toronto to encounter a modern, English speaking city teeming with immigrants from all over, residing in harmony, refreshingly making a go of it. We notice how clean Canada is. The lack of litter is a glorious sight, but we discover that although this land is spotlessly clean, it's not exactly exciting.

Returning to the States, we sail through American immigration without a problem and heading south, we avoid major cities, relishing the exuberant spring foliage of the East Coast. A mandatory stop at Gettysburg is on the agenda to reflect on scenes from the Civil War. The canons are still in position, to the delight and endless fascination of my man. This isn't exactly my idea of entertainment and my interest is on the wane, my mind drifting back to the shallow pleasures of the frivolous London life I left behind.

A food bonanza awaits us in Savannah and Charleston. We would have lingered longer at these charmed spots if more aware of the vast culinary desert that stretched before us. A period of endless days of nothing else available but a tough tasteless Howard Johnson hamburger and iceberg lettuce served with a variety of dubious dressings, the supposedly French dressing, a substance totally devoid of Gallic origins. Astonishment greets my request for oil and vinegar, recognizable condiments, not an evil mixture of undecipherable ingredients.

The meals are humorously large, the contents nondescript at best. We witness everywhere the endless flow of a harsh brown liquid labeled coffee, which bears no resemblance to that answering to the same name in Europe. We're intrigued how the moment the cup is empty a waitress appears, pot in hand, to refill it. This beverage is obviously a necessary cog in the American wheel of life.

The year is 1971, gas is thirty-nine cents a gallon and McDonalds has sold thirty six million hamburgers. A sign saying that it is so, proudly hangs outside each restaurant they operate.

In the south our accents from the old country are warmly and widely received. Invitations to stay abound. The friendliness is unimaginable and buoys us on our journey. How quickly life can change, "Britishness" now being our prime card. Of course Peter plays it up to the hilt.

When no offer of accommodation rears its head, we try camping out in far flung deserted areas, sometimes only to be rudely awakened by flashlights beaming in our faces and instructions by the local police to move along.

An official campground is a unique experience to savor at least once. As we pull in, looks of disbelief greet us, judging us to be obvious novices at this lifestyle, laughably lacking the convenience of a Winnebago, a virtual house on wheels. Wanting to get some sleep after hours on the road, we get a spot and whip the sleeping bags out of the "E," rolling them out on Terra Firma before settling in for the night, surrounded by our fellow humans barbequing, drinking beer and enjoying all the paraphernalia of back home. Waking up after a fitful sleep, I have difficulty opening my eyes, my face is puffy and swollen, ravaged by marauding insects. I vow to skip camping out in future, Motel 6 from now on... but I have yet to encounter the bed bug!

Back to Reality and Beyond

Florida is now racing past under our wheels. After picture perfect Saint Augustine, we quickly tire of the retirement home atmosphere and beaches where motorcars are allowed to roam. The smell of bad air conditioning in cheap motels will always be with me. Visiting in the month of May, driving a car not suited to such climes, we travel with the top down to avoid frying on the black seats, now covered with towels to stop our bums from sticking to the perspiring leather. We make the acquaintance of the big black honeymoon flies that mate mid air at this time of the year, not able to tear themselves apart for several days. Many meet their doom on our windscreen while copulating as we plunge down the peninsula, flying past palms trees.

After a brief glimpse at Miami and deciding to avoid this seedy slice of life thriving beneath the sun, we drive out of town, park the 'E' in a field paying the farmer, the owner of this piece of planet earth, for the honor. We need to take a break from the endless driving and North America.

The Caribbean lies at our feet. St Thomas a haven for shopping and duty free is not to our taste, the pristine stretches of Tortola and Virgin Gorda are gorgeous but cater exclusively to yachts and the well shod, others we soon grasp, need not apply! Disembarking from a light aircraft in Anguilla, a British enclave, a few ramshackle huts emerge out of the dust, we have stumbled across a diamond in the rough, years before being cut, polished and suitable for the upper crust tourist.

Taking stock of our latest dilemma, deliberating our next move, a jeep careens past, lurching to a standstill when catching sight of us. The jeep is full of British cops, patrolling the island. Anguilla is having a war! The U.K. is trying to unload their colony and foist it on the neighboring islands of St. Kitts and Nevis. The Anguillans are up in arms wanting nothing to do with the idea, wanting to instead grab their independence. Rumors of unrest and bad behavior had reached the British shores, growing in size and ferocity as they crossed the oceans resulting in an elite London police force being sent to quell the restless natives.

"Want a lift to the pub? the coppers ask. Two drinking establishments have been strategically installed at opposite ends of this three by sixteen mile island, separated by a dirt road. Racing between the two effectively encompasses the whole territory and a cold beer is just the job to keep cool between shifts.

Our new heroes are thrilled to be missing yet another grey dreary English summer, trudging with their truncheons on the cold wet streets of home. They aren't sure why they are here but then neither are we! We solemnly promise not to utter a word about what is actually transpiring lest the controlling powers in Westminster cut short their vacation!

The natives are few and low key, only one diagnosed as off her rocker is temporarily confined to the tiny jail, apparently more of a risk to herself than anyone else and inside for her own good. Additional hammocks are strung outside the make do police headquarters, providing us with a place to stay.

New recruits fresh from England are scheduled to arrive, a big event in these parts as not much happens here, besides carousing and taking it easy in hammocks after a hard day drinking.

We dress to greet the new crop of cops consigned to duty in paradise. Standard uniforms are not suited to this clime and have been replaced by flowered shirts and shorts, a variety of hats including a French policeman's are worn. A squad of pigs are rounded up, secured by leashes and accompany us to the air-strip. This war, after all, has been dubbed "the bay of piglets".

The heavy cargo aircraft looms in the distance and drops onto the dusty strip, immediately qualifying as the most exciting recent event in Anguillan history. Witnessing this bulky giant landing in such a small expanse is an amazing sight, the pilot screeching the brakes to stop this monster from plowing into the surrounding scrubby landscape and nearby ocean. As the cloud of dirt subsides an opening in the undercarriage reveals the latest offerings from London. Neatly turned out, they look confused, as if they have arrived in the wrong place. They hesitate, but we, although not clad in official uniforms speak the King's English and soon they are initiated into the clan and the war that never was.

In the end, maybe it's because of the fun loving coppers that the Anguillans demand they remain under British rule rather than be subjugated by their neighbors or themselves.

Island hopping is the name of the game. Sitting in an English garden, steel drums blasting, the roses bobbing in the breeze, in the shadow of Nelson's dockyard we take advantage of Antigua's beverage of choice, the local rum. An expat American seems happy to see us. He makes a living exporting tropical fish. An invitation to stay at his place is offered and happily received. It's a cottage set high on a hill of equatorial splendor, overlooking a beach of white sand, the warm pellucid waters lap invitingly below. Peter is delighted to be amongst so much history. I'm ecstatic to slow down and enjoy the overt sensual attributes of mother nature.

We drop in on Saint Lucia and Barbados, the latter already fully aware and equipped to cater to the foreigner. The Barbadians are sophisticated, sleek and glamorous, so perfectly in sync with their exotic surroundings.

Running low on funds, we need to return to America to work, to replenish our bank account, to finance the remainder of the traipse across the North American continent. We have stayed away longer than anticipated, captivated by the steamy, slow Caribbean lifestyle.

The 'E' still graces the turf where we left it. Thrilled it's still there, that it has not been sold for ransom, we pay the farmer off and head up the West coast of Florida. Disneyland in Orlando is set to open its doors, maybe we can land a couple of jobs? Two long-haired types with a strange way of putting words together - Mickey Mouse with a foreign accent? No way, we don't even get to procure an application, getting the shaft before we even get in the door!

Realizing that we are not blue eyed, blonde thoroughbred Americans, we pick up our lives and move on, only to be greeted by the red tide, an unbelievable stench all along the Gulf of Mexico between Florida and Louisiana, a phenomena created by sea dwelling plants that spiral out of control and produce toxins that harm and kill other residents of their watery domain. Millions of sea creatures have been annihilated and thrown up on the beaches to rot, the smell is overwhelming. There is no chance of avoiding this obnoxious odor. The relentless heat precludes closing the top on the Jag unless we want to expire and melt in the bucket seats.

After a long nauseating six hundred mile drive, New Orleans is within our sights, materializing invitingly on the excruciatingly flat horizon.

Twisting and turning in the hot interior of the 'E', an itch that will not subside erupts on my backside, jumping and spreading, it's keeping me awake at night, I'm tearing at my flesh. Consulting several doctors en route, this affliction is a mystery to all who inspect my rear end. They have no clue as to what this might be! In agony I writhe on the black leather, these formerly sexy seats now intensifying my dilemma. The long, long bridge to New Orleans goes on forever before we finally reach this fabled terrain and head straight for the emergency room at the public hospital.

The waiting area is vast, people of all ages and colors mill around or sprawl on the hard utilitarian benches, some in pain, others bleeding from gaping wounds. Chaos and distress is everywhere, and no one is paying any attention. The heat is unbearable. It's August and air conditioning has yet to arrive at this sad institution, the last resort for people trying to get by. I reach for a paper cup at the water fountain to revive my diminishing powers and collapse.

Regaining consciousness, I'm vaguely aware of a man in a white coat hovering over my now naked body asking me whether I mind if a group of students look and learn from my hapless state. He has identified my problem, a condition he hasn't seen in forty years! I agree to all terms, anything to be released from this torture and am soon surrounded by a group of highly interested young men bent on scrutinizing my behind. The prognosis is that probably while sitting on a tropical beach, my rear end had been invaded by worms from fluid or other bodily waste deposited from a pig/dog? onto the sand.

I apply topically the prescribed lotion and after days of misery, I can now sleep at night. My body is released from the tumult and turmoil of tropical infiltrators.

In the French quarter we rent a room in an apartment and set about roaming the streets looking for work. Peter secures an engineering stint, I get to be a hostess at My Father's Moustache, a Jazz club on Bourbon Street where I make yet another cultural faux pas on my first day innocently requesting a rubber, which to an English ear translates as an eraser, causing much mirth from my new colleagues. Staying for six weeks in this multi erogenous zone, we are happily and without question accepted and included. In this one square mile, whatever the creed, color or sexual preferences, everyone is embraced.

Soft shell crabs, gumbo and jambalaya, a carnival of cuisine awaits any traveler to these parts. We stock up hungrily, knowing that a leaner menu awaits us on the road to California. Steamer Tramp ships ply the waters of the Mississippi, jazz cruises drift nightly up and down the river against a backdrop of long pale green moss dripping from the live oak trees. Pumpkins glow in the outdoor street market where the air is starting to have a slight chill. It's time to climb into our yellow friend.

Back on the road with enough cash to finance the last leg of our expedition we surge into Texas, briefly taking in the Houston Astrodome, a break from rolling through flat, flatter and the flattest scenery with oil derricks dotting the landscape or lack of it, instead of trees!

Forging through this desultory scene we take only the absolutely necessary breaks to gas up and piss. We slow down going through small towns, making sure we do not go over the speed limit, noting that there is always a cop to hand out a ticket if you do. Having to consume something edible on this mad dash through no man's land, we entertain questionable venues to assuage this human requirement. Entering a coffee shop in rural Texas I'm impressed by the men decked out in their best cowboy garb. Passionate about clothes, I'm thrilled to witness these Texans dressed and pressed to the hilt, a splendid sight in cowboy boots, jeans, hats, all the attributes of western glory—so well and conspicuously turned out that I wonder if they might be playing for the other team. Poor sods watching us emerge from the depths of the primrose Jag to quench our hunger and thirst, they just have no concept of what we might be. Life has been too cruel to allow them much insight into the real world beyond their small frontier. They whisper, plot and watch as we gnaw on the offerings of the day. Mean eyes dart, distasteful remarks are launched in our direction.

Back to Reality and Beyond

Surmising that we are not particularly welcome, that to these eyes, strangers are a suspicious breed and not wanting to find out more, we eat and get out of town. Thanks, guys, for making us feel so at home, and happy trails to you, too. May you drown in your own natural resources!

With relief we escape Texas and breeze into New Mexico, stopping to visit the Carlsbad Caverns. Taking the elevator down to the depths of the earth, the stalactites and mites are totally and wonderfully mind boggling. We, in comparison, are small fry.

Santa Fe is so low key we almost fail to notice that we have arrived. Trekking up to Taos to catch a glimpse of the Pueblo Indians, a group of stucco flat buildings greets us. It seems we are the only people interested in climbing the ladders onto the roofs to visit. It's cold. The children are playing in tattered clothing, snot flowing from their nostrils. A sense of abandonment and sickness, rejection and unhappiness permeates the air. No one appears to mind as we mingle with their strife. It's as if the clock is stuck motionless in their backyard as the rest of the outside world moves on.

We head back to Route 66, a stretch of tarmac often fondly celebrated in songs. It's the fastest route to take, not yet abandoned, bypassed by so called prosperity, and relegated to the status of an historical relic. We are on course for Flagstaff. Snow falls as we approach. A big rig, pristine and shiny, a well maintained truck manned by a dapper cowboy challenges us to a race into town. He ploughs ahead, we resist the urge to join in the scuffle, letting him streak ahead. Following in his tracks, we later unfortunately discover his rig overturned and wrecked by the side of the road.

It's Saturday night - a time to boogie at the local dancehall. I'm spellbound, totally enthralled by the women in cowgirl attire, wide skirts with billowing petticoats, boots, hats and frilly blouses cavorting with checkered shirted, jean encased, cowboy booted males. I have never seen anything like it. I pinch myself. Is this the twentieth century? I realize that I am very far from home.

The Petrified Forest crosses our path, we have to take a break for a quick look. To a European acquainted with small, organized environments, these expanses of the planet are vast and terrifyingly magnificent, basking in their state of natural wilderness. In this sea of dead, fossilized wood, we lose our way, visions of our corpses starved, dehydrated, mutilated by the residents of this untamed desolate expanse start to fester, as our imaginations spin into high gear. To the rescue, a park ranger. He's doing a last check before locking up and heading for home.

The Grand Canyon is shrouded in fog. We stand and strain to appreciate this wonder. The fog does not lift and we move on.

We are now hell bent on going full throttle to San Francisco. Enough is enough; We need to arrive. Exiting the Bay Bridge when entering this much lauded oasis, the first thing I notice is the Hills Brothers billboard depicting a man in a flowing tunic and turban advertising their product, coffee! I marvel that an ugly concrete freeway obstructs the magnificent bay view.

Back to Reality and Beyond

*British coppers ready to greet a new crop of cops to Anguilla
and the war that never was, circa 1971*

Finally California

CHAPTER SEVEN

The Land of Opportunity

A fellow Englishman, a friend of Peter, has organized an apartment for us on Pacific Heights, owned by a certain Daisy Upham. We had already encountered Daisy in Boston, where she appeared on scene to research her ancestors who had arrived from Plymouth, England on The Mayflower. We had duly escorted her around town, wined and dined her. Now we are on her turf and that is exactly what it is!

Ensconced on the second floor at Divisadero and Jackson we soon understand that Daisy pulls the strings. Peter's friend resides on the first floor, his girlfriend in the basement and Daisy reigns supreme on the top floor. Never married or having borne children, Daisy is now seventy-five years old. In her youth she played tennis, perfected her swimming skills at the Sutro Baths and had inherited the building we now call home on the demise of her father. Her only living relative a niece, she finds annoying and refuses to see. We duly note that Peter's friend seems to be grooming himself to take over her considerable worldly wealth when her departure time arrives.

Every evening it's mandatory to ascend to the Daisy apartment, where she prepares dinner whether or not you like or want it. We're required to attend, it's part of the deal for cheap rent and a great location. She needs company and we provide it. Other friends drop by. It's an international crowd. Claude hails from Algeria, a French national who had grown up in this former colony but had been forced to flee during the Algerian War, which had greatly diminished his nervous system, resulting in a twitch that has become a permanent part of his range of facial expressions. He recalls, when pressed, scenes of women raped, pregnant females having their stomachs slashed, fetuses spilling onto the ground, tales of blood & guts flowing freely in the streets. He always arrives clutching his own bottle of salad dressing, often accompanied by his diminutive ami, Jacques, as well as a few girlfriends in tow. Daisy puts up with the females but we are relegated to the back of the bus as she bathes in the male attention, which is amply provided by all the young stallions she has gathered in her salon. They dutifully deliver the charm, stroking her feathers in the right direction, while feasting on the free food.

At dinnertime, the television continually hovers in the background, the news showing footage of the latest action in Vietnam, flag draped coffins returning home. On Thanksgiving and Christmas, we dress in festive attire, the air thick with the aroma of marijuana. Daisy appears not to notice; she is so thrilled to have a few young studs around to regale with her history. After dinner the girls are dispatched to the kitchen to wash and dry while our hostess slurps up the testosterone.

Needing to find work I draw on my secretarial skills and sign on with the Pat Franklyn Agency. Pat another Englishwoman runs a tight boat, catering to a potent string of companies. She sweetly informs me that I need to tone down my London look. "Try and be more subdued, dear. The mini skirt has not yet reached these shores. That lacy see-through shirt is too much of a distraction."

Following her advice I land a few temporary assignments, the most notable of which is aboard the Walter Landor boat, The Klamath, docked next to the Ferry building in San Francisco. Walter, of German descent, aspires to be the perfect English Gentleman. Anything English is top hole! Advertising is his game, promoting products, creating logos and packaging. I struggle with the endless differences between the American and English languages and nausea from the perpetual motion inflicted by the sea, my desk and typewriter gently swaying in sync with the movement of the waves. I have arrived just in time for Christmas and on board the Landor boat is where society gathers to celebrate the occasion. Perfect timing on my part! The local elite appear to be friendly and chatty, not at all similar to those strutting on such an elevated level in England, where the correct accent and pedigree are required to breathe such rarified air.

After the seasonal distractions, tied once again to my old enemy, the typewriter, and the prospect of endless letters dancing in motion, I decide to apply for a nighttime job at my old acquaintance, the Playboy Club, here in San Francisco. I'm readmitted into the Hutch but have to endure another round of indoctrination before deemed fit for show time. The release from dining with Daisy is worth the inconvenience.

People are experimenting with various sexual roles. It's fashionable for heterosexuals to experiment with same sex encounters, and mate-swapping orgies are trending, none of which entice or interest me. Terry, Peter's friend is always ready for a walk on social ground not yet tried. Unwittingly, at least on my part, my dear husband and I get drawn into a suburban house to behold naked couples in various stages of intercourse, littering the sofas, floors, any available space. Terry sheds his garb wanting to join in the display, inviting me to do likewise. Peter, excited by so much action has disappeared in the confusion. Maintaining the clothes on my back, I decline the advances of our British comrade and repulsed by the sight of so many middle aged unappealing bodies exploring each other's intimate anatomies, I take refuge in the garden, preferring to smell the roses rather than rear ends and seminal fluid.

The invitation to a cocktail party in Sausalito sounds like an innocuous diversion. As usual at these contrived events the guests stand around, glass in hand, making polite conversation, this particular entourage are sporting jaunty hats and racy bow ties but below the elegant neckwear bare skin is the order of the day. If only these partygoers had been of more interesting proportions, portraying beauty rather than unattractive attributes it might have been more rewarding! At least, once the room becomes crowded, what loiters below the raised arm is not so conspicuous. I guess it's construed as titillating. To my mind it appears a banal stab at Bacchanalia.

San Francisco is so much smaller than its reputation, and quite provincial compared to London. I'm too young to realize that is its charm. I tire instantly of the bar scene, Isn't there more to life than this raw girl meets boy saga? Many of my peers spend their spare time, bums draped over a bar stool at Henry Africa's fern bar on Van Ness guzzling down Gallo wine in the throes of the meat market pick up scene, waiting for some action. Lazing spread eagled in a chair clasping a drink at Enrico's on Broadway is more my style, after an evening hustling at the nearby Bunny Club, sitting outside on the sidewalk, jostled by tourists from the Midwest and big breasted babes on their way to work at the strip clubs which dominate the bustling strip. "Hey isn't that Carol Doda strolling by – the all American cultural icon – one of the first women to dance topless and to have her twin peaks augmented from size 34 to 44?"

Two skyscrapers dominate the downtown scene, the much hated and contested Bank of America building, which appears massive in scale and the much loved Transamerica Pyramid.

As a pair, Peter and I succumb to the lure of Tahoe, our German colleagues persuading us to join in the fun, and invitations to stay at their rustic log cabins are not refused. These stalwart members of the ski brigade rise at the crack of dawn, are fed, bright and shiny and by 7 a.m., they're ready to attack the slopes, to get in a complete day of snow. We English types prefer to loll and linger getting a leisurely late start, paying more attention to the après ski.

We dance our arses off at Bimbos on Columbus Avenue, imbibe Irish coffees at The Buena Vista Bar. We freeze in the fog attending the concerts at Stern Grove, boat on the bay, down English beer at the Pelican Inn at Muir Beach and barbeque our bodies on Stinson Beach. But in spite of all the above diversions I want to fly again, to shed the caul of claustrophobia suffocating my aura when planted securely on planet earth.

In Boston, a colleague had mentioned a company called World Airways based in Oakland California, a charter company with flights worldwide. Forget the tedious duties of domestic flying, taking off and landing several times in a day, I long for the long haul flights, international flying. I had applied to World Airways immediately on my arrival in San Francisco and now they are hiring. My interview is imminent.

When filling out the application I waver at how to approach the box marked married or single, knowing that if I tick the former, my quest will automatically be garbage, an airline industry nasty dark little secret. I tick single. Damn, I can get a divorce if necessary.

ESCAPE FROM ENGLAND

I pass the first and second interviews and am duly awarded a date to commence my introduction, yet again into the world I wish to rejoin.

Driving the Jaguar still bearing English number plates to and fro destination Oakland airport arouses a virulent desire in many a macho male to chase, race and squeeze this yellow interloper off the road, especially truckers. With the top down, my long hair flying in the wind I'm obviously vying for their attention, offering an open invitation! Being hauled over by the California highway patrol is also routine procedure.

The "E" type constantly needs tune ups to sooth it's temperamental soul, parking on the street is a lesson in peoples' disregard and disrespect, the back and front of this glamorous beast getting dinged and dented beyond belief. But the moment of pure disbelief is discovering the convertible top slashed and lying in a sad black heap. We need to fix this monster up and cash it in.

The term stewardess is ancient history. I'm now training to be a flight attendant. The emphasis this time around is strictly about safety, mechanical in nature. How to handle the equipment, the fire extinguishers, open the doors in an emergency, inflate the slides, how to get all those pesky passengers out and away from the craft before considering one's own mortality. This is now presented as the real purpose of a flight attendant, why we're on board, not just to smile and smooth ruffled feathers. The British approach had been all about customer service and pleasing the clientele with polished charm.

On purpose I let slip, that I'm married. I hate to lie. The prospect of having to offer up my passport and alien card issued in different names, important pieces of paperwork in this line of work when traipsing through immigration frontiers and being confronted with questions makes me queasy. Knowing that President Johnson passed the Act of Non Discrimination in 1964 makes me confident that termination on those grounds, from a company that relies heavily on government contracts to keep afloat, is not a rational possibility.

A shudder of horror rattles through the classroom. The lesson continues but I'm extracted from my seat and chaperoned to the office of Vice President Bailey Raines, who in blistering terms informs me that I lied on my application and pronounces my dismissal. I let him bleat and bellow and watch the veins on his neck bulge while his index finger wildly jabs the air. When the ranting subsides, I inform him that the mere boxes regarding status on the application form are illegal. This cuts no chaff with the man in charge of my demise.

If they want a fight, they'll get it. A visit to the offices of the Equal Employment Opportunity to file a complaint is the next move. Peter and I also file a dissolution of marriage just in case. We write letters to the President of World Airways, the Chairman of the Board and to Richard Nixon the residing American President, covering all angles to resurrect the future of Ms. Crimp.

I now have a lawyer, a charming African American man from the Equal Employment Opportunity Commission, and the Fair Employment Practice Commission is investigating too. All the guns are loaded – we're ready for action.

I hardly have time to collect my unemployment pay or enjoy trips to the nature reserve at Devil's point South of San Francisco to join the other jobless on the beach sunbathing nude. World Airways crumbles before the case ever reaches court obviously taken by surprise that a mere female wanting to be a waitress in the sky would actually contest their decision.

Prior to resuming my training, I have to report to V.P. Bailey Raines. He informs me that World Airways has decided to give me another shot at the training course but lets me know emphatically that the first time anything contrary to regulations occurs, I will be out the door. He spells "out" for me with much feeling.

Not wanting to let me off the hook so easily, lusting to see me squirm a little before letting me sail out of his office, he inquires as to whether I'm getting a divorce. "I'm seeking a dissolution of marriage" I respond, "as this is the procedure in California." "Are you living with your husband?" inquires my interrogator. "I'm complying with the California law regarding this matter" I reply. He shoots back "I have no idea what the divorce laws in California dictate but I've asked you a straight question and want a straight answer." Irritated, I coolly retort, "you have no right asking me personal questions about my private life. Do you question other flight attendants with regard to their intimate affairs?"

V.P. Raines stiffens at what he considers the insolence of a woman actually answering back, spittle forms at the corners of his mouth as he blasts "I know the activities of all the flight attendants under my control. Their parents thank me for looking after their daughters." He adds: "I do not want such virtuous girls corrupted by a usurper lacking integrity."

I raise my eyebrows and tighten my lips at this latest disclosure to suppress laughter. Mr. Raines says I "smirked" and wants to know why. Having never before experienced such degrading comments, I let him know. "I consider my morality unquestionable. My principles, integrity and values are of a high standard and any insinuations to the contrary are not appreciated!"

He can't let go - he tries to squash my spirit or at least make me feel guilty, he needs to regain his supposed stature, to appear to be the big man in the room. "Are you and your husband willing to commit perjury to obtain a divorce – so that you can be employed as a flight attendant?" "We are getting a dissolution of marriage in order that we might both be free to follow the way of life and be employed in the capacity that we desire."

The Vice President continues to waffle on. "The airline industry requires people of integrity (even the validity of this word is losing its integrity), who can be trusted." Presumably to illustrate this point, he informs me that when he initially joined the industry he had witnessed an airplane burst into flames on the runway, that all the flight attendants had panicked, failed to function as required and as a result everybody perished. "What do you have to say about this?"

I proffer the standard by the book response, " I'm well aware that the primary reason for flight attendants on aircraft is for the safety of passengers, and it is of the utmost importance that flight attendants know what to do and how to react in an emergency." Attempting to diffuse the angst filled atmosphere and wind down this session I mention, "I'm exceedingly enthusiastic about becoming a flight attendant once again and I will try to prove to the best of my ability that I am worthy of the position." Just to charm the old sod I apologize for causing so much inconvenience.

Leaving his quarters I feel mildly unwelcome but during the course of that first day, several training instructors come up to me saying that they're glad to see me back. On June 16, 1972 I graduate from flight school, I'm ready to perform the duties of flight attendant for World Airways.

On Friday September 14, 1984 I read in the San Francisco Chronicle that a federal judge has awarded $37.9 million in back pay to female flight attendants who were fired by United Airlines in the

1960s because they were married. U.S district Judge James Moran ordered the award in a class action suit that accused the airline of discrimination because of its "no marriage rule" since rescinded, which had resulted in the dismissal of about 1500 women between 1965 and 1968.

At B.O.A.C. we were ambassadors for our country, we flew around the globe and were handled with kid gloves. Luggage was picked up and positioned for us, thus avoiding the sight of an exhausted stewardess in high heels dragging herself and that suitcase through the airport for all to see after a long flight. Separate rooms were assigned on layovers. We were treated with respect. We responded accordingly.

Now I find myself in the company of an impressive band of globetrotting rip off artists. I stand back aghast, amazed at such entrepreneurial spirit. The unscrewing and removal of wall fixtures in hotels to be carted back home and resurrected, the luxurious German goose down comforters that had graced the hotel bed in Frankfurt, removed and stuffed into a garment bag. Drinking the contents of the alcoholic beverages from the hotel mini bars and refilling them with urine. Where is Mr. Raines when we need him? Probably tranquilizing fathers regarding their delinquent daughters. World Airways is a fly by the seat of your pants, fly by night operation.

I have to wait ninety days for my probation period to expire, before I can become a proud member of Teamsters and can join in the fray! I fly the minimum amount of hours, take advantage of every available furlough and aim to spend every possible moment I can visiting planet earth on discounted tickets. The least amount of time I spend hustling in the aisles and in America the happier I am.

Desperate to escape from Daisy and her increasingly servile

retinue, husband and I relocate to California Street just around the corner from Chinatown. The cable cars rattling past of a morning remind us that it's time to rush into the street and re-park the car rather than be rewarded with a parking ticket.

A man in Tiburon teetering on the cusp of a middle age crisis buys the 'E,' inviting us to his home, where we meet his wife and two adorable offspring. Recognizing the writing on the wall we are not surprised to notice after the sale, the Jag frequently parked overnight opposite our abode, the proud new owner now parading a more appealing piece of talent on his arm. The four thousand dollars we receive for the Jag, about what we paid for it, provides the deposit on a house in Mill Valley California, the start of our real estate empire. We replace our classy ride with a blue Ford Truck.

We move into this newly constructed, three bedroom piece of crap in the spring of 1973, It has a gold shag rug covering most of the floors and cheap white linoleum, but it's all ours! The bed fits in the back of our new set of wheels and we install it in the living room, which provides an unparalleled view at night of the moon as it appears from behind a mountain. We watch it climb high into the sky as we succumb to the wonders of being young and together. We're on track, moving towards our goal of financial success balanced with sun in the bank, dividing our assets equally between fun and investments.

Part of the glamour of the flight attendant life circa 1972 is to be assigned to work in the back of the aircraft, the smoking section. A permanent blue haze hangs over this area of the cabin and gives the fearless flight attendant the opportunity to politely remove a patron's food tray, while smoke is puffed in her face (obviously a sign of gratitude), the butt of this evil addiction often extinguished in the remains of an inedible entrée!

Most of the flights are full to the last drop. World Airways is a charter company. The cramped quarters, the cattle car atmosphere work in perfect cohesion to bring out the worst in people, making them even more demanding than your average wild beast in a cage or human trapped in a tube. Any small malfunction or altercation potentially has the power to blossom into an epic disturbance. Unlike a scheduled flight, a charter flight is a one off deal, an expedition subject to many unforeseen circumstances, anywhere on the globe.

Days are often never ending. Our contract allows the company to schedule sixteen hour work shifts but this time frame often balloons into many more hours on the job and it's all entirely legitimate. If you ever think you're flying with a load of flight crew zombies – you're probably correct! The airline is professionally astute at overlooking overtime, lack of flight crew, any violation on their part of the Teamster book of rules which any flight attendant worth her salt keeps with her at all times. Special pay requests have to be filed for any infraction, a lot of paperwork often changing hands before the dough is forthcoming.

A perfect example of just another typical day in the life of a World Airways indentured serf unfolds as follows. On a flight to Asia from Oakland, while transiting in Anchorage Alaska, the captain informs us of a problem. A new part is required which has to be flown in, as it's not available right here on the ground. It's mid winter, we sit on the tarmac with the passengers, the generators providing heat and any electrical power have ceased to function. Braving the freezing temperatures we calm the passengers with the customary platitudes. "It shouldn't be too much longer. We will soon be on our way."

Flight attendants are often kept in the dark, oblivious to the cause and when it will be resolved, the catch being that if the actual length of the delay is estimated to be more than four hours - crew and passengers have to be removed to a hotel. It's advantageous for the airline to keep knowledge of extensive delays on a minute-by-minute trajectory with only the pit knowing the real scenario.

On this particular mishap the passengers are eventually transported back to the terminal, but the crew are left to stiffen, huddle in blankets onboard. After four additional hours, we too are carted off and housed overnight in a hotel. A perfect illustration of how an innocuous flight can transpire into a twenty-four hour odyssey and beyond.

Consigned to ferry a plane over to Iran, I narrowly avoid ending up as a shish kebab on a Persian dinner plate. We are on our way ostensibly to pick up American and British expats attempting to flee the scene in the wake of the ousting of the Shah, the last King, a puppet of Britain and America, the controllers of bountiful Iranian oil. The Shah has been deposed by the Islamic high priest Ruhollah Khomeini. Mechanics are on board, just in case of a glitch. Maybe they can patch the craft up in a hurry if required!

We are to land at night in a desert, in an undisclosed location, where the expats are gathered for their escape. The moon has taken the night off, the night is black. Not a light twinkles on the ground. There's no sign of a control tower to guide us in. On our final approach just before the wheels touch the dust, the pit abort the landing. For some reason it's not safe to land. The pilot turns the nose upwards, the craft around. Mission interrupted – we're heading back.

On descent into Charleston, the DC8 starts to pitch wildly from side to side, seesawing out of control. The rudder has apparently failed. The Captain instructs us to prepare for an emergency landing. The cockpit door is wide open flapping on its hinges, affording an intimate view of the men up front, ties slack, sweat cascading down their faces as the tarmac ricochets beneath us. The Captain lets us know that "This might be it – the final flight." Sitting in the front rows, some of the cabin crew hold hands and pray, while the more astute members brace for impact, grabbing their ankles.

Somehow the pit brings the bird down with a thump, heavy but in one piece. The tires screech, the rubber smokes. The guys up front emerge from the flight deck totally wasted, pale, shattered, apparently amazed at the outcome. In a state of dazed joy that night Charleston seems more beautiful than ever, the cobbled streets never more glamorous, the food even more divine and everyone feels the need to get totally blasted in celebration of our survival.

I go out of my way to avoid involvement in further dubious adventures, sick leave is an option if everything else fails. Just sitting, sipping pernod by The Seine, the possibility of being whisked away on course for Angola always lurks behind every potted palm, a flight to salvage oilmen wielding guns, firing shots at pursuers as they scramble onboard, the stairs shoved aside for a speedy take off, bullets flying. No thanks, I don't get paid enough or any more for such sorties, in spite of being placed in a scenario, which could make front page news. Staggeringly this is not a volunteer situation.

Vietnamese refugees incarcerated in Thai camps for over two years need to be transferred to Hong Kong, World Airways is awarded the government contract. I'm installed for three weeks right on the waterfront in Kowloon across from Hong Kong Island, as part of the team to shuttle these people between the two spots before they are air freighted to the U.S.A. Many are sick, with only the clothes on their backs. They carry the currency with worldwide appeal, gold, to finance their future wherever they might land. The galley is a hot position to work on these flights away from the rampant pulmonary tuberculosis and tiger balm fighting for airspace in the aisles!

The Land of Opportunity

We transport the military. No alcohol or fun is allowed on these missions. Most of the boys and girls are so exhausted they just sleep the whole trip. World Airways, the purveyor of government troops worldwide, stations flight crews in Belgium to operate turnarounds to Doha, positioning troops to partake in the Gulf War. We drop them off in the desert and pick them up when they are done. We crew members have just enough time on the ground between these back-to-back flights to take in the endless sand and buy tee shirts that some entrepreneurial type is marketing out there in the grit, a hot item with the flight attendants, a breed known for its ability to drag something home from every corner of the planet.

A World Airways flight attendant's home has papasan chairs from the Philippines, Korean chests, ceramic elephant seats from Vietnam, installations illustrating their illustrious globetrotting careers. In Thailand, it's mandatory to purchase a gold bhat chain. In Jeddah, Arabic inscribed gold discs and gold chains are a 'must have" souvenir. Some of these golden trinkets end up being ripped off when worn on other trips, (especially on the beach in Rio de Janeiro), or disappear when left in an ashtray in the hotel room for safekeeping. (The maid, no doubt, is unable to resist the temptation.)

Servicemen and their families are frequently on board. These guys often hook up with ladies from all over, resulting in the offspring being cultural mixtures that provide endless fascination as I welcome them on the aircraft.

Long flights produce a multitude of garbage, we humans have such a talent for creating litter. For the cook and food slinger it presents yet another fun challenge, another glamorous aspect. The garbage can is pulled out into the galley when overflowing with gobs of plastic, beer cans, bottles, all the stuff we caste away without a thought and to create more room for more trash the versatile galley performer climbs on top and jumps up and down to compact the contents under the in-flight flats, of course not forgetting to smile if caught in the act by an astonished guest. I strive to be galley queen, mistress of my lowly domain, so much better than mingling with the riff raff belching and farting in their seats.

Working the skies seems like an exotic occupation to many a person trapped on the ground. A flight attendant must encounter so many exciting individuals. Au contraire. The flight attendant patrolling the aisles usually just sees rows of heads sticking out from seats, needing to be fed and watered and serviced when they squawk. It sometimes doesn't even register that these are actual humans with love, hate, sweetness and avarice all wrapped up in an airline seat. Hopefully wrapped up in an airline seat, we have seat belt extensions just in case.

I learn to pace myself, to never get personally involved with any of the squirming morass of erect primate mammals squeezed on board in seats arranged to be profitable for the airline but guaranteed to dent personal demeanor. The interference, the bickering, the neediness, the inescapable nature of a flight, to survive such an ordeal I discover is always to be pleasant, to smile and be gracious. I give a passenger whatever is within my ability to provide, lay on the charm and pour large drinks. Why bother pouring just an inch and a half of wine in a glass? Fill it up the first time around. Don't be cheap. Get them drunk and snoring. Rise above the fray. Remember the passenger is always right. If they are abundantly out of line reference the guy in charge, the one up front in the left-hand seat.

On a flight from Paris to Newark off duty and luxuriating in the first class section the flight attendant servicing the cabin provides a stellar example of a woman overstaying her time in the air, her unhappy plight shining through in the worst way. Barely able to perform the basics of service, she finds it so hard to let go of the amenities that are rightfully due the inhabitants of her zone. Her acetone looks and manner sour what might have been at least a pleasant ride. Time to retire, bitch; time to throw in the towel, if you can't refrain from spreading your curse throughout the aisles. On the same airline, the purveyor of the friendly skies, I have experienced outrageously wonderful service in economy by a lady of equal longevity, who had a great time making sure that we did too. Attitude is everything.

We flight attendants, men and women have been handpicked for good looks and charm. The ambiance onboard an aircraft is defined by the personalities of the crew. If they are having a good time working together, so will the passenger. An unhappy crew leads to a painful ride.

Flying is my first encounter working with African Americans. Taking to the skies with a crew of eight, all women, two white and six black, we two crackers find ourselves working the aisles as our six compatriots take over the lavatories, locking the doors, settling into their personal offices and make up parlors for the rest of the flight. I see another angle when on a layover in Charleston, South Carolina. When I step out on the cobbled streets to shop I am welcomed as a visitor from the Old Country, but my companion, a striking African American is viewed as straying from her strata in society. Delving a little deeper I ask some of the local airline staff what gives? "People in this part of the country realize the difference between being black and white, what they can do where they can go and where they can't and to do otherwise is a breach of conduct- some things are just plain unacceptable" is the reply. A way of thinking that is news to me.

Flights are long and often nocturnal. Long hours are spent on the jump seats or embedded in the galley behind tightly drawn curtains exchanging news, gossip, tales and jokes. I bend an ear to listen to the self proclaimed Austrian princess who dreams of leaving her flying shackles behind and launching herself into society, way before she actually becomes Mrs. Austin Hills of the coffee clutch, the San Francisco coffee moguls who had used a man in a flowing robe and turban to advertise on the billboard I had first laid eyes on when entering San Francisco.

All the dirt that can be squeezed from our ranks is divulged and dutifully distributed during these long night hours, providing an antidote to sleeping on the job. Tales of the latest romantic intrigues linking the cockpit to the cabin are always of keen interest, starring the married guys up front who love to philander with the babes in the back of the bus, augmenting their flight schedule by infiltrating any available warm body. Some of the pit when leaving their land locked wife to fend for hearth and home have an understudy on the road, a member of our flight brigade to soften the bumpy landings on far-flung layovers.

We revel in the escapades of a first officer when stationed in Indonesia and dating two women, one a flight attendant the other a native flower, each one fully aware of the other, the animosity between the two women creating a deluge of crew dialogue, as the dust and daggers glint and whirl. Bets are placed on who will win the duel. The flight attendant's passport disappears without a trace and her clothes are mysteriously slashed to ribbons while she is out of town. The dragon lady strikes again!

We are verbal encyclopedias of all the extra marital affairs and any of the sexual intrigues that continuously swirl in our midst. Wide eyed, we listen to the stories of the gay stewards laying over in Amsterdam spending every minute in the hot tubs, having anonymous sex with multiple partners. Heading out to the baths after a flight, they appear back on the airplane, bright and shiny, not having even creased the sheets on their hotel beds. We marvel at their capacity to fit twenty encounters in a one-night layover! The gory details are relished step by step, the agony and ecstasy of so many wet, writhing males shooting off so many rounds of ammunition and our own stewards, the AK-47's of the air, provide every lurid, numbing detail.

Sometimes just to break the monotony, we each pick a passenger we think is pretty hot and discreetly give them a little extra service, making a point of prancing by their seat frequently, attempting to make eye contact to see if they are alive, if there is any reciprocal interest wafting in the dry atmosphere. We let each other know the seat number of our target and progress reports are made as we stifle our laughter, not wanting to disturb other sleeping beauties. After all a snoozing passenger is a wonderful thing. For a few of our rank these are serious maneuvers, a way to hook up later, to provide sexual services after the flight, a way to boost a bank balance.

The mile high club is in full swing, an opportunity to fly high on many levels and not notice the tedious minutes as they tick by. The lavatory, although small and cramped, provides a private space to consummate a sudden onboard attraction or a venue to fill a necessary requirement to join the club. If a W.C. has been occupied for a long time, it's our duty to check to see whether a passenger has perhaps got his head stuck down the bowl, is using the latrine as his own covert closet or is up to any other tricks. With time on their hands most passengers are only too thrilled to report any suspicious activity, a rest room they consider has been occupied for too long or sightings of couples emerging from or entering the inflight pissoir. Bodies found in bathrooms contorted in strange positions trying to perform acts of love or lust usually suffer from a rapid decompression of the necessary tools of the trade when the door is flung open and the gaze of other eyes interrupts their privacy. Personally I think it's none of my business. At least they aren't complaining about the food!

What's happening underneath those blankets? Leave it alone. It's dark. Let sleeping or active dogs lie is my motto. Just remember as a passenger, blankets usually get cleaned between flights but sometimes they are just folded and given to the next unwitting soul.

Many consider I'm lucky to have survived without disaster, spending so much time suspended thirty seven thousand feet in the air in an aluminum tube flying into dodgy airports and dubious destinations. On board a flight attendant is so busy just getting through all the duties and requisite gossip, the possibility of death and destruction doesn't even cross the mind. Maybe it's also the lack of oxygen at that altitude, the brain becomes comatose. Turbulence is almost an enjoyable experience, enabling a flight attendant to sit down, to take the weight off the feet that have enabled her to walk many times around the globe. As the aircraft bounces back and forth, we relish the fact that the passengers are being put in their place, strapped down in their seats, immobilized, maybe even a little terrified.

On a flight out of Jeddah, Saudi Arabia transporting pilgrims back home to Indonesia, the captain, in a generous gesture gives the left seat, the driver's seat, to the First Officer so that he gets some hands on experience. We flight attendants, sitting on the back seat for takeoff notice an ear splitting thump as the nose of the bird starts its climb into the sky. Not having sampled much airtime, our clients probably think it's just business as usual. The pit has no way of knowing of any possible damage, which might result in an emergency at the next port of call.

The Land of Opportunity

We prepare for the worst on the approach into Colombo, Sri Lanka, fortifying the cabin, making all our guests, already secured by seat belts, adopt the brace position which entails bending over and grabbing the ankles. Due to lack of verbal communication we posture and pose in the aisles to show how this is done. The pilot flies around the control tower a few times to see whether they can detect any problems. The runway is foamed; the fire trucks are in position, but by the time we finally come into land, the pilgrims have tired of grasping their ankles, probably thinking, *What inane western torture is this?* Who knows if they still have their seat belts on. We're strapped in waiting for the wheels to kiss the landing strip, ready to jump out of the bird. After so much preparation, we land without a hitch, but further inspection reveals that the tail has been severely bruised from hitting the ground on a too steep takeoff. Hey, instead of landing up as a withered tea leaf on the tarmac— I get to buy a pound of the best black tea money can buy at the airport shop to send to my Mum, the avid consumer of tea!

If a plane suddenly drops ten thousand feet, as members of the flight brigade we realize that one or more engines have decided to take time off, but know that they can be restarted if the guys up front are awake. As a stiff working the aisles, especially if out there doing your duty watering, feeding, and smiling at the hapless human cargo stowed in their seats, you know to hang on for dear life, grabbing any available seat and the protection of a seat belt. That stuff can fly off in-flight tables and food and beverage carts can take aim at the ceiling. We know that flesh and blood has died, thrown against the cabin or ceiling along with the carts just like pieces of driftwood in a storm.

Some of our esteemed clientele even know more about flying than we do, which we find out when escorting a load of Air Force guys out of Japan back to their home base in Hawaii. The chief pilot of World Airways, a management man, is heading up the flight deck. He's a guy who likes to take all the risk, leaving nothing for the rest of the pit to accomplish. He sidelines the first officer, knowing that only the captain can perfectly perform the checks and balances, the flight load and the fuel requirements, preferring to fly with his figures rather than be subjected to theirs.

Two hours out of Japan heading towards Honolulu, our leader realizes he hasn't enough fuel to make it. We will have to turn back. The cast of characters on board, Air Force pilots, won't be content with the usual lame excuses for this change in plans, a face losing situation for the man in charge, who will also have to own up to the company about the big mistake, so expensive in terms of fuel and landing fees too! We hide our pleasure while racking up more flight hours and extra pay.

Getting ready for a trip out of Anchorage to Asia, after clambering on the crew bus we learn that a World Airways cargo plane has just flown into a mountain in Alaska with, of course, no survivors. Life is Russian roulette but we all know that flying is the safest way to travel. In spite of which, when we hear of a crash, we wait on tender hooks for the next aircraft to bite the dirt or water, well aware that crashes usually occur in groups of three.

On a steamy July night in New York City my crew is scheduled for a midnight pickup. The lights go out about 9.30, a few hours before show time, and we're told to stay in our rooms. Lightning has closed down the entire electrical grid. It's pitch black. Sirens wail outside. Firecrackers explode. Carnage is taking place on the streets below, shops ransacked, violence, vandalism and arson— a free for all! Pick up is moved to 0900 hours the next morning.

The Land of Opportunity

Donning the uniform, exiting into the dark corridors, we discover the elevators are at a standstill. It's time to use the back passage, the emergency exit, the one you see if you ever bother to glance at the fire escape map on the back of your hotel room door when you check in, but probably don't. After hauling our suitcases down twelve flights, we stumble onto the crew bus, failing to notice the romance of our jet set lifestyle! On reaching the airport everything is once again up and running.

Even in Sicily where the mafia run the show, after another never ending day of in-flight extravaganzas, safely tucked up for the night, I'm jolted, thrown out of the bed and left dangling halfway to the floor, an earthquake has decided to shake us all up. I grab at a piece of cloth to wrap myself in and rush outside to find other people in similar disarray. Glancing up, we are rewarded by the sight of the volcano Mt Etna spewing magnificent, fiery balls of molten lava up into the night sky.

The flight attendant training includes instructions on what to do if an in-flight emergency occurs. Of course, we never dream it will happen to us— until it does. On a flight to Saudi Arabia, the aircraft stuffed tight with those abiding by their creed, making the flight of their lives to view the birthplace of their leader, Muhammad, a pilgrim, an Indonesian woman comes up to me in the aisle, a small slight figure maybe four feet tall. She's coughing, blood oozing from her wrinkled lips as she collapses at my feet, passing on before I even have time to consider CPR. We place her back in her seat, there is nowhere else to put her, covering her with a blanket, the flight continues. At least she was on her way to complete her requisite duties to her faith. That must be a plus! She appeared to be in her seventies but she was just forty-three. A hard life had etched so many furrows into her tiny face and body.

As plodders of the planet we have also been primed as to how to deliver a baby while aloft. First a row of seats is cleared and covered with in-flight blankets so as not to soil the cushions, then the pregnant woman is placed in position and we let nature take its course. Where to put the displaced passengers if the flight's full is a mystery and luckily, as yet, I have not been blessed by having to deliver a naked, wet pile of flesh into the friendly skies. But the question does persist; would such a babe have dual citizenship if born flying between two countries?

When a flight is approaching the runway after yet another ball buster, there is always an exquisite feeling of relief that the finishing line is in sight, the glorious conclusion to yet another marathon. I'm strapped to the back seat of a DC8, a plane with rows of three seats each side of a central aisle, approaching the landing strip in Newark, New Jersey when we fly straight into a storm. The plane is tossed up and down and side-to-side as if a used candy wrapper, torrents of rain whip and batter the bird as thunder booms and crackles, letting us know how small and dispensable we really are. A stupendous streak of lightning blazes down the aisle, delivering a free light show. Is this the spectacular finale to yet another red eye night flight? The passengers, pale and sweaty, cling to their arm rests as Mother Nature once again shows her supreme ability to shake us up and fill us with awe.

Many events have less than perfect endings but the World Airways pilots, almost to a man perform stupendously, displaying great skills in difficult situations and especially when under stress. A real professional group of men who really know how to fly an aircraft hands on, many having tested their wings in and survived Vietnam. Thanks guys!

CHAPTER EIGHT

The Aroma of Clove Cigarettes

"Apakabar/How are you?" ... "Where are you going?" ... "What have you bought?" ... "Would you like shares in my monkey?" ... "Rent a mosquito net?"

This is Bali, Indonesia, a place where an earth dweller is never totally alone, social interaction being unavoidable. The whereabouts and actions of all are known, although a stranger in paradise might not be aware of it. Balinese love company, they live communal lives. If they have broken away from their village they must return for the myriad of ceremonies that are mandatory, that keep the Balinese way of life flowing in harmony with the gods. They believe Bali is the center of the universe and find it hard to understand the Western need for peace and quiet and solitude, the requirement to retain a decent distance between the flesh, when not between the sheets. Their lives are played out in the midst of an ever-present throng of humanity. Individualism is not a desired commodity. Proximity with family, friends and enemies is the fabric of their existence.

Disembarking from the DC8 aircraft, sultry thick air engulfs us, air tinged with the aroma of cloves from the cigarettes passionately and frequently enjoyed by the inhabitants of this archipelago. I sense that I am in for an exciting few months based in Jakarta as a flight attendant. Flight crews and aircraft have been chartered by Garuda Airways, the Indonesian flag carrier to transport Muslim pilgrims from their Indonesian homeland to the birthplace of Muhammad, their spiritual leader in Saudi Arabia. This pilgrimage, namely the Hadj, takes place every year, the timing dictated by the lunar system. Muslim pilgrims from every corner of the globe flock to Mecca, heeding the call, a journey to be performed at least once in a lifetime if financially possible. The more times the merrier no doubt makes for a more comfortable segue when arriving on the other side beyond the grave.

We are installed at the magnificent Borobudor Hotel in the heart of Jakarta, which circa 1976 is the best thing about this city of intense heat, dirt, traffic, extreme money and agonizing poverty. Luxurious high rises soar above families squatting on the street seeking protection from the elements with strips of corrugated metal and cardboard. Open sewers are their only source of running water. This lifestyle is covered up with barricades when protocol cannot afford to lose face on a state occasion. An immense one-way road system services the incessant, suffocating traffic. To miss an exit the first time around results in an extensive detour to correct the blunder. Negotiating this writhing, steaming jumble is not for the faint hearted or those prone to heat exhaustion.

Our flights take place at night, the coolest time. The humidity makes the requisite flight attendant support pantyhose into which

The Aroma of Clove Cigarettes

Map of Indonesia

Saudi Arabia

we had previously poured our legs before commencing a possible twenty-four hour work day, feel like sticky wire netting. The polyester orange and brown uniform sends rivers of sweat coursing down our backs.

We are on the tarmac, the pilgrims are boarding. Many have only previously viewed an airplane flying high above, out of reach over their heads, this is a sudden ascent into the twentieth century. Many are peasants who have saved over the years to make this trip of a lifetime.

The women are dressed in colorful sarongs, lacy kebayas, light gauzy or fine cotton creations through which underwear is often visible. No headscarves or heavy duty cover up for this crowd. The men sport the Islamic black velvet hat. They scramble on board clasping pots and pans, food, and prayer mats. We Western flight attendants tower above them. Prior to the flight while still on the ground, the pilgrims have been introduced in Indonesian to the art of utilizing a western toilet, seatbelts and flying but some of these people do not even speak Indonesian only their local dialects.

We are ready to depart, everyone is belted in, every seat is filled, the baggage stowed and the doors armed. Due to the heavy air and the full load, the DC8 staggers down the runway, lifting off the ground at the last possible moment. The pungent aroma of Tiger balm, the all purpose salve, the ten thousand uses ointment for headaches, stomach aches and influenza to name a few, explodes and dominates the cabin air.

We fire up the ovens. Many of these people have been waiting hours and even days in the terminal for the flight. A few ready their pots and pans and attempt to ignite fires in the aisle to rustle up some food. We hastily extinguish these culinary experiments. I soon figure out that working the galley is the way to go, thus avoiding the fray erupting in the aisle. Dinner is served, chicken and rice. Indonesians, it seems, cannot live without rice three times a day. Rice and chicken are soon everywhere including the floor, some is even neatly stowed away in the seat pockets. I discover that cold, congealed rice is almost as solid as cement especially when stuck to the bottom of an in-flight shoe.

Devout Muslims are required to pray five times a day. This performance entails rolling out the prayer rug and prostrating the body in the direction of Mecca. Even though such a call to duty is difficult to accomplish on a DC8 with only a central aisle and blocks of three seats each side providing minimum legroom designed for a maximum payload, some of our zealous believers achieve this goal.

Before such prayer, it is necessary to cleanse the body, resulting in long lines for the bathrooms. We flight attendants are initially horrified to observe future Hadjis emerging from the rest rooms shaking blue water from hands that they have obviously just washed in the toilet bowl!

Our pilgrims are used to existing in a communal manner, are not familiar with locks, consequently when using the facilities even if they remember to close the door they often fail to bolt it. When performing another glamorous aspect of being an airborne skivvy, the art of restocking and revamping the restrooms, we frequently find ourselves unwilling spectators of personal functions in progress. You can imagine our amazement when attempting to fulfill our duties, we inadvertently discover pilgrims performing the task at hand, executing the elimination of waste matter while standing up on the toilet seat! I would later discover that in many areas of South East Asia a hole in the ground is the only form of latrine, above which one hovers and delivers.

The tiger balm grows more intense. More chicken and rice are deployed and water by the bucketful. At least we don't have to perform in the aisles with the beverage carts as our charges do not drink alcohol, at least not on this flight!

After eleven hours, an interminable time, we start our descent. Everyone is belted in and buttoned down. Sitting on the back jump seat for landing, we find out, poses a potential disaster, such a long flight, so much water used for purification as well as bodily functions, the toilets are filled to capacity. As we graze the tarmac on arrival into Jeddah, water and other lurid waste blast forth and cascade down the aisle! We flight attendants, initially unaware of such possibilities, vow in future to wear plastic bags over our in-flight flats and land with our feet in the air. We would have time when the deluge recedes to discard our synthetic booties and squeeze our tired feet into the de rigueur heels so as to appear once again as professionals when the doors open.

The early morning thick dry Saudi Arabian air sweeps through the cabin singeing our skin. Men in flowing thopes (robes) and headdresses appear on scene to check the manifest and contents of the craft. As the pilgrims leave the cabin each one shakes our hand with the limp Indonesian style shake, a mere touch, then the hand is quickly dropped and a "terima kasi" ("thank you" in Indonesian) is uttered. They are almost as astonished as we that they are once again on terra firma.

Saudi customs is a breeze unless you have a copy of Playboy or such in your luggage, which you will quickly be relieved of, a forbidden treasure to be read at the back of the customs shed later, sure to be handled by many furtive fingers.

We crew take lots of bottled water off the craft when deplaning. Certain fearless individuals replace this basic fluid with another more potent potion of the same color, not wanting to forgo the pleasures of alcohol on the layover. On one flight into Jeddah, the captain, prior to landing, requests a glass of water, only to be handed a glass of straight vodka. The unfortunate galley worker had not been informed of the maneuvers of some of her more subversive cohorts. Luckily the captain has a sense of humor.

People from all over the Muslim world are arriving at the Jeddah Airport, many wear just a rough white cloth draped over their frames, great waves of Muslim humanity joyful that they are commencing the most important trip of their lives. On the ground, the pilgrims wait and wait for transportation, buses provided by the Saudi government to shunt them to low cost housing in Jeddah and then on their final trek to Mecca. Those who do not cling to Islam are not allowed to set foot in the birthplace of Muhammad. Accordingly we are restricted to the delights of Jeddah.

Our Indonesian crusaders, unaware of the dry burning heat by day and the cool desert nights, are prone to fall sick in this climate and on the return trip cough and wheeze. Many do not even return at all, dying in the dust and sand. Most of the passengers we transport on board are the poor trying to make the necessary trip on a shoestring. The less money paid for this honor the longer the stay in Saudi Arabia. Some of the faithful are sentenced to a two-month expedition. The rich play it differently, of course, arriving at the last minute and staying only the mandatory ten days, spending the pilgrimage in the luxurious surroundings that money can buy and so soften the experience, while performing the crucial, grueling, religious stunts.

We crewmembers have been briefed on the rules of dress and conduct to be adhered to when catching some rest and relaxation between flights on the ground in Saudi Arabia. These apply mostly to the women, recommended attire being a floor length loose tunic, which completely covers the upper torso and arms. If female, driving is out of the question. Even going out of town unless accompanied by a husband, brother or father is off the books. Absolutely no alcohol is allowed and, most importantly, we women are gravely informed to "not even consider inviting a man into private quarters." We find out that hotels have men stationed on each floor to survey the activities of all the guests. Any infraction of the above regulations, we are warned, "could land the culprit in the local jail." In spite of such warnings a few souls have to test the limits only to find themselves duly arrested and behind bars for their improprieties, World Airways having to pull strings to pry them out and dispatch them home in disgrace. Last but not least, photographs are not to be taken on Saudi soil.

With all these restrictions digested, we set out to make the best of it. It's too hot by day to even venture forth. Nighttime, when the air is bearable, a visit to the souk is the place to go, to sit outside and indulge in one of the many delicious fresh fruit juice drinks and soak up the scene. The men in flowing white with their women totally swathed in black, the hijab and yashmak covering the head and face with only the eyes revealed, their wrists bristling with stacks of glittering gold bracelets. Many of the shopkeepers in the souk are purveyors of gold, operating out of tiny kiosks stuffed with the precious metal fashioned into articles of adornment. Necklaces, bracelets, rings are strung haphazardly, in great abundance on string across the glass shop windows. Bare light bulbs shed a harsh, brilliant glare, giving the displays a cheap garish allure. The Saudi women are here to add to their visible wealth.

Money changers are perched cross-legged on a cushion next to their safes in the street. They offer to change dollars into Saudi riyals or Indonesian rupiah and happily cash checks, always at a better rate than elsewhere.

The souk is the place to find scrumptious fast food Saudi style, made to order right before your eyes, superb crispy chicken wrapped in light flaky dough, the biggest, oiliest black olives and all manner of the sweetest desserts. Local women are not to be found sitting at the tables and chairs enjoying the fare. It's a male only stronghold except for a few foreign females. The Souk is the place to buy lampshades made out of camel skin, carpets, gaudy velvet bags with gold designs, the latter a must have item for every female crew member.

As mere mortals haggle under the cover of the velvet night, as a parade of Arabian characters stroll by, draped to conceal which in its own way reeks of sexual overtones, a deep resonant voice booms through the darkness, bouncing off the crumbling walls, demanding attention as it permeates thoughts and lives. The call to prayer dominates, commanding the faithful to fulfill their duty. Business deals are left dangling, trading is dropped as the devout respond, heeding the voice soliciting their presence. Forgetting worldly pursuits, they stream to the mosque. Shopkeepers desert their shops, leaving their displays and wares unlocked, unattended, abandoning the bazaar. Pagans and followers of other dimensions are left to wait for their return, for the intrigue to continue, they have already heard that the punishment for thieves in this land is the immediate amputation of the guilty hand.

Asking a shopkeeper if he has anything antique, he guides me to the rear of his tiny emporium. Copper coffee pots abound, beads, weavings from many parts of the Islamic world, a yashmak from the Bedouin people, a tribal treasure embroidered and dripping with silver coins. It smells of the heavy perfume oils so popular in Arabia and substantial evidence of life as a nomad in North Africa is ingrained in the cloth. A piece I have to have.

ESCAPE FROM ENGLAND

I feel a hand from behind on my gown, no doubt having lost its way. Surprised, I fail to notice whether it is the left hand or the right, the right in the Arabian world being the clean hand, the one to eat and shake with, the other is for lesser unclean functions. Spinning around I see that the merchant is under the impression that having accepted the invite to see his stuff, I must also be interested in other opportunities. A frosty glare makes the hand recoil from a further voyage on my person as I resume the business at hand, the price of the yashmak. Having been rebuffed on one front he is only too ready to battle on another and so am I.

Leaving with the piece in my purse I'm ready to hightail it back to the hotel only to find that the crew have already left. I'm solo for the first time in Saudi Arabia. Not wanting to try my luck at walking, I hop in a taxi. At least I know the way back but soon notice that is not where we are going. Rather than go with Inshallah (god willing) a convenient saying in these parts, an excuse for any deed good or bad, not willing to wait for unforeseen events to occur, I open the door and flee on foot, a trip to the local branch of the white slave trade headquarters is not a trip I want to make.

The only other diversion on this sacred Saudi soil are men involved with oil but they keep to their respective compounds away from the cloak and dagger exploits, until news of our presence reaches their ears. These stranded gentlemen, thrilled with the prospect of digging for something other than liquid gold, demand the pleasure of our company and we become the willing benefactors of parties and imbibers of their homemade moonshine. A few of our tribe even staying over longer in the sand than required, rather than taking time off in Indonesia, happy to have found familiar dishes to dine off, rather than Arabic or Asian flavors.

For the first three weeks we escort the Islamic adventurers to

Saudi Arabia then ferry the empty airplane back to Indonesia. The devotees have to stay in Saudi for at least ten days to fulfill their Hadj requirements, which means we, the flight crews, are free to roam. The second phase is ferrying the aircraft from Indonesia to Saudi and hauling our passengers back home. In all, a flight attendant only has to perform seven or eight 'live' flights in two months.

The Borobudor Hotel is the only place to be in Jakarta with its tennis courts, Olympic size pool, lush tropical gardens and fancy restaurants. The centerpiece is the extensive lobby where musicians from the various parts of the Indonesian archipelago serenade the clientele as they sit in colonial splendor, enjoying their beverage of choice or a pot of tea that is served in the afternoon in memory of a different era. The expat crowd and much of the local wealth descend. It's the heart and soul of local society as well as the home away from home of many flight crews, a breeding ground for non stop opportunity and intrigue, where many a fleeting affair is consummated and bid a fond farewell, never having to deal with the basic realities of washing a pair of fouled underpants or utilizing a toilet brush.

Navigating the interior, I come across an antique shop bursting with cultural curiosities, procured from the fourteen thousand or more islands that are Indonesia. Growing up around art, my parents suffocating in a lifestyle of stuff, I loathe the need to acquire. Now I feel myself getting sucked into the lure of strange new sights, the excitement of an imminent rollercoaster ride into foreign fields, intuitively recognizing a fork in the road, a jaunt down a new path.

The man at the helm is from Sumatra a member of the Minangkabau people, a matriarchal society where women control the land, where husbands move into the households of their wives. Where in the event of a divorce, the husband collects his clothes and leaves, an arrangement any woman could appreciate!

The Minangkabau are surprisingly also Muslim and strictly adhere to many Muslim traditions. They are outgoing, open to new ideas and are addicted to playing chess. Foreign traders historically trod on their soil, contact with these pioneers no doubt resulting in the great Minangkabau entrepreneurial spirit that produces many of the leading lights of Indonesia. Many of the men leave their homeland, maybe fleeing the domination of their women, although it is never mentioned, many becoming successful art dealers. Dhody Munir is one of these and has cornered the antique market in Jakarta as well as making and exporting batik kimonos to Japan. He's a world traveler, a highly respected ceramics dealer in Europe, and this is just the tip of his talents. He no doubt eyes me as a potential client, and seems willing to nurture my budding interest, but not without noticing that I am a woman. But the only card I play is the equal card, gently brushing off any inroads into other distractions, despite his attempt to deliver a strange swipe with his nose to my cheek.

He offers a ride to Ciputan on the outskirts of the city, where lesser art dealers ply their trade. Dhody watches as I sift through the stuff, not offering any direction but noting what catches my eye. Is he ingratiating himself with the other dealers so that he can reap the benefits at a later date? Am I the prize at a carnival side show where everyone just might get lucky and strike the cash jackpot? He invites me to his house, decorated with crystal chandeliers, plush carpets and European furniture, the mark of a wealthy man in these parts, to meet his family and have lunch. Ushering me into his private showroom, masks leer and peer down from the walls, finely carved dancing masks from Java, abstract wood images from the outer islands mingle with renditions of dead ancestors. I feel an instant connection to values as yet I know nothing about. I get the feeling that my days by the pool are numbered!

The Aroma of Clove Cigarettes

Opposite the Borobudor is the main Jakarta bus station. On leaving the hotel, throwing caution to the wind, I stroll past the offers of "Taxi! Taxi" and stride onto the bustling streets where people jostle, fighting for space on the sidewalk. Men armed with long wooden tweezers troll the pavement picking up cigarette butts. After accumulating a quantity of these discarded remnants, they sell them back to the tobacco company to be reused, the tobacco repackaged into brand new packets of fags. Women squat along the way, their palms outstretched. Many have a sarong fashioned into a sling around their necks which tightly holds a baby to their breast as the rest of their brood, clothed in tatters, play in the dirt. The crowd rushes by, used to this familiar sight, they have grown numb to the ever-present poverty.

I convince myself that negotiating the chaotic bus system is more honest than riding in the relative comfort of a taxi, a real taste of authenticity. Sampling the grimy heat, crushed with the locals on a lurching ancient bus, to be part of the throng stuck on the insufferable Jakarta streets with a cacophony of motorized two-seater wooden chariots, Mercedes luxury sedans, motorbikes and bicycles and to breath the rampant pollution is the only way to get a feel of the pulse of the city. On reflection, returning to the Borobudor makes it all bearable, to be once again in the midst of cleanliness and order!

My new passion I am finding out is a highway strewn with potholes. The Jalan Surabaya Flea market offers stall upon stall of stuff, every one manned by an eager salesman with no scruples, willing to promise anything for money. I need to bone up on my knowledge, to develop an eye and to follow my intuition, if I want to play this game.

On the way back to the sanity of the hotel jammed on the bus, my Mexican coarse string bag is slashed, but I'm holding it too tightly for anything to disappear. Another member of our flight brigade is not as fortunate, while sitting in a taxi, with the window rolled down in a street teeming with people, a hand emerges from the crowd, equipped with a knife and yanks a fat gold chain from his neck, the assailant disappearing as quickly as he had appeared, back into the mass of humanity swarming on the street.

In Yogyakarta, just a short flight away, I find streets plied by becaks, wooden chariots for two, powered by men with extremely strong legs peddling a bike. Motorbikes, horse drawn carriages and the occasional car share the road, all promoting a very gracious pace of life. I check into the Batik Hotel just around the corner from the main drag, Jalan Malioboro, the exotic central garden, makes up for the basic accommodation.

Needing to feed the inner man, at a nearby restaurant I order the local delicacy, fried pigeon accompanied by a fruit and vegetable salad in hot sauce topped with coconut ice cream, sweet, spicy and salty all at the same time! Returning late to the Batik Palace the doors are closed for the night. Banging on the hand carved wood initially seems useless but eventually sets off the alarm system. Two disheveled men crack the door open, assigned to sleep behind the bolted portals to deter unwanted intruders, I realize I have rudely awakened them!

In Yogya aka Yogyakarta (everything in the Indonesian language is shortened in conversation, as the lengthy names and words in the formal context take too much time to use) I head for the "pasar," a vast indoor expanse offering every edible feature of Indonesian life, pots and pans, medicinal potions, spices, piles of batiks and antique keybayas, wedding blouses, superb white lace concoctions. The women vendors sitting cross-legged in their kiosks take great delight in practicing the art of bargaining and making a deal. The pleasure of negotiating is part of the fun and entails a lot of laughter and astute business moves on their part. Falling victim to their charms I walk out with a stack of stuff. These women know that the secret of selling is that everyone enjoys the deal and the outcome. I feel the rigid social structures that had stifled my early life under the rule of the British Empire dissipating into the equatorial breeze as I learn to play by a new set of rules. Here you can buy your way into a deal or buy your way out of a fix. The ordinary guy realizes the system is rigged and survives by his wits. There are no handouts in this land. A smile is the takeaway everywhere. Amusement constantly hovers on faces, even when looking at death and destruction.

A visit to view Batik is mandatory, to see how these sophisticated designs are spawned. The factory turns out to be just a backyard where women crouch over their current masterpiece, intricate, precious designs flow from their brown lithe hands guiding the primitive metal container of hot wax used in the process. Batiks are all around strung up on lines, these future works of art in one of the various stages performed in the process—designing, waxing, dyeing and cleaning. They are part of Indonesian life, to be worn on every occasion. Signed antique batik in good condition can also be an investment, part of an art dealer's inventory.

"Want to buy a Chinese wedding bed?" It's an Asian style four-poster, a frenzy of red and gold carvings depicting dragons, bats, flowers and a multitude of mythological good omens. What a splendid way to wake up and start a day! Rumor has it that whole families share these magnificent quarters of a night. It's the perfect answer in the tropics for an insect free snooze shrouded by mosquito nets hung from the framework or curtains can be used in colder climes to keep out the draughts. It won't fit in a suitcase, but I'm assured by the enthusiastic antique dealer that this masterpiece can be broken down into fourteen parts and shipped to the country of my choice,

Wayang Kulit water buffalo leather puppets Yogyakarta, Java depicting maidens in ritual attire 19th/early 20th century

Mask Cirebon, Java depicting an aristocrat 19th/early 20th century

each piece numbered for easy assembly! It's a marvelous example of mortise and tenon workmanship, every piece fits together without the use of a nail. How can I resist? Apart from needing a forklift truck at the other end, it's a breeze.

The budding art dealer in me feels the need to dig into who these people are, what makes them tick, fuels their furnace, tickles their fancy? To explore the real meaning of wayang kulit, the buffalo hide puppets, hand carved and painted with buffalo horn or wood handles, an institution in these parts. They can be as fine as lace, exquisitely adorned with gold leaf and vibrant colors and viewed by an artful eye as desirable. The beauty of these hues is invisible in the actual wayang kulit performance, an example of an Indonesian idiosyncrasy, the creation of beauty, which is not always seen. Memories of Punch and Judy performances from my childhood resurface, this is a medium close to my soul.

Puppet shows can last all night, the themes originating from Hindu epics, the characters evolving with the times. Performances are used as purveyors of propaganda and class distinction, as a tool in resolving local conflicts which are brought to life by the puppets, shadows of which are projected by a lamp onto a sheet and manipulated by the puppet master as he spins the story. People come and go, talk, smoke, eat, sleep and kids play, it's all about the super good against the super bad and the good guys always win. The characters are known by heart, household names and often used to describe an individual in conversation.

I visit the Kraton (palace) and meet the sacred white turtle, who according to mythology bestows unending springs of good fortune upon anyone he meets. He has resided in the pool for longer than anyone can remember. The original buildings, dating from the eighteenth century, are a stellar example of classical Javanese architecture. Visiting the Hindu Temple Prambanan and the Buddhist temples of Borobudor, headless Buddhas gaze down on the plateau below, ripped off maybe when Islam swept across Java or perhaps flogged on the art market by the unscrupulous to the unscrupulous.

Enough of the ancient; time for some fun! I plan a trip to Bali - only to discover that the Indonesian government is in the midst of moving troops to East Timor in an attempt to suppress the Timorese on that part of the island. These people having been under Portuguese rule since the 16th century have just achieved independence and want nothing to do with becoming Indonesian citizens. After being subjected to foreign whims for so long, they want to have a shot at governing themselves. The subsequent maneuvers by the Indonesian government result in all passenger planes being commandeered in the effort to take them over. Thousands of Timorese are being killed in this exercise. The male population is being decimated and many others are dying from starvation and disease, as the rest of the world ignores this reality. Indonesia is, after all, viewed by the West as a democracy.

Travel by bus or train is the alternative. The train sounds a little less threatening. The trip to Bali from Jakarta is a distance of over 700 miles and traveling at a steady slow crawl allows intimate viewing of life along the tracks. People cooking over wood fires, children playing happily in the trash, the lean-to shacks they call home offering basic protection from the weather but no relief from the stench of the locomotive as it dawdles by. The gentle pace of Javanese village life seeps through the train window. We amble past the duck herder leading his long line of feathered flock through the rice paddies. People in vivid sarongs and batiks toil in the fields, their heads down and backs straining, cultivating the all-important rice crop as they sizzle under the relentless sun. Java is one of the most densely populated zones on the planet. After a billion palm trees seen through eyes glazed over from the reflection of water on rice paddies and twenty four hours, the train eventually reaches Banyuwangi on the other side of Java and hopefully the ferry to paradise.

My husband by the grace of a reduced rate ticket has flown in to spend the hiatus between flights with me. These are the best moments, traveling together, as he is an inordinately social being in any climate, outgoing, spontaneous, ready for any event or change that chances to cross our paths, not that we have a plan to tether us to the straight and narrow. Peter has an innate ability to become part of any environment wherever he lands.

The journey unfurls slowly, we are beginning to understand that here things happen when they happen, there might be a schedule but it does not really apply. After a few hours spent surrounded by dry brush straining to survive in clouds of swirling dust, the ferry puts in an appearance and we clamber aboard, followed by the luggage, livestock, and the staples of life, until the craft is loaded up to the gills.

Having only recently arrived in Indonesia, we are blissfully unaware of the high incidence of ferries sinking due to overcrowding. The old boat creaks forward through the night and delivers us safely to a dry expanse of no man's land on the west coast of Bali. This is not the stuff that the tourist brochures depict. Where are the swaying palms, golden sands and bare breasted babes of the travel posters?

An ancient Mercedes bus to the rescue, we gratefully hoist our backsides on board and watch the now familiar sight of worldly goods being stuffed to bursting on board, those that don't make it on the bus are strapped to the roof. We're off on a spine-tingling

Indonesian bus ride, straight into the humid Balinese night, windows without glass the only source of air conditioning.

It's early morning when we arrive in downtown Denpasar, the capital. The bus station bustles, hot and grimy, engines are running, gasoline fumes rising. Women in sarongs arrive from market balancing overflowing baskets on their heads, they clutch live chickens in woven straw containers. Peddlers are pushing cigarettes, soft drinks and sweet sticky rice. The buses share the space with a smaller form of transport, the bemo, a truck with wooden benches thrown in the back. "Taxi! Taxi!" so much confusion, so many choices. Immediately spotted as tourists its open season. People joust for our attention and money. The bemo drivers send out their assistants to drum up business, especially targeting the weary, overwhelmed white variety. We are chatted up and led to one of these contraptions. We haggle over the price and scoff at the alternative, the comfort of a broken down taxi. A lengthy rally of differing prices ricochets back and forth before we settle on a seemingly appropriate fare and are allowed to load our bodies and bags aboard a bemo heading to Kuta beach.

Stuffed cheek to jowl with the inhabitants of this fabled island we traverse Denpasar, a town few visitors visit unless under duress or by mistake. We hurtle past stagnant rivers, poorly constructed, rundown buildings, and luridly illustrated billboards featuring the latest romantic saga to hit the only screen in town. Imposing statues portraying the glories of war and spiritual entities revered by the Balinese function as centerpieces at roundabouts where roads meet. The ceremonial burning grounds used for cremation, people selling peeled pineapples and all sorts of edible distractions line the way. A cremation tower is taking shape in a front yard, the gold paper glittering in the hands of the many helpers. Young boys, eight or nine years old, sell newspapers. It's a continuous parade of brightly colored humanity.

The landscape softens. Resident flora sprouts abundantly on either side, attempting to take over the crumbling road. The sea shimmers intermittently. Arriving in Kuta we heave our fatigued flesh off the bemo to be greeted by a dusty strip. The losmen is the local cheap accommodation, a room with just enough space for an uncomfortable bed. There's a mandi out back, an Indonesian style bathroom consisting of a tank filled with water, a bucket and a hole in the ground, which serves as a repository for human waste. The plastic bucket is to dip into the cold water before sluicing it over the body or to flush the imaginary toilet.

The mosquitoes are thick and friendly. Bananas and hot tea in a thermos suddenly appear and we feast on these offerings outside our room on the porch sitting in bamboo chairs. We are close enough to the next room to know that we will soon get to know our neighbors more intimately than we want to.

We have arrived at a quiet fishing village where Balinese have for centuries lived off the land and sea when not pacifying and worshipping their gods with endless offerings and ceremonies. A solitary dirt road lined with untidy shacks displays the beginnings of the garment industry that will later flourish and be found in every closet worldwide. We take a seat at Made's Warung. Made is holding court, strategically positioned behind boxes of cash, eyes focused on every move, choreographing every employee. Her name tells us that she is second in line amongst her siblings, a first born babe on this terrain is automatically named Wayan, Nyoman and Ketut follow suit after Made. This of course is limited to those of lesser stature, priests and royalty pontificate under the burden of more flamboyant titles.

And here is Made bang in the middle of this dusty strip to

personally welcome us. Having once been part of the swinging London scene we instantly recognize that it's the pivotal place to be seen, where people parade their stuff. Slurping up a Gado Gado, a steamed vegetable salad with a boiled egg dancing on top under a creamy peanut sauce, accompanied by crunchy Krupuk, a giant shrimp flavored starchy cracker, conversations with our fellow diners erupt spontaneously. Our companions are munching on plates of Nasi Goreng, fried rice with all sorts of familiar and strange tidbits thrown in to liven it up. Made has created a refuge from the grit and glare a few feet away, a space to quaff down an ice cold Bintang, the local brew.

We duly observe one bare breasted woman squatting on the sidewalk offering snacks to passersby. She has obviously overindulged in her product and is too old to realize that times are changing, that the previous lack of adornment on the breasts of Balinese women is heading for extinction.

Bemos and motorbikes race back and forth, vying for attention, trying to cut a macho image as they churn up the dust on Jalan Pantai the main drag, the ocean pounds at one end and the way to Denpasar looms at the other. At first glance that seems to be it—all there is—but lurking behind the grubby facade we find mazes of footpaths, native houses, losmen (cheap hotels) and portable warungs (kitchens on wheels) dishing up tasty local cuisine for small rewards, fast food to be eaten while squatting on the edge of the path if all the few well worn stools are taken. There is Poppies Restaurant, the brainchild of a fellow Englishman and his Balinese partner, the other staging area where expats preen and proffer their goods. At Made's the hot topic is the mysterious disappearance of the Brit. It seems that after the birthing pains and putting Poppies on the map his presence was no longer required. This might be

The Aroma of Clove Cigarettes

paradise, but apparently it's a good idea to skip across the surface and not get involved with local politics.

Beyond this sprawl, rice paddies and scattered village life trickle on as in the past, the beautiful Balinese cows graze, their wood bells rustling melodically as they chew. Palms sway and tropical flowers caress the green fields that roll right down to the sand. (Just beware of the steaming cow pancakes from which the magic mushroom springs overnight.)

Bronzed skin is a prerequisite when making an entrance at one of the places to be seen. At the beach attempting to acquire this superficial need, we notice that white skin is an immediate signal to a host of individuals who spend their days braving the grit and rays, trolling endlessly up and down the beach, that a new arrival, potentially with money to spend has just dropped out of the sky. "Massage, sarong, kite"... "Pineapple ready to eat in plastic bag, cigarettes"... endless chatter and choices. These hustlers parade up and down, merchandise piled on their heads, with always a sad story to relate, heartbreaking cameos of their hapless lives, in an effort to make their prey, ostensibly on the beach roasting their bones, feel sorry for them.

A woman vendor lowers the bundle from her head pulls out a sarong and demonstrates the many ways it can be worn. A hand carved bamboo wind chime is thrust before our eyes. Sticky rice cakes are pushed in our direction. We shake our heads declining the endless barrage of pressure to buy, which motivates our assailants to try harder, like mosquitoes attracted to fresh thick blood that has just arrived in the tropics from colder climes, blood that takes a couple of weeks to thin out and adjust to the heat.

To show any kind of encouragement is lethal. Some, when realizing that success is not on the cards, just give up and squat besides their quarry, wanting to chat, aspiring to improve their English, which can provide an excellent chance to try out some Indonesian. Besides, once you know some of this tongue you can tell them to "bugger off" in the nicest possible way.

For a change of pace, we flee to the cleanliness and order that prevails at the Hyatt Hotel, where the wealthier more exclusive visitor resides, swaddled in an atmosphere they can understand, without having to actually sample the life teeming outside their tropical paradise, their swimming pool and room service. A cold beer buys us time within these pristine walls.

Getting around on a bemo, which constantly drops off and loads passengers whenever a shout or signal is seen or heard, enduring the tight sweaty quarters offering such cozy proximity to our fellow humans is becoming a drag, so my spouse rents a motorbike, much to my surprise. He hasn't been on one since his tussle with a car in London at the tender age of twenty-one.

A visit to Ubud is on everyone's list. "You haven't been to Ubud, the cultural center of Bali?" is asked with incredulity, in a tone used by those who consider themselves superior because they have been to a place you have not yet visited and feel the need to impress upon the uninitiated the "must see" angle. We slog up to Ubud to find another dirt central track with a few shacks purveying all manner of art and artifacts clinging to the edges. Magnificent temples and lily ponds lie behind the scruffy façade.

We suck up cool lassis, a delightful yoghurt concoction in what appears to be the only joint in town. Ubud is where expat artists abound cashing in on the Balinese scene, a bountiful posse of native models continually available for their inspiration. Here at last we discover the poster kids, the well endowed, liquid smooth, brown skinned women wrapped tightly and brightly in vivid sarongs from the waist down leaving the rest to swing in the sultry breeze.

The Aroma of Clove Cigarettes

Ubud, higher and cooler than the beach areas, is a place to heal the Bali kiss, the so named wound acquired on the leg from the burning tailpipe of a motorbike, a place to recuperate from hitting the ground in one of the frequent collisions. Forget a trip to the local hospital, it's a place to check into and die.

An event of great consequences is about to unfurl, an important cremation and we are invited. In fact, everyone is invited! Such ceremonies marking the departure of the dead to another realm are expensive affairs. To make them more financially palatable, bodies are often kept for a few years, until there are enough corpses to have a joint ceremony, thereby splitting the cost and not bankrupting any one family.

The bodies are placed in caskets, the gold paper and mica decorations glitter defiantly as the midday sun relentlessly hovers overhead. We watch as the casket of the most important deceased clan member is placed inside the voluminous belly of a bamboo

Balinese Village, circa 1937

Balinese theatre, circa 1937

The magnificent Hindu temple complex in Ubud

The Aroma of Clove Cigarettes

Ubud with banana tree

Fan tree

Making offerings at a shrine

and papier mache effigy of a magnificent black bull, sporting a gold leafed necklace studded with mica and matching earrings, the horns and tail soar upwards, a spectacle created by family and friends, as a fitting way to transport their kin on his last ride.

Everyone turns out for this extravaganza. The streets are lined with onlookers, all gathered to give the dead a happy send off. We find the perfect location to watch the event atop a moss covered stone wall, which we share with a few other guests. It has the feel of an epic movie production, but on this set the supporting actors are dressed in batik turbans, ceremonial sarongs with a keris, the dagger with magical powers at every man's waist. The only one wearing black is the bull.

The burial chambers are placed on platforms of sturdy bamboos laced together. It takes a bevy of Balinese men to raise each casket aloft and onto their shoulders, when securely in place a last stroll through town to the cremation grounds is required, a ritual that cannot be achieved in an orderly fashion but requires a zigzag journey, swaying back and forth to confuse the evil spirits that lurk on this Island. The pallbearers carrying these precious cargoes groan under the weight and perspiration flows as they perform this exercise under the broiling sun. The parade passes, a giddy aura sizzles in the air as one of the flotillas spins out of control, lurching towards us. The crowd in front of us springs back to avoid the onslaught sending the wall, crashing to the ground and us leaping to safety.

The burial caskets proceed on, dipping and reeling, until they reach the final resting place, the cremation grounds. We follow in the wake of the procession, morphing into the crowd celebrating the looming liberation of the dead into the cosmos. At the site vendors of food and drinks are set up and doing brisk business. People relax on the grass, socialize. Kids fly kites, as they wait for the event to further unfold. As with everything in this corner of the world time is expandable. There are words for this oblivion to the clock ticking, "jam karat" (rubber time). Peter is in his element, being a man who finds it difficult to stick to timeframes in any society.

The cremation chariots containing the corpses are doused in gasoline and set alight. The chamber enclosed in the gleaming bull initially ignites, but the flames fizzle. More gasoline is poured and as the Balinese feast and fraternize, enjoying the ongoing drama, flames burst forth. This is a happy time, a reason to rejoice. The dead have completed their life cycle and their spirits are now to be released to return as reincarnation dictates in another form. Propelled by a lurid fascination we are rewarded by the macabre sight of the bottom falling out of the fiery bull and as the sarcophagus hangs suspended in mid air, the body stark naked and bloated with heat comes into view. The penis standing stiff and straight up in the air for the last time before being demolished by flames. A glimpse into Balinese culture, a celebration of life, the acceptance of reality-a much better idea than our own stilted perception of sadness.

As we sail on two wheels through the vivid green, the sides of the roads are strewn with stone compounds, where three or four generations of a family live together and die. They comprise many separate dwellings combining indoor and outdoor living, platforms on which to lounge and entertain and the mandatory personal temple for ceremonies, a place to give offerings each and every day.

Poking our noses into a roadside temple, images of demons and gods glare and smile as we are gently informed that a sash has to be worn whenever entering a sacred spot, a mark of respect in this land, like donning a hat when visiting the Vatican. Women sit preparing offerings, laughing, luxuriating in the social aspect of working together, nimble fingers expertly weave square baskets from green leaves they have just plucked. Baskets to be filled with rice, maybe part of a banana, a cigarette, a one hundred rupiah note, anything that might please a god. Offerings that have to be distributed three times a day to keep the flow of life proceeding in the right direction. To be strewn at appropriate places, the entrance to a building, where a path splits into two, then sprinkled with an elegant flourish with holy water and a prayer.

Just breezing around, keeping to the straight and narrow, it's part of life in paradise, avoiding such gifts to the gods that appear anywhere and everywhere. The dogs that roam the island but belong to no one are happy to graze on these sacrificial donations. Bali dogs lope through life tortured by skin diseases, gaping sores, fleas and malnutrition, they interrupt the night with incessant barking and fighting. After a nighttime brawl, their bloodied flesh hangs in tatters off their bony frames. A frequent sight, a cause of much fascination is to see these beasts standing hindquarters to hindquarters still joined together, after a sexual escapade, unable to break free.

Back on the road a procession of women, their dark, luxuriant hair coiled and coiffed, a long stemmed bowl perched on top overflowing with food for the gods, wind their way in a column to the temple, gold leafed, fringed umbrellas undulating overhead. Forced to make way for the whims of the spirits, we are happy to stop and stare.

Continuing on, we climb higher, passing a Banjar, a raised platform, where men congregate to smoke, to sort out the state of their community. The kretek cigarette is an indispensable accessory it seems for any man. People appear not to care or notice us churning up the dirt, enjoying the view, as they bathe and eliminate waste matter in the streams that course by each side of the track.

The palatial open air courthouse of KlungKlung rises up from the side of the road, the rafters and eaves graced by sumptuous gold paintings of Balinese heaven and hell, no doubt to impress upon those subject to scrutiny here, the destiny that might await them. A collection of seedy markets and streets portray a tired version of Island life. Warungs offer dishes of dubious food, rats scuttle underfoot jumping at any edible sliver that falls to earth.

Most travelers rarely bother to investigate these upcountry distractions not being able to tear themselves away from the easy living down south, but we are not satisfied to just mingle with the bar, beach and boobs scene; we want to dive into the meat section!

We press on up to the mother temple of Besakih, through poverty stricken Kintamani, where mean grey houses float in the clouds, the tropical pageantry of Ubud replaced by somber, drab rock formations strewn haphazardly in untidy heaps. The weather is cold, the gaiety and laughter of the lowlands nowhere to be seen.

The onslaught of frigid temperatures is enhanced as the motorbike climbs upwards, a blast of reality. On arrival at Lake Batur a wood burning fire is blazing in the room we rent, providing a chance to thaw out. The view of the lake we have been told is magnificent, but a swirl of clouds and mist persist, denying us the vision. Clambering on the bike we flee back to the easy life down south.

Traveling for the husband and I is an aphrodisiac, bonding us as a team, we feel the need to jam as much experience as possible into our souls. Sulawesi an orchid shaped island a two hour plane ride north of Bali tempts are restless natures.

Ujang Padang is the capital at the southernmost tip. We glance briefly at the birthplace of the Bugis, the indigenous people of the area, a name from which the term "bogeyman" is derived, and decide to hop on a bus while we still can and head up to visit Torajaland, the real reason to visit this island.

The road is unmade, the bus ancient, a long, bone-rattling ride seems imminent. It's crammed with local flora and fauna. We are the only alien species. Two hours out we stop at Pare Pare for the necessities of life, food and excretion. Sitting on hard seats in what we assume is the waiting area, we look forward to departing as soon as possible, but word of our arrival circulates and the whole village turns out to see the spectacle. They form a semi circle around us and silently stare. It's somewhat intimidating and not particularly friendly, one of those moments to be exceedingly glad to have a traveling companion.

The bus lurches forward into the night. By morning we reach Rantepao. It's Christmas day! Unfortunately zealous Christian missionaries have arrived before us and spread their creed, not that this fact is evident on this birthday of Christ. No trace of Christmas tackiness rears its ugly head, and for that we are grateful.

The market is in full throttle. Women squat, thick wads of betel nut in their mouths, their teeth red and rotten from the habit. Enormous woven rattan hats protect them from the elements, rain or shine. They sit behind small bundles of produce, shouting their wares.

We try hiring a jeep but have to settle for a motorbike and head up into the mountains. Gorgeous shades of green glow and illuminate our path, swallowing us up in verdant clouds as rain falls and the flooded rice paddies glisten. The vegetation undulates gently back and forth as if in an underwater movie, a pristine environment broken infrequently by small groups of Toraja houses with sway back roofs soaring up into the heavens. Hand carved panels in rust and black decorate the exterior walls and racks of buffalo horns hang over the entrances, defining the wealth and rank of the occupant, a display of age and artistry that I have the luck to view in situ.

Pausing to wander through the houses and granaries, people stare in disbelief as we pass. They pull my hair and pinch my bare arms. A man with hair completely covering his face ambles by, the feeling that we are pushing our luck is all around. This might be the place but it is not the time to inquire whether any ancestral wealth is for sale.

Back on the bike, we plough through muddy ruts on the way to Loko Mata, to find sheer mountain walls into which a myriad of horizontal resting places have been excavated to house the dead, past and future. When life ceases to flow, the body is manually lifted up towering bamboo ladders and deposited in the final resting place, next to other kindred spirits, all now dwelling high in the sky for eternity. The cavity is sealed with a wooden door carved to depict the departed ancestor within and stating their rank in life. At a later date many of these facades will be ripped off by robbers or sold by a clan member to service the ever-hungry art market, exported to the other side of the globe, to be viewed gazing down from a felt covered wall at a Tribal Art show in Paris or New York.

Balconies have been hacked into the rock with wood railings fashioned at the edge behind which stand images of the departed, ancestors clothed, looking out, still managing and advising their descendants going about their daily struggle far below. Images which will perhaps resurface on another day at a museum in the company of historical elements from Ancient Greece and Mesopotamia.

As night falls we retrace our steps by moonlight back into Rantepao. We celebrate Christmas with a greasy Chinese dinner, just the two of us in an otherwise deserted dive. We are just happy that something is open to service our appetites.

CHAPTER NINE

Under the Thumb of The Money God

In spite of Peter finding the confines of marital bliss restrictive, our relationship is still intact, although the wedding ring that once adorned his nuptial finger has now lost favor and been discarded, but for some unfathomable reason I still feel this is the love of my life, not realizing as yet, that life can be long and many options dance on the horizon. It's prudent to have the antenna erect and functional to get a clear, sharp picture of the world and the opportunities swirling in the mists of everyday life. To be aware of such distractions is always advantageous in equalizing the gender game.

    I'm stagnantly immersed in the delusion that we are bound together as Brits in an alien land. I remind myself, heroically in retrospect, that we speak the same lingo and revel in the same brand of humor. Surely such bonds compensate for a few departures from the beaten track? Caught in the web of coupledom I strive to retain my identity as a complete package not just an appendage to the guy in charge, I see myself as an equal player. We have so much going for us I reason, I can afford to overlook a few deviations from the straight and narrow.

We jump into the real estate bonanza, acquiring two more houses in as many years, property is affordable and can even be rented out at a profit, it seems a solid place to put our dough, and perhaps will finance a splendid conclusion to our earthly experience! We are painfully unaware of how much time we will spend maintaining our budding empire and in pursuit of renters able to pay the price, while we juggle three mortgages. Even though ruled by the money god we fail to grasp that we might be pressed to take on less than stellar tenants just to fill the monetary void, resulting in ugly consequences.

As a lackey in an aluminum tube much of my existence is spent away from the nest but I have no qualms leaving our latest investments in the capable hands of my dashing husband, a man who somehow never succeeds in loosening his grip on his British accent which he considers opens many otherwise closed doors in this land of opportunity! Oblivious to the savvy required to be a landlord, we naively believe that as a team we can rise to the occasion and conquer.

Our marriage was not an arranged agreement where the prospective partner is thoroughly vetted for any disquieting qualities by the matriarchs and patriarchs on both sides of the tribes involved, a marriage viewed as a family affair, not just a couple of love struck babes getting hitched! Who in the Western world considers when diving into connubial bliss such unromantic functions?

The first few years are a wondrous calm. The properties are relatively new, the rent is forthcoming but as the houses begin to age, to need more upkeep, our views of humanity will be in for a jolt of seismic proportions. Around the corner lurk a pack of parasites sporting beneath superficial attractive exteriors, manipulative blood sucking proclivities.

Under the loving care of husband dearest our investments start to sprout problems, which left unattended blossom into disasters. Tales of blocked toilets imminently poised to overflow, of rain cascading through a roof, or plugged sinks, all demanding immediate attention, before evolving into the extinction of the species are prone to arrive at dinnertime. Mother-in-laws fall down flights of stairs. Soon sad excuses instead of a rent check will be delivered at our door, along with the ploy that "the check is in the mail - please hold it for a week or two as it's not bankable right now!" We plough on relentlessly until the next fiasco.

One property in particular attracts seemingly delightful people who metamorphose into horned demonic fiends. A lovely young couple with a preteen daughter and Afghan hound in tow, answer our advertisement. After much deliberation and in spite of the 'no pets' clause in our rental agreement, we allow them and the Afghan hound to rent. To quell our fears of doggy debacles they agree to have all carpeting professionally cleaned upon their eventual departure.

Moving in, they are happy as pigs at a trough, delighted to be in marvelous Marin, their daughter able to attend an award winning school! Four months later without our consent they rent out half the house to another couple, undeterred by restrictions allowing only three people to reside in the property. Their entourage soon includes two more furry canines and a parrot!

After the initial phase of geniality the sub tenants astutely realize that the rent they are paying to their housemates is not reaching the landlord, that a tug of war is imminent and it might be time to evacuate. The roomies have already ruined the clutch on their car and clocked up 400 miles on the speedometer, but then what are so called friends for?

Things continue to spin out of control. I've had enough of slaving thirty seven thousand feet up in the air to finance the lifestyle of cretins, and vote to remove the remaining gang of four, who at this point have accrued $10,500 in rental arrears. The ultimate weapon, a three day notice to quit is delivered and we wait in great anticipation for the view of their backsides and stuff disappearing into the sunset.

Two months later the impervious group, pick up their threads and depart, declaring bankruptcy a year later. We, the sagging financially impoverished recipients of their bad behavior file suit in order to be a creditor in the case, during the process of which, we learn that the delinquent family in the interim have acquired a further debt of $5600, money owed to their current landlord victim.

In the courts of law we're victorious, we win the motion but learn the important lesson that if the debtor has no collateral, it's impossible to collect any of the money we have been bilked out of.

Still stinging from our less than glorious sortie into capitalism, our money tree now dwindling in the dust, we, the tenacious team, stride onward on our quest.

The next tenant for our spiffy townhouse, which radiates the Marin lifestyle, privacy, and ravishing views is a middle-aged lawyer sporting a shiny new flight attendant wife. What an adorable couple, so happy in their new-found bliss! After a brief honeymoon of several on time rent payments, we inconveniently discover that our glossy new tenant's specialty is writing bad checks and eventually not even delivering these. Instead, he attempts to placate our monetary demands with stories of his latest business ventures, an array of creative formulas always teetering on the cusp of fruition, promising that a tidal wave of dollars will soon be flooding through his life. He swears that the big deal is always about to materialize, just minutes from smashing through his portals as portrayed by his fertile imagination running on overdrive.

My dear spouse, not one to rush in and wield the action club when excrement starts to fly, waits in the wings much to my discernible anguish until this con man is $23,042 in rent arrears. Not willing to tolerate this circus of rising debt at my expense any longer I demand that the three-day notice to pay or surrender possession be put in place. Why fund this lifestyle to the detriment of our own. Why support the bad behavior of a rental demagogue at our expense? Do I have to explain this in more simplistic terms?

The Flight attendant bride works for United Airlines. Let's garnish her paycheck. Let's get some cash flowing into our diminishing bank accounts! Her husband picking up the scent of this forthcoming knife between the shoulder blades, without hesitation divorces his latest blushing acquisition in order to subvert our attempt. He, of course, is self employed with no obvious assets to lien. We are unaware that he is also duplicitously in arrears with spousal and child support to his first marital casualty to the tune of $26,000! Or that our erstwhile entrepreneur is on course to be disbarred, prohibited from practicing law in California by order of the California Supreme Court for committing acts of moral turpitude as well as professional misconduct!

This stained excuse for humanity and his second ex-wife love the area so much that they purchase a house in her name just around the corner from their former unpaid pad. I can only hope that Karma is as good as advertised!

After such disturbing contact with the human race in the name of attempting to be self sufficient in the capitalist system, we stagger monetarily along, scraping our way out of this latest financial quagmire.

Unfortunately, people who avoid paying their way in life are prone to vacating their former nests in a trail of filth and destruction. We aspiring landlords, now spiraling down the ladder of success and into the light of impending doom, spend long hours revitalizing this hastily abandoned forlorn dwelling, endeavoring to resurrect its former glory. Etching this blot from our portfolio entails much time spent balancing on ladders and on all fours stroking and cajoling our investment back to life, far from the glitter of romantic trysts. My skills with the paintbrush, toolbox and structural knowledge expand in the wake of the chaos left behind.

A single, conservative, white collared, employed man with great credentials and references signs up to be our next tenant. A few months after paying the now vastly enlarged deposit and coughing up three months rent in advance, his freshly graduated Harvard girlfriend moves in to complete his happiness.

We relax. The rent checks arrive on time. At last the future looks more cheerful. Then he seems to tire of her presence. Indeed, the tantalizing body which she moved in with has now blossomed into a larger version of the original and despite her highly touted schooling attributes, this same package seems content to loll around the house, not using any of her much vaunted skills. She chooses the couch in preference to the call for cash, drifting through life, her expanding body attracting a series of mysterious afflictions, only too happy to take up residence in her burgeoning corpulent carcass. Whether real or imaginary, the invasion takes over her life.

Unfortunately lover boy finds that the only way to get rid of this no longer wanted attachment is to flee, leaving us with a cesspool of human waste powered by a mind ready to suck a free ride out of any creature within her vision. Oh lucky dynamic duo. Life is never easy, and neither is riding the wave of entrepreneurship on the great American rollercoaster! We're left with the unwanted task of dismantling or diffusing this lethal human grenade, a hot potato, a promising source of disruption and destruction.

Halloween is nowhere in sight but a witch has risen out of the sewers digging in for the kill, demanding that the lease be transferred to her name. '"Get the bitch out; no contest," is my adamant view, "Why deplete our sanity by lingering in the depths of her stinking depravities?" This aspiring tenant, although extremely smart, is manipulative, conniving and also unemployed, even though she still assures us that her prospects are brilliant. I argue that if the boyfriend had to abscond under such circumstances, we're looking at big trouble.

Peter, a man totally lacking in female intuition and the knack of divining the true nature of the beast (a proclivity that is of utmost importance to females on the scent of a worthwhile mate who will bring the horseflesh back to the cave to feed the neolithic family), decides to give her the benefit of the doubt. As usual things go smoothly at first.

Our shining honor student after such a brilliant rise in the firmament, with prospects propelled by scholarship accolades now disembowels any noble ambitions seeking instead a free ride on the back of disability benefits. Due to her boldness and fraudulent mind, she becomes a recipient of free money and starts her career as a slug on society's landscape, sucking up and living off the sympathy and stupidity of others. The house has to be inspected by the Disabilities Board to make sure that they consider it suitable to accommodate her growing proportions and supposed sickness. The changes necessary to accomplish this have to be made, of course, at our expense.

Even though she is now on the government payroll, the rent checks became harder to collect and eventually evaporate. She becomes a hermit boarding herself in the house, disconnected from the rest of the world. Peter, the still hopeful landlord, when attempting in person to collect the requisite rent, is accused of harassment. She sees herself as a victim of persecution and unwanted visitations by an aggressive predator. She files for a restraining order, then takes him to court, pleading that he is stalking her.

Again the judge rules in our favor but the endless tiresome maneuvers strain the now scarred threads holding our mutual bliss haphazardly together and although we receive the blessing of our righteousness from the court, financially not a penny is forthcoming. Our former Harvard graduate with superb potential, has to be forcibly removed by the boys in blue in order that we can repossess our now demoralized hunk of a house, leaving us with the task of removing the demons and stench left by her sour soul.

An abundance of crap and garbage greet us after this untenable tenant is hauled away, streaming, cascading down the stairs, overflowing into the sundrenched courtyard in pools of torched trash, the sum of a life destroyed by an evil force. There's not a trace of the hot tubs and peacock feathers attributed to the Marin lifestyle, only a wide swath of human debris.

Coffee or a similar brown fluid appears to have been hurled at the bone white walls, or maybe she has a hidden artistic streak. More likely the devils that dwell in her flesh have released their brown inner slime, daubing it on the landscape, painting portraits of the hate that courses in her veins. The synthetic ply of the beige carpets has been welded together in clumps by what appears to have been extremely hot appliances, but more likely from the waste from her thwarted talents, unused as so many talents are on futile ugly endeavours, if at all.

CHAPTER TEN

As Fools Rush In

The DC8 rises into the night sky, flight crews and luggage heading for the other side of the globe. The Borobudor Hotel awaits us. The beds embrace our jet lagged souls, soft and welcoming like a long lost lover. The sheets, crisp and perfect, are changed every day by gentle discreet hands. We have to save our strength for the chaos in the aisles, our pilgrims on their way to redemption.

Leaving the entrails of domestic bliss and exploits into capitalism in my wake, I'm back to pursue my tribal mania. With the flight regalia stowed in the closet and one ballbuster trip to the birthplace of Muhammad under my belt, I race back to the airport accompanied by a small bag of body concealing clothes and a toothbrush.

Just a short ride away, a frisky jump over the Sunda Straights, the city of Palembang in the South of Sumatra shimmers beneath the craft. At first sight it appears to be a flat, dusty stretch, exuding a lack of redeemable features. On closer inspection, after an elderly motorized relic has spewed my perspiring rear end out onto the hot earth, as the wind blows dirty particles up my nostrils, I notice that nothing about this place has improved. None of the hustle and bustle of normal street life course through the dry arteries of unmade roads and broken concrete. There is only an oppressive feeling of despondency.

Clouds of litter dance in the sticky hot air around decomposing architectural eyesores. Men in clusters hang in shadows cast by uninviting structures that sprout haphazardly. This, I assume, must be the welcoming committee. They are here to greet the misguided traveler who has strayed into their web, a stranger that maybe they can manipulate to boost the coinage rattling in the folds of their sarongs. Black velvet hats perch over dark looks. They peer in my direction obviously wanting to be of service!

An uncomfortable sensation of doom washes away my initial excitement at touching down, prompting me to consider forgoing the uncertain pleasures of Palembang. My intuition tells me to get my booty on a bus to Lake Toba, the home of the Batak people, my real reason to be in Sumatra, far from the glances of the throng who have eyed my arrival and followed me on my jaunt downtown. Sorry to dash your hopes so soon, boys!

The bus lurches, climbs and speeds through stunning curvaceous vivid green jungles. We stop periodically for refreshments and visits to the local hole in the ground to accommodate other human functions. We reach Bukittinggi a distance of over three hundred miles, a town perched high in mountains where mists swirl and rain glistens on the corrugated steel, sway back, pinnacled roofs of the dwellings. The market place seethes with activity. I sense a very different ambiance, as the locals go about their business, allowing a stranger to wander at whim. This is the land of the fabled Minangkabau people, the matriarchal society.

As Fools Rush In

After another four hundred tortuous miles, crammed like baggage on this ancient beast, we arrive at the rough, bustling port city of Medan in the north, Arabic smells and faces float in the air and wander in the streets, carts pulled by horses amble by.

I find an old Dutch style hotel above a restaurant downtown and collapse exhausted on a well worn mattress, clasping the contours of the Dutch wife provided to keep a lonely visitor company, the tightly stuffed body length bolster. Feeling strangely insecure, memories flash capriciously through fitful hours of sleep as the raspy antiquated fan twirls above.

The sun streaming through shutters reminds me that I am still alive and thankfully alone, except for my Dutch friend. Time for a breakfast of hot chicken curry soup accompanied by the obligatory pile of rice, the spicy dish burns my throat on its way to my gut, washed down and tempered by steaming tea.

After being mangled and squashed in an Indonesian size seat the previous day I'm happy to wander down to the streets to join the crowds milling around beneath my hotel window. Encased in my body-concealing outfit I'm ready to absorb the flavor and feel of this distant outpost where ships from Arabia, Persia and India landed at the end of the 14th century in search of spices to satisfy the growing demand in Europe and China, bringing with them great wealth, new ideas and the teachings of Islam. Sumatrans' highly developed entrepreneurial skills and their obsessive love affair with chess were no doubt acquired from these early merchants.

Medan is bereft of the smiles of the Javanese and the Hindu celebrations of life. Furtive glances enhance the sensation that I'm being followed. A few lackluster art shops materialize, maybe concealing a hidden gem, but the best has already disappeared to more lucrative markets, and the rest has been left to accumulate dust. Malevolent clouds hang in the sky as the evil eye darts from behind and out of unkempt streets and dwellings, following my movements and every step. Not to be deterred I skip on a pony and trap and bolt out of town, securing a bus to complete the ride to Lake Toba.

Native eyes view me as an alien species, I'm a woman on my own, a weird new phenomena in these parts. Deposited at Prapat on the lake's shores I'm an instant curiosity. This is the price to pay for traveling budget style in obscure parts. So many would love such attention, to be with the real people of this universe, otherwise run by corporate decisions and greed. Just smile and bare it I confide to my inner woman, not that I have much choice as I am far from a more comfortable alternative.

After haranguing over the price, a small boat takes me over to Samosir Island on Lake Toba. The missionaries, it seems, have already put in an appearance equipped with their various brands of Christianity, which the local Batak people, having survived the earlier onslaught of Islam, succumb to peripherally, recognizing this new god, no doubt in exchange for commodities and services they consider worthwhile to access. Animism and ancestor worship are more their style, black magic, poisons and spells their way of operating. Pupuk, magic potions prepared from the cooked brains of a kidnapped or murdered child, are more their line of functioning and one of the rather unique aspects of their culture. Shamans heal and medicate, determine auspicious days, foretell fortunes and officiate as mediums between the living and the dead—like combining a doctor, priest and clairvoyant all rolled up in one, not a bad idea!

Installed in a Batak style house with a soaring swayback roof, below which intricately carved wood rooms straddle on precarious piles, I settle into a delicious solitude, torrential rains cascading on

Traditional Batak house, Sumatra

the tin roof, great sheets of water falling past the windows. I pull the lone blanket over my head and sleep until noon the next day.

The deluge continues, the world outside turning into a soggy, brown bog. Starving, I breakfast off a bowl of what seems to be pork stewed in spices and sauce, only to discover it was probably dog drowning in a mixture of regurgitated cow's cud.

I'm here on a tight schedule, so with no time to waste I wade out into the squall. Freshly created art, acquiring needed patina in the steady downpour, materializes before my eyes. Hungry dealers slosh through the waves in my direction, proclaiming the wet wood to be heirlooms of great age. Amazed at their tenacity and sense of purpose as they jostle for my attention, water dripping from their faces, I avoid the sales pitches and subsequent free fall into a monetary pothole, my rudimentary knowledge saving me from a plunge into fakery. They unintentionally educating my eye with their badly made imposters and my ear with their scurrilous lies.

ESCAPE FROM ENGLAND

My exploits curtailed by the elements, I'm ready to jump back on the bus. Jammed in with the throng, I head to the airport and Jakarta, arriving just in time to shed the accumulated grime from my escapade down the pipes of the Hotel Borobudor, on schedule for my next flight. What a magnificent oasis to return to after seven days of lurid latrines and the cold joy of sluicing the body down with buckets of frigid water. I slip into the uniform and climb aboard the crew bus, on track to execute the eleven-hour flight to Saudi Arabia, ready and able to replace the land of sarongs for thopes and red-checkered headdresses reminiscent of tablecloths at a French Bistro.

Bouncing back again into the land of chicken sate and humidity, my new reason to be takes hold. While my comrades flop by the pool hands wrapped around a cool drink meticulously rotating their flesh, I take to the steaming hot pavements in search of the arts of the ancestors. Flights to Bali have returned, it's only an hour away, easy to access between my schedule.

Seated at the Made's Warung, lingering over a mango yoghurt liquid lunch, a fellow diner sporting a billowing Afro while munching on a good looking fish dish accompanied by large clouds of krupuk, catches my eye. Yamin Makawaru introduces himself, he's a man from Sumbawa a few islands away, a land of honey, horses and sandalwood. He lounges on the hard wood bench skinny as a rail, dressed in jeans, a sought after foreign delicacy that confers instant status when worn in these parts, especially by an Indonesian. Having not yet found any leads to service my art obsession on this Island, I mention my quest. "You must visit my house" he smiles, displaying a great set of pearly whites, "it's just around the corner."

Finishing lunch, I take his advice. A couple of American dealers are waiting for him when we arrive at a thatched cottage with bamboo

Winged Goddess Bali 19th/early 20th century

walls and a mud floor. They are just checking in to view any new arrivals and demand immediate attention. Not particularly happy to see another potential competitor, they ignore me, I take a back seat and watch the interaction, ready to pick up any cues. I notice they have no interest in a classical piece of fine art, a gold winged goddess gazing down from the rafters, they want primitive wood.

After their welcome departure I garner center attention and together Yamin and I dig through the stuff. Wood pieces, baskets, cloth much of it dusty and dishevelled. I have not yet reached the heights of knowing what I am looking for. Mentioning the other lady in the room, the one surveying the scene from above, surprises my host. He is not sure whether he wants to sell and puts what seems like a high price on it, maybe hoping to avoid a sale.

ESCAPE FROM ENGLAND

He sends out for two cups of grainy black coffee, I ask about other antique destinations, are they all secreted behind similar facades? He is coy on this front, I fathom he prefers to keep this newly acquired prospective cash flow in his own back yard. He volunteers the notion that he is the first to make a living redistributing the art of his ancestors to the rabble of western entrepreneurs beginning to show up on these shores. I switch back to the winged wonder looking down from above, she almost looks Egyptian, sitting like a sphinx on a platform of lotus blossoms. The face of a Balinese woman. a gold leaf headdress and ear plugs, breastplate and armbands, the lower arms reminiscent of a resting lion but the hands are human, the wings soar upwards and a tail sprouts from behind. Yamin does not waver from his original price, his confidence shines through, he knows he is good at what he does, that he is on solid ground. I leave with the winged lady under my arm and the knowledge that I will have to forage and find on my own, this chance meeting at Made's was just luck.

But I remember seeing in the deplorable depths of Denpasar on my initial deployment on the island, a shop front that looked like a possibility. I brace myself for a dash into town. Yes-it's a gallery with a glass case no less. Relieved to be proven right and as I mingle with the art, an older gent with a kretek cigarette stuck on his lower lip makes an appearance, cups of the ubiquitous coffee appear and he invites me to take a seat. Here there is a social aspect to every deal that might transpire, coffee to be drunk, clove cigarettes to be smoked. He is happy to engage this alien tripper in conversation. The wife brings forth sticky rice cakes and another packet of fags. When the one already engaged between his lips dies, it is instantly replaced. He too is the original prototype, the first to try his hand in the art field. He's on a roll, enjoying a willing

As Fools Rush In

Beaded betel nut bag Timor Indonesia early 20th century

ear, taking off on tales of his happiest moments spent afloat sailing on the China Seas looking for artifacts to shanghai back to paradise, fighting off pirates, bobbing in the ocean, thrilled to be far away, at least for a while, far from his Christian catholic wife and five daughters, escaping from a house submerged in femininity. Having not produced a son, which is crucial in this land, he needs to show his masculinity in other spheres.

I'm dying just to dive into the stuff, but realize it's best to take a seat and indulge in the sweetmeats offered, to arrive and just look at art might be considered an affront. Such bad behaviour, I am learning, might even ruin the chance to glimpse at the freshest and the best material, to be revealed in due course if in favor and fortunate.

A few hours pass, he is a Buddhist—a painter from Java, gradually some of his latest acquisitions emerge from behind closed doors, beaded bags from Timor used for carrying ritual betel nut paraphernalia, the opiate of choice in many of these islands. He throws them out and watches my reactions. Even though I haven't seen such pieces before, I intuitively recognize they are special, the

217

sense of design, abstract in form, announce that these are prestige showpieces, the former property of a man of position and wealth. He states his prices but seems open to a little back and forth on this topic. With him there is room for adjustment.

Having inhaled the smoke from a pack or more of cigarettes, addictively smoked by my new friend, I squeeze back into a beamo, the beaded bags stowed in my satchel. I feel honored to have encountered Verra Darweiko, at least one of the first in his field!

Eyes on stalks perched maybe on the back of a motorbike or loitering in auspicious places have spotted my movements, news is circulating as to what might be, perhaps a victim, subject to further scrutiny. Word is out that I'm staying at the Three Brothers Inn, a gathering of ramshackled dwellings featuring cold water, outdoor bathing facilities and the basics of bedding. Where the western toilet is still a foreign instrument prone to constant malfunctions, not yet quite understood. Where bamboo poles cover the open windows allowing air, mosquitos and wandering fingers to penetrate, illustrating the need to never place anything of interest within reach. Where shoes are to be left outside the door even though armies of ants march fearlessly through on their eternal search for anything edible.

I arrive back at base camp to find a slew of men camped outside the room in a haze of clove, the kretek cigarette a fixture in every hand. Not knowing what might materialize, I figure dinner can wait.

Word is out and the runners descend, some who spend their days sniffing out material from all over the archipelago and have arrived to exchange their stash for cash, local lads get stuff on the arm, acting as a middle man, hoping to make a killing, while masquerading as the real thing. So many entrepreneurial souls ready to provide entertainment along the acquisition highway.

As I sit in state on my tiled patio in a bamboo chair, each

vagabond takes his turn. Textiles are rolled out at my feet, wood masks are pulled out of rucksacks, gold and silver used in traditional ceremonies lie glittering in the fading light, the dusk providing cover maybe for many defects, holes and repairs. It's not a good time to part with money, I need to wait for the light of day. Most of the stuff has seen better days, if even authentic—but who knows what might emerge.

The men operate in groups of two or three, but one is solo, he has a suitcase and is wearing socks and real shoes. The footwear is impressive, here the shoe de rigeur is the honorable flip flop, secured in position between naked toes. He is Ferri, a man from Sumatra, he shows cloth from his island and strands of glass beads he says were interred with their owner in the eleventh century, recently dug up and now ready for another life. Even without a roof over their heads to deal under, exorbitant prices are thrown into the air, they obviously believe me way too fresh on the scene to understand how much something is worth.

Luckily I have learnt the art of making a deal from my husband, a man never shy about getting the best price, in fact the first to relish the challenge to a verbal duel whenever the opportunity arises, be it in India or Venezuela, slashing asked prices to a third and maybe getting it for half. It's a tightrope, a fine line to tread, in order not to cause the opposition to lose face by going too low or adopting an aggressive stance. To never walk away when the prices merge in the middle, or an unpleasant interlude might be waiting around the next corner.

Show and tell over, I'm ready to concentrate on a plate of rice, maybe adorned with a fried egg. Native drums signal the death of a clan member, a constant beat from dusk to dawn. Walking through the surrounding gardens in the shadow of dark I make the acquaintance of fire ants patrolling their turf, obviously irritated by my presence they attack my feet and ankles piercing the flesh with what feels like red-hot needles. The restaurant sprawls under a thatch roof in the depths of an oasis of green, the sides open to the elements. It's a great place to unwind from a day spent interacting with the Indonesian mind and frequented by the business tourist, here on the daunting task of seeking quality control in contemporary designs, clothing and jewelry to name a few, a place to take a break from the constant need to monitor work in progress.

The Three Brothers Inn

The restaurant at Three Brothers

Retiring to my hard mattress, I pull the sheet over my head, hoping my rented mosquito net will protect me from the flying menace screeching and circling, knowing that if there is a hole in the net, they will find it. Most of the night I twist and sweat, searching for sleep, their constant drone a pneumatic drill in my ear.

At five in the morning the rooster starts strutting his stuff and lets everyone know that his day has begun. I lie above a kaleidoscope of green, trees laden with cloying odiferous flowers used in offerings or placed behind an ear. I breakfast off a bowl of sweet black rice while watching the rats running along the rafters above, on course to raid the freshly placed offering, put in place to appease the gods. The rats dropping pieces and other waste onto the unsuspecting guests lounging on pillows below, maybe adding a little extra something to their nasi goreng. The green and red tokay, a lizard over a foot long who lives behind one of the ornamental mirrors jumps out rattling the glass on his search for insects and small vertebrae or to take advantage of a plate of chicken sate.

A bevy of green clad workers manicure the plants, using scissors to clip the grass attempting to deter the ever encroaching jungle. A man is waiting outside my door, he wants to take me to see a certain Daeng Iskandar, newly arrived in town and setting up shop in rented rooms. I jump on the back of a motorbike and we stream past beamos belching fumes, past caged cocks placed by the side of

Mamuli heirloom gold jewelry Sumba, Indonesia 19th century

the road, their owners under the illusion that the roar of the traffic will make them more ferocious when encountering their next duel, to fight for their lives.

Entering two dismal rooms where textiles have been pinned to the peeling painted interior is not impressive, and as I wonder how to gracefully escape a man in a plaid sarong motions towards worn chairs and a makeshift table. A woman appears and in a sequence that is becoming familiar, steaming cups of the local bean are presented with a side of oven fresh mysterious bundles which melt when put between the lips into pools of excruciatingly divine nutty flavors. This pair have just arrived from the Isle of Sumba hoping to cash in on the art market, Daeng having swallowed a bait thrown in his clean Sumbanese air by one of the current rajas of tribal art, Yamin Makarwaru. Yamin had hired him as a guide when visiting Sumba seeking treasure.

Daeng is a man of no particular education, he realizes that he has to be a gambler to survive and art dealing maybe one way to get ahead fast. No schooling is required, just a good eye and loads of charm which comes naturally to so many of these people. Daeng is a change of pace, as yet he has none of the slick manoeuvres of the already established dealers, he is still trying to pick up the art of the English tongue. I throw in a sprinkle of Indonesian that I am attempting to learn and know I must acquire to flourish on this side of the equator. He is already missing his island where his many siblings still live and his mother who was lost in one of the many ferry disasters that occur. He is refreshingly straight forward. I wait for the good stuff to make an entrance.

A gold piece is placed before me, each side depicts a tree with human skulls hanging from the branches and rows of buffalo horns at the base all worked in what appears twenty karat gold surrounding a central opening, reminiscent of female genitalia- or is it male?

Maybe part of the lure of this business is the explicit nature of the material, bodily parts being a fact of life and not as I had been brought up to believe safely kept under wraps until the proper moment arrives. The gorgeous golden ornament is a mamuli, an exquisite example of heirloom jewelry formerly owned by the big cheese of a village in Sumba and previously stored in the rafters of his house, only to be taken down and worn ceremonially on auspicious occasions. Sets of enormous ancient ivory bracelets are placed alongside. Daeng is another man who states his price, is open to a little back and forth, one always has to put a paw in the water, to see which way the wind is blowing.

Exiting with my newly acquired loot a man just climbing off his motorbike and about to make a grand entrance, introduces himself as Jogya John. Suspecting I might be an interloper, a new threat on the scene, he lets me know that the Indonesian art market has already been divided up, that each island is already presided over by a foreign art dealer landlord and not to waste my time. This makes me even more thrilled to be in on the chase.

Not accepted by the reigning studs already in the field is to me of no consequence, I view these latest exploits by my future peers as pure insecurity, just part of the shifting sand beneath the feet of any dealer. I'm more concerned with understanding the Indonesian mind which seems ready to accept cash from any quarter and finds it amusing to watch the foreigners squabble. The Indonesian mind that is often only too happy to sell a beautiful copy as the real thing. A scenario which while a little disturbing, keeps the foraging foreigner on his toes. Even the nicest people seem willing to play this game maybe they know, maybe they don't - it has always been thus. It's up to me to know. I'm on my own and have to see through the charm offensive. It's the only way to sink or swim, to differentiate between the crap and the killer piece and the marauding imposter. To look at many pieces, to handle them, to feel their surface, the edges. Do they feel worn with age or fresh out of the workshop. Does the piece have a life of its own or is it just a chunk of dead wood or metal? To spend time with a piece, to spend time with the people who made such things or their descendants, to know why it was made and for what function. Hopefully if attuned to the medium, like any other, an awareness develops, a familiarity. An ability to spot repairs, flaws, the ability to approach a piece with a discerning eye. An ability that evolves over time for some but not all.

On my way back to the Inn, past new concrete eyesores springing up around the edge of the road, creeping further into the green beyond, a group of men in a circle are animatedly shouting, hands gesticulating in the air. They don't seem to notice my presence, there is so much action taking place on the ground in front of them. Two roosters are having blades strapped to an ankle. Bets are being made and money is changing hands. The birds are positioned face to face then released, flying at each other in attack mode. A wild brief flurry ensues, before one is lying dead or dying in the dust. The women folk are nowhere to be seen, they are probably out planting rice, digging a ditch or carrying cement bricks on their heads. They know their place in paradise and that only the men can deal with the more important issues of the day.

That night at Made's after listening to a posse of young studs describe all the intimate details of catching waves, I meet up with a band of guys working on an oil rig exploration project. Happily off the rig, they're indulging in a few weeks of relaxation after a spree of dangerous deep-sea assignments. They introduce me to Long Island Tea, a lethal concoction of equal amounts of vodka, rum, tequila, gin and triple sec with lemon or sour mix all topped off with a splattering of coca cola, a drink I instantly loathe. These boys like living on the edge and drinking I gather helps banish their underwater experiences. An older Indonesian man introduces himself, apparently a former ambassador to the United States, he invites us home to meet his American wife.

I find myself strapped on the back of a bike, heading out of the jungle floating over a moonscape of white boulders, to arrive at a house hanging off a cliff overlooking the runway at the airport. For me the sight of planes taking off and landing never loses its allure, the rush, the speed, where are they going, the romance of the unknown.

Watching glowing aluminum rise and fall in the velvet black sky, we join a party in progress listening to early jazz vinyl and drinking the deadly tea. A delicately magnificent Balinese woman is draped over one of the sofas, obviously a woman of consequence and proves to be an irresistible attraction for one of the deep sea divers, who is drawn to her side as a moth to a light bulb. Together they radiate an aura of being in another world, as if the only people in the room, captivated by each other.

Apparently she is the wife of a local prince. On an island plagued by masculinity, infested with good and evil spirits and the need to save face, this is not a romance to consummate unless testing the forces of black magic. As woven into the Balinese Poleng textile, squares of black and white depicting a balance that has to be maintained for harmony to exist. I find that it's best not to become involved with the spirit world according to these people, strange inexplicable events might occur. Hair, nail clippings even underwear procured by vengeful hands can wreak havoc in a life, used as an instrument for revenge.

Just as I feel that I am getting the hang of operating on this part of the map or at least getting a toe wet, my progress is interrupted, another flying mission to Saudi Arabia has to be flown. But the time away will give me the time to reflect on progress made. Back jammed on the airplane with another load of pilgrims on the trip to their holy land will be a dose of another reality, a cold shower, away from the incestuous art circuit. It's always good to put a little distance, to take a look from another point, to fully understand what's happening. But on returning to Jakarta, I'm ready to jump back into the fray.

Returning to the center of the world, as the Balinese refer to their island, a sarong and dagger drama has just played out and the news is sweeping down the long table at Mades. Legend goes that as another day had sprung into action, as a houseboy delivered a flask of hot steaming tea and the mandatory bunch of bananas to the room of his guest he noticed that the door was ajar. Pushing it a little further he sees a man lying face down in the rented room. A Keris, a sacred ceremonial dagger, an instrument imbued with mystical, magical powers having pierced through the gap between the collarbone and shoulder blade severing the subclavian artery had entered the victim's heart. There on the white tiles, now splattered with blood, lies the American oil explorer.

Secrets are hard to hide on this isle of many ears and ulterior motives. Word had reached the enclave of the cuckolded spouse. His property had been infiltrated and soiled, whispers had swirled, to save face if nothing else, he needed to show strength, to maintain his position.

Needing a distraction I hire a car to escape to Ubud. Driving is an experience most visitors avoid. The village elders had placed a car wreck on a platform by the side of the road at one point, just as a reminder to anyone considering such a feat, of damage done when performing dangerous tactics behind the wheel, but it vanished after a few years, probably deemed too frightening for the fragile foreigner, there to witness the beauty not the seamy side of life.

I find that Indonesians who are so polite face to face, when they take to the roads are without scruples, adopting a style of driving I name surge and smile. The imaginary rules imply never give the right of way to anyone and drive like a bat out of hell whenever possible. When emerging from a minor road into a so called major road, surge full volume into the ongoing traffic, to wait for an official opening will be to wait all day. But always remember to smile when cutting in front - it's local protocol.

Of course I have to participate in this egomaniacal circus. Tailgating is a favorite sport, honking the horn is a way of life to be constantly embraced, just don't forget to grin and laugh when being a complete asshole! On the few stretches with double lanes the fast lane also serves as a turning lane to the left. Road works that are frequent alert the driver of their presence about thirty seconds before the fact. Road signs are just arriving but scant, it's so easy to take a turn to all the wrong places but at least it provides me with a chance to use my Indonesian patois to unravel my misguided wanderings. Everyone enjoys my plight, the opportunity to meet a stranger in an unhappy situation.

I carry cash in small denominations. When stopping at an intersection or one of the few impressions of a traffic light, I make sure that I don't go over the imaginary line. The police in their very smart uniforms, received in lieu of real wages use their official garb and authority to make up for their lack in pay. If pulled over for a real or invisible infraction, it's best to keep it friendly, a game to be played, to never protest. Bargaining is the way to go. The equivalent of two dollars seems to settle any problem and it's over quickly. I try not to run over chickens or other personal items that I might be sharing the road with, but a little cash always softens the blow if a dead bird is my fault. I become aware that raising the voice, arguing, pointing a finger or putting hands on hips, are all gestures considered offensive to the Indonesian. And even though I hate to bribe, I always remember to tip the vagabond on the street, the guy who lets me know that he will look after my car when I park. If I don't or ignore him, he will be sure to extract revenge.

I stop in Celuk, a cluster of dwellings on the road to the utopian republic of Ubud, a place where generations of silver artisans follow without hesitation in their ancestors footsteps, crafting by hand one piece at a time of wearable art, working in a room furnished with ancient wood benches, naked light bulbs hang in the air. This I find is a factory, I'm here looking for smiths to make some designs for my future inventory of silver jewelry as well as to purchase some of their productions. Darweiko, my kretek puffing new friend has recommended a family. They live behind the shop and factory, just off the main drag in a compound, grandmas, aunts, brothers and wives, all together.

Even though my main interest is in 'Tribal Art' I realize that this field has a limited audience as well as a limited supply of artifacts and I feel the need to have other ammunition to sell to a wider swath of humanity, to cash in on a different front. Besides, I've always loved fashion and the art of adornment.

I cautiously place an order asking my new crew to make a few prototypes, I need to see what they are capable of, having heard many a disaster tale from my buddies down at the Three Bros., the trial and error pathway to the perfect design, even saleable merchandise.

A tooth filing ritual is about to take place in the family private domain in the rear, a right of passage from puberty to adulthood and I'm welcome to join in. In the Balinese world teeth have to be smooth and level, pointy or uneven ivories are thought to be akin

Ceremony Legian, Bali

Balinese tooth filing ceremony. Suitably attired to commune with the spirits.

to an animal, associated with lust and greed, perfectly aligned teeth make a person physically and spiritually attractive. Besides how else would a god recognize a soul knocking on the heavenly gates, know whether it be man or beast?

The family reappear exquisitely attired in layers of gold painted cloth, tightly and ceremonially wrapped. Confined in such magnificence, they swelter under the tropical sun, groaning under the weight of the stunning gold headdresses, moaning about the headaches that will ensue. They let me know about the burden of having to fulfill these duties, the tremendous cost!

I come face to face with the local specialty, spit roasted turtle flesh, a greasy nauseating dish, luckily there's lots of rice to disguise my disgust and the heaviness of this delicacy. Gold leaf umbrellas flutter, a musical gamelan troupe plays and a theatrical dancing performance springs into action. As a spectator, I can just enjoy the scene without the overhead, the stress of having to look fabulous and vow to avoid the slick turtle dish at any future event.

Our flight duties successfully concluded it's time to ship out of paradise. The plane waits on the tarmac in the shimmering heat. Climbing aboard we stake our claim, a row of seats per person, a niche to camp out for the next seventeen odd hours, a myriad of accumulated souvenirs stuffed in the belly of the bird. My stash, I hope, will translate into a sideline career, but more importantly, a reason to return to these shores. Indonesia is an addiction and, like any other, it's hard to resist.

In San Francisco I approach the gallery of a veteran in the field of tribal art to get a feel for the market, but the local boy is not impressed enough to be interested. His assistant/girl friend however discreetly hands me her card conveying the idea that she might have viable clients. Another dealer, Richard Gervais of The Manila

Trading Company, an elegant successful haven on California and Polk Streets for Tribal art enthusiasts and decorators generously takes some pieces on consignment.

Then I discover the Sausalito Flea Market, a great arena for budding art dealers, providing a backdrop for not only meeting clients but an environment to practice the art of selling, bargaining and dealing directly with the public. People of every description gather to buy, barter and sell. It's billed as the greatest show on earth!

Flying in from a trip, I load up my car and line up for hours in order to get a much sought after space. Every Sunday is show time. At 6 a.m. the air bristles with anticipation. Buyers dive into freshly unloaded boxes, flashlights zooming in on a possible find, struggles erupting when two people spot the same thing at the same time, and this is even before the vendor has time to set up!

At the flea market

As Fools Rush In

One never knows who will show up

For many it's a Sunday ritual, a religious experience, where true art mingles with socks selling at three pairs for three dollars. People travel far and wide to attend this rite. Its reputation is a planetary statistic. The Flea is a place to get a corn dog, shoot the breeze and take in the latest antics of the Dirt Man dressed entirely in black leather, his head enshrined under a cowboy hat as he wanders through the dust laden strip shoeless and encrusted with a coating of real, proudly acquired down to earth filth.

Rain or shine, It's a huge outdoor party. Bill Galvin aka "Mr. Philippine" if he's in town, can be found selling in the Tribal zone with a barbeque set up smoking on the side, burgers and chicken cooking, fodder to feed the tribal flock. It's an incubator for dealers who will later grace the halls of elite shows in Brussels, Paris, San Francisco, Santa Fe and New York. The Flea is where they find their legs buying and selling. It's a basic set up, just a table to throw the material on, no frills just straight forward fun. Pedestals and polite conversation are not required! Snatch it up while you can before another reaches out to grab it! Repartee cuts through any acquired attitudes. Worship at the Flea Market altar, but don't expect your sins to be forgiven. The era of political correctness has not yet been invented!

There is, of course one individual who attempts to stir the shit, muddy the waters, and is apt at killing merchandise with faint praise or launching a ploy to dissuade a likely buyer especially if a piece is already in other hands and being enthusiastically viewed, hoping that he can, after doubt has been caste, wiggle in and obtain it at a lower price. There is always some pig trying to raid your trough, a malevolent fixture relentlessly willing to sabotage confidence in a piece or a person, a foul fish contaminating the bubbling brook, manipulative and deceitful.

By two o'clock the wind barrels in and whips up the dirt, a signal to pack up and leave before displays crash to the ground and the filth infiltrates even the most personal parts of the human anatomy. Cars and trucks jostle to exit. Vendors of used frying pans and ancestral art slink back into reality, hopefully with more bucks than when they arrived.

CHAPTER ELEVEN

A Beautiful Arrival - A Traumatic Finale

Showing up at the airport for a trip, I casually call my gynecologist for the results of a recent pregnancy test and receive confirmation of what I have been trying to achieve for the last eight years. I immediately pull sick leave. To continue the grueling flight attendant schedule while carrying such precious cargo is out of the question. Kaiser, my health care provider, refuses to issue the paperwork stating that I'm unfit to fly, but another doctor for a fee deems it necessary for me to forgo the joys of waitressing in the sky for the duration of my growing state of being.

    A trip to Indonesia on the other hand is an unavoidable necessity! I need to stock up for life after birth! As I sprawl on the Indonesian sand enclosed in a thong, the Balinese lady beach vendors are full of questions and advice about my obviously swelling situation. I have never felt fitter. Luckily my pregnancy is the sort that makes me glow rather than throw up.

ESCAPE FROM ENGLAND

Nine months after a Mexican adventure in a dollar-a-night bare bones shack on the beach in Puerto Escondito, Alex arrives, a much longed for and anticipated event by both of his new parents, a great source of joy and for me, a tremendous achievement!

On arrival at the hospital for the big event, the clerk asks why I'm here, the evidence of my increased girth concealed in wraparound purple Balinese jodhpur pants, a matching purple with silver threads mohair sweater, and with gold shoes on my feet, I'm ushered into the birthing quarters.

Spread eagled on the bed the next question is, "Would you like medication?" Unaware of the painful drama about to unfurl, I naively reply, "No thanks," no drugs or injections to lessen the agony for me. What is a little pain after having been attacked by a band of feral dogs on a Mexican beach, or narrowly escaping being trampled by water buffalo in the mountains of Nepal and stoned in Morocco?

Three hours pass and for the first time in my earthly existence I totally lose control, screaming along with all the other women attempting to restock the human population. Those slender hips, I have always enjoyed are not such an asset when performing this task! I plead for any kind of relief. Peter, kitted out in blue shoe covers and headgear, is here at my request to make sure that nobody screws up, but he's busy chatting up the nurses, cracking jokes, enjoying the moment.

Alex makes his appearance on the world stage just four hours after the first indication of his imminent arrival. At eight thirty on a Friday night he arrives, just in time for the weekend.

A huge, muscular African American male nurse appears by my bedside. He lifts Alex, now washed and cleansed, and places him in the palm of his hand, which is large enough to accomplish this amazing feat. Then, very gently, he places Alex in the appropriate position and instructs me in the ways of breastfeeding.

Having just pulled off the most phenomenal accomplishment of my worldly career to date, surviving almost certain death and receiving a present in the form of a wonderful boy baby, I'm not ready for the barrage of decisions thrust at me. "Do I want my new prize circumcised?" "No thanks. I'm British. We don't inflict such barbaric procedures on the innocent and newly arrived!" "What are the names to be set in stone on the birth certificate?" Not having yet come up with a definitive winner, I take a rain check. I just want to relax, but it's time to get up and walk around. I'm ecstatic to have been relieved of my bodily burden.

The next day, mother and child are discharged into the arms of a sunny November afternoon, I'm ready to do what it takes innocently believing that it's a natural chain of events. As my dear husband insists, a woman instinctively has great insight into motherly minutiae. My own mother is six thousand miles away, having shown no desire to rush over for the event and I'm somewhat relieved she didn't insist, knowing that I would have to look after her as well as the newborn babe if she did. But the first time diaper rash erupts on that pristine white bum I immediately panic and rush us both to the doctors.

With the hospital behind us, all three in the car, I'm primed for the ride back home. Peter on the other hand has other plans, a site visit to one of his projects, followed by a brief tour of downtown, during which I almost collapse, having to rush to a restroom to recover, not that a water closet is ever an easy place to locate in any American city. Finally reaching home, I tuck Alex into a basket with handles I had converted into a cot and place the babe in the great red and gold Chinese bed standing center stage in our living room to get him off to an artistic start. This motherhood excursion is a great learning curve for me and happily Alex survives in spite of my inadequacies.

I finagle and delay my recall to the skies for a year. Then I'm given an ultimatum: resign or return. I hire an au pair, a French girl, her style is slow, but that's a plus when looking after a one-year-old. I envisage a clean house filled with French cooking aromas as being part of the deal, but none of these dreams materialize, Sam is totally devoid of any culinary skills but in caring for Alex, she's on the right wavelength.

Although not particularly ravishing Sam, like most French women, knows how to make the best of her assets, transforming mundane into radiant mystique. We spend many a night around the dinner table (She doesn't seem to mind my cooking), accompanied by red wine and Franglais, a French and English combo.

A year later, speaking English like a native, she returns to the Basque lands of southwest France. I'm not quite ready to quit the skies, so I sign up for the dreaded Honolulu turnarounds as a last resort, which entails rising at four in the morning for destination Oakland Airport on cue to transport a load of humans ready to break loose in the tropics. After a couple of hours on the ground spent gazing at the airport koi gracefully gliding in pools and stocking up on macadamia nuts, we return with a fresh load, the seats filled with yards of sun kissed flesh, straw hats and floral necklaces, arriving back late at night. Six or seven of these nightmares suffices for the month in terms of flight hours.

With a growing inventory paired with the desire to continue my equatorial flings I inspect the Tribal Art Show in San Francisco. Many of the players from the Sausalito Flea Market are there, flogging their wares in more illustrious surroundings. The show is friendly and casual. Art is a vehicle to finance trips. Potential clients have bucks to splurge, a superfluous cash flow. These are giddy times, we will find out later! The people of Indonesia, Nepal and the

A Beautiful Arrival - A Traumatic Finale

Philippines are just beginning to realize that their everyday old junk is actually worth something and can be exchanged for cash! That they can then replace it with new bright and shiny stuff and plastic!

I'm in the door, accepted as a bona fide art dealer. As a graduate of the Sausalito Flea Market, I know the drill. "It's show time and you're on, the world is your oyster and the future is a vivid shade of rose."

I sign on to more shows in Los Angeles and San Francisco, juggling to avoid conflict with my flight schedule. To fund the ever-growing financial requirements of houses and home, I continue designing and buying silver jewelry, handmade by the artisans of the island of Bali, covering every willing inch of the local scene with my taste and acquisitions, leaving no stone unturned.

I realized on stepping foot in America that it was all about loot. Now I'm bending over backwards to worship the money god, the quest for gratification in the sales circus nipping at my ankles. Or maybe I'm beginning to realize that without my financial success, my current lifestyle is in danger of crashing and burning. Just as well, as other areas of my sphere are starting to implode!

World Airways sells its Oakland Airport location, offices, hangars and all to United Airlines. The crew bases are relocated to Charleston South Carolina and Philadelphia. Flight attendants are now required to relocate or commute to one of these new bases, a strategy no doubt to dislodge high seniority crew members, those with the union book of rules firmly tucked under their armpits, who know their rights, fight for every penny owed to them for gross overtime infractions and other abuses, those who squawk and demand retribution for all and every strike against them.

Many of my peers have married, bought houses, produced children, stuff that normal people do with their lives. The company obviously hopes that these crewmembers will throw in the towel and save the company a lot of money, rather than commute back and forth to the East Coast at their own expense.

Philadelphia is now where I show for a flight. Reduced rate tickets, ten percent of a first class ticket fare, can be purchased but reservations cannot be made. A flight attendant has to show at the airport and hope that a seat will be available. Even if already installed onboard, a flight attendant can be dragged off the plane if a passenger shows up with a higher priced ticket. Only when the aircraft doors are closed can a sigh of relief be allowed, a chance to relish a five and half hour flight before actually clocking in for work!

Airlines are consolidating and canceling flights, trying to squeeze as many warm bodies aboard as few aircraft as possible. The glamour is wearing pretty thin.

I have a flight out to Europe and beyond late at night, I show early at the airport in San Francisco but the flight is overbooked. I secure a seat on a later flight and still arrive on time at Philadelphia airport to meet the crew— but I have to sign in at scheduling, a few miles down the road! Instead I call, they let me know that "the rules cannot be bent" to accommodate my plight, I'm removed from the flight. Do I hole up in a cheap hotel or catch the red eye back, all, of course, at my personal expense?

I receive a disciplinary notice documenting that I have failed to comply with the company rules, failed to show for a trip. I'm suspended from all duties without pay or allowances. But "due to a perfect record for the past twenty years the usual fourteen day suspension will be reduced to seven days and will be administered at a later date due to present company requirements." I'm overwhelmed by their benevolence.

It soon becomes clear to even an oxygen deprived, jet lagged individual that the price for commuting is similar to, or less than,

A Beautiful Arrival - A Traumatic Finale

the pathetic remuneration being received for the honor of operating as a sky bound slave for this bunch of despots.

The Gulf War is in full swing. Thanks to George Bush senior I'm temporarily based in Belgium taking troops to Doha in Qatar. Dropping them off in the desert, we crew get to spend a few hours admiring the sand dunes and stocking up on tee shirts flouting palm trees and camels, silk screened by some entrepreneurial spirit out there in the void. Then it's back to Belgium with another batch of boys and girls. Although we signed up for a two-week assignment, the schedule is TBA (to be announced), potentially never ending and morphs into a month long saga! My flight career is winging into oblivion.

"Those wretched crewmembers and unions are ragging about having to fly in and out of a war zone?" our Chief, Ed Daly, states, "No one is held here at World in bondage." No, we just enjoy being inhumanely chastised and our lives put on the line in some foreign conflict without the thrill of being monetarily rewarded.

Ed Daly, the Commander in Chief is still living in a different era in the 1970's and fondly remembers himself as an action figure as portrayed in the scenes of him standing on the steps of a 727 aircraft on the last flight out of Da Nang Vietnam as the aircraft attempting to take off swerves on the runway to avoid men firing bullets and hurling grenades, one damaging a wing. When armed deserting Vietnamese soldiers pushed aside women and children trying to mount the stairs, determined not to be left behind, only to encounter Ed wielding a pistol in one paw striving to control the surging stampede.

When people in sheer desperation climbed into the wheel wells, some falling back to earth as the plane gained altitude, when at six thousand feet, the stairs still hanging from the side of the craft, Daly pulled one last man into the cabin. When the plane had to be flown at low altitude as the door where the stairs used to be would not close and the load was so heavy. When seat rows meant for three were stuffed with five or six and the hold was bursting with even more bodies.

When the pilots had no idea how badly the plane might be damaged or whether the wheels would descend for landing as people and bodies might be stuck in the wheel wells hindering the deployment of the landing gears, when the pit brought the craft in delicately but successfully into Saigon.

Ed Daly is and was a man who lives rough and tough and expects his employees to be made of the same stuff. "The Teamsters Union leaves a rancid taste in Daly's mouth," states the San Francisco Chronicle. Another newspaper notes, "He's arranged mercy flights to disaster sites at his own expense, yet fired stewardesses who can't find his brand of steak sauce." As one World pilot, who like most of World's employees asks not to be identified, confides, "He's an extremely difficult individual - the way to survive around here, is to stay out of his way. You're fired is the method of operation." As yet I haven't had the pleasure of encountering this dashing entrepreneur.

As serfs in the sky, we strive to improve our conditions. But even when we strike, the company by law, conveniently, has to execute military requirements for the government, and naturally, World Airways is delighted to comply. Management men and high seniority crew members man these trips, but World Airways employs any warm bodies, virtually straight off the street to fill the void. The company, continuing to feather its own bank account, can afford to hold out indefinitely while hoping the striking crewmembers will be brought to their knees. We who picket at the airport receive $37 a week from the teamsters union. Unfortunately, most crewmembers live on the financial edge, a few weeks away from bankruptcy, and

A Beautiful Arrival - A Traumatic Finale

the company, aware of this, waits for the Teamsters to cave in, to accept a new contract offering little more than before.

I resign in October, 1991, handing in my wings, the metal pin worn by all people of flight, and my cockpit key, receiving in exchange $2000 severance pay, which I immediately invest in a magnificent Philippine tribal head ornament a wild array of rattan, mother of pearl, feathers and a monkey skull, later sold to the De Young Museum a world renowned fine arts emporium in San Francisco dating from the nineteenth century. It's just as well that I've been practicing for my future role—self-employed.

CHAPTER TWELVE

The Most Important Part of Life is Death

Free of flying the increasingly malevolent skies, no longer an employee with a paycheck I feel the pressure to replenish my dwindling inventory and bank balance, another trip to the other side of the equator is, I hope, the answer.

Arriving early in the morning instead of sensibly grabbing a few hours in the bed, which I notice now has two sheets instead of just one, I feel the need to check up on some chatter about a new place in town. Taking a shower to revive a little of the aura I lost in the sky, warm water instead of cold sprays out of the faucet at the Three Brothers Inn. Starving, having avoided the donations handed out in the aisles, I'm ready to grab a bite, only to find that the gloriously ramshackle restaurant has been replaced by a more sanitary specimen located close to a new jostling road at the back. Hovering over a bowl of Bakso Urat, meatballs suspended in noodle soup, motorbikes blast past, the brush man pedals by seated on his steed piled high with feather dusters and the toy man interrupts demonstrating his latest cheap trinket, guaranteed to break within a few days. I'm just happy to see that at least bratwurst is still on the menu.

Polos is a small shop front on a nasty expanse of Jalan Legian coexisting with shacks that have recently sprung into action catering to the latest lurid form of tourist with just enough expendable money in their pockets to effectively destroy any pristine landscape. Hole in the wall kiosks, purvey all the tacky souvenirs deemed necessary by this breed to take back home as evidence of the great time had while capsizing from the Bali Belly. There in the middle of this stickiness is Polos, an unassuming passage leads to a garden of vivid green where banana trees flourish, providing a great escape from the endless parade of vendors now pushing their wares on the streets outside. Furniture, textiles, sculpture and jewelry are skillfully displayed. In the rear, busy hands restore, reconstruct and resurrect.

Uninterrupted I wander through many rooms, devoid of the usual haphazard piles of stuff, here every piece is thoughtfully presented with style, chairs and tables provide lounging areas to sprawl in while absorbing the presentation. In the distance a woman sweeps the floor with a native reed broom. A slight wiry guy appears, to inspect what has strayed into his domain. Barefoot, in shorts and a tee shirt, a halo of black curls reveals an enigmatic countenance, not easy to read. A soft boyish voice welcomes me, as two steaming cups of the local brew are gently placed between us. He is interested in why I am here, who I might be, rather than impressing upon me who he is. On this front I have met my match, always preferring to listen rather than prevail. I am used to males stating their case, extolling their virtues, he veers away from that tack, a refreshing change of pace. Just as we are delving into who we might be, word arrives that an event of magnificent proportions, a once in a lifetime ritual of

The Most Important Part of Life is Death

passage, the funeral of the last Raja of Waikabubak on the island of Sumba is about to take place and I'm invited along for the ride.

After a twenty seven hour trip, seventeen spent in the air and ten just waiting on the ground, I'm looking forward to chilling out slowly as my internal clock readjusts to the fifteen-hour time change. An, my host, gently lets me know that "this is a chance of a lifetime."

The next day I find myself sitting at the airport with Daeng our leader, the man from Sumba, now our guide, An, Daniella an Italian freshly arrived that morning, Jogyja John and a wealthy married Javanese collector and his girlfriend. Daeng's wife, not willing to put her comfort level on the line, knowing that a trip to this outlier island is a hard landing strip, has come to see us off and prepared a moveable feast for our journey.

After a few false starts, commandeering seats on inter island planes often requiring patience and a lot of graft, we eventually take to the air. Waingapu, the main town is a scruffy cluster of huts scattered along a dirt road, but a few nasty antique stalls need to be inspected. The horns emerge from art dealer heads as we rustle through the stuff, ready to engage in a rut if anything of consequence emerges.

A friend of Daeng has offered us a place to sleep. The cool night sky provides a riveting display of stars as we sit outside, goat, rice and raw garlic are on the menu. I share a bed with Daniella, the newly arrived Italian, we both pass out when we hit the straw mattress still wallowing in the throes of jet lag.

Stuffed in a jeep with Daeng our anointed leader at the wheel, we fly past wild scrub, where feral horses still roam. A village crosses our path, a man splendid in a turban, sarong and batik shirt comes out to greet us, he is ready to lead his kinsmen on foot to the funeral. Invited into his home, we stoop under an enormous thatch roof to witness a single room with a central fireplace used for cooking, pots and pans hang down from above. Art dealer eyes soar up to the rafters, where they know the heirloom treasure is stored. It would be inappropriate to enquire as to whether it might be for sale at this point in time, as it is necessary equipment to be displayed at the upcoming ceremony, we will get to see it then. One can only guess what art deals might take place behind the scenes, furtively in the shadows of death. A pair of ancestor figures stand on duty, not of great age or beauty but they will later appear parked in a booth at a tribal art show.

The clan voraciously chew the betel nut, a mild narcotic, no doubt to get in the funereal mode, to give them strength on their upcoming safari. Umbu, the head man is delighted to pose for a photo, a natural exhibitionist, who would be just at home on a film set in Los Angeles or lighting up the Bollywood circuit. He wants us to stay so that he can get to know us, especially the women. We drag ourselves away amid fond farewells.

On arrival at our destination, we're invited to view the Raja's body by his widow. He has been resting up in the attic of his house, embalmed and wrapped in many expensive ikat cloths for two years while his family amassed enough cash to perform an impressive farewell, suiting his status in life.

Here death is viewed as a successful conclusion to the earthly life circle, the most important part of living. It's of paramount importance for the mortal soul to be sent out of this world with the prestige appropriate to its' rank, to journey into the superior spirit world to join the ancestors in style.

Sitting cross legged on the floor, sirih, the betel nut is presented, a sign of peace and unity, the seed of the areca palm. Just the nut, lacking a betel leaf or lime powder to activate the nuts effect when chewed. We graciously accept, to refuse would be a show of disrespect. It's tough and gritty, like chewing aspirin, I hope not to break a tooth in my show of gratitude.

Guests arrive settling in for a possible two week stint, camping out, cooking over fires, there's not enough roof to cover all these heads. We are assigned to sleep on desks or the floor of the schoolhouse. The river is our bathroom, trees and bushes providing cover for other functions. A gift of a goat arrives, to be cooked on a makeshift spit, luckily this is men's work, Daniella and I look on with enthusiasm.

Maidens wrapped in hand woven sarongs embellished with wild horses and chickens dance meditatively in a semi circle, the carved turtle shell combs perched in their hair signifying that they have reached puberty but are not yet wed. The Raja's wife takes part, wearing a similar comb, a privilege displaying her nobel rank. Huge gold mamuli hanging from ears, breastplates and headdresses sizzle in the sun. Mourners, presumably overcome by grief and not from an overdose of the constantly available nut, fall into a trance like state, flailing and wailing until they have to be carried away. Guests sit in the dead Raja's house, chants of shamans fill the air. The betel nut tray circulates continuously.

The night before the big event heralds the slaughtering of the animals that will accompany the last Raja to the next world. This practice used to include wives and slaves but is now outlawed by the powers that be in Jakarta. Limits have also been set on the number of animals sacrificed under the pretext of preventing families from bankruptcy. But Jakarta is a long way away. Human headhunting is still rumored to be practiced here and this is 1988!

The first buffalo is led to its' destiny by two ropes attached to a ring through the nose. In sacrificial position, six men each side of the beast grip the ropes, the creature's head is raised high in the air, the whites of the eyes flash, he tries to bolt, the men hold on. Machete man swings his weapon aiming for the throat, hoping for an instant death from a single blow. Blood spurts, the beast staggers, writhing, putting on a final show of strength before dropping to his knees as life ebbs away. It seems like eternity before another thrust mercifully finishes him off, he collapsing in a pool of his own blood.

The other animals smelling death, panic, try to break loose, ready to charge anything in their way to freedom. This might be the time to shin up that tree you have already earmarked for such an occasion. Many onlookers have died when events went awry at similar ceremonies.

Umbu head man of a village on the Isle of Sumba

The Most Important Part of Life is Death

Arriving for the last rites of the last Raja of Waikabubak

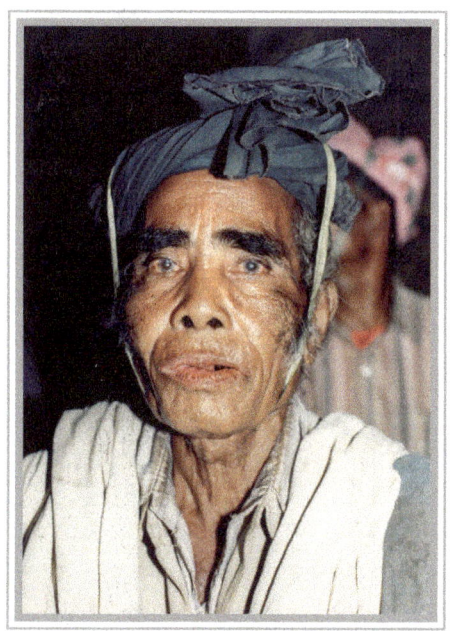

A guest at the funeral

Maidens wrapped in handwoven Sumbanese sarongs dance

Guest wearing an heirloom gold headdress in a trance

The Most Important Part of Life is Death

Guest carried away by emotion

Sitting in the dead Raja's house as the Shaman chants & the betel nut circulates

ESCAPE FROM ENGLAND

The first buffalo being led to his destiny

Machete man takes aim

The Most Important Part of Life is Death

The final cut

The first sacrifice

ESCAPE FROM ENGLAND

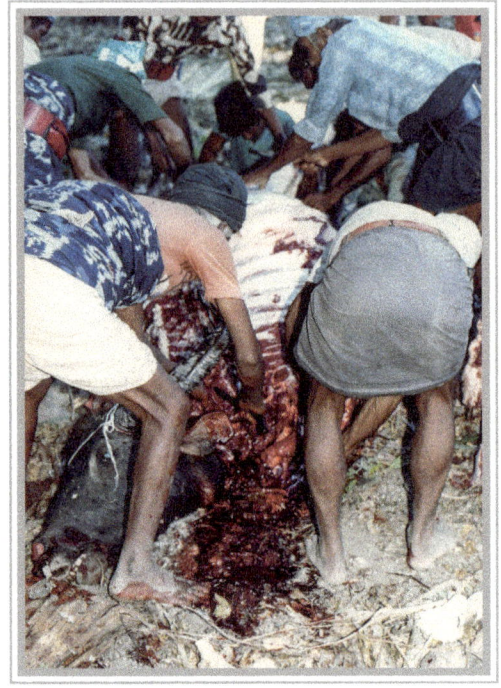

Food for the ensuing feast

The dead Raja makes his final journey

The Most Important Part of Life is Death

Wearing the tortoiseshell comb while contemplating life

Traditional village

Megalithic stone tombs & altars

Megalithic stone tombs & altars

The Most Important Part of Life is Death

Woman weaving the ikat cloth

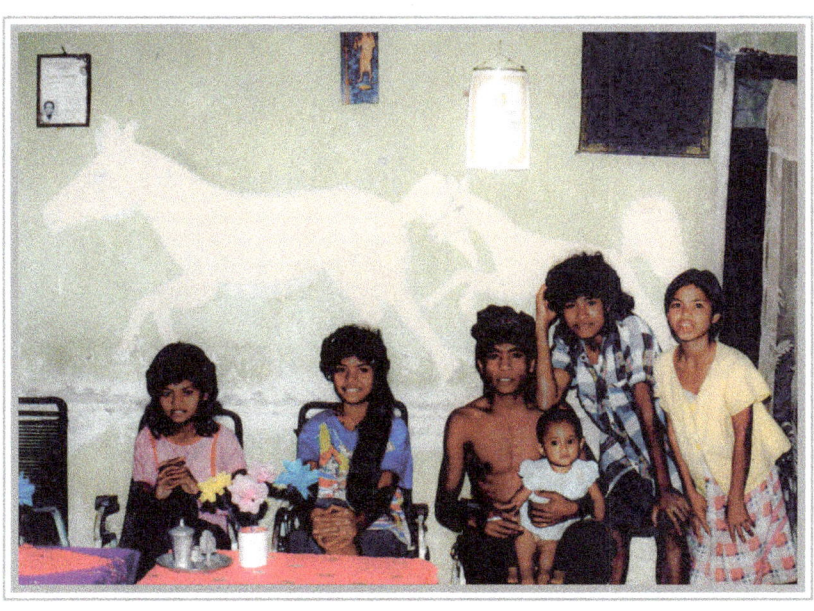

Some of the locals we were lucky enough to meet

ESCAPE FROM ENGLAND

The Most Important Part of Life is Death

Ninety nine more executions to go, the view macabrely fascinating proves too gruesome for our palates, the crowd is getting higher and higher, electrical currents surge through the air, the joint is hopping, Jogyja John is out in the throng with a vodka bottle sharing the good spirits.

The following day, the sarcophagus containing the Raja draped in prestigious ikat cloth is transported from his house on the shoulders of twenty men to his final resting place. Protecting the cortege, men flank either side ready with shield and spear. The ground is littered with blood and guts from the buffalo and horses, following the Raja into the next world, the carcasses are being cut up to provide for the ensuing feast.

Foregoing such culinary treats we set off to explore megalithic stone altars and tombs, to watch women weave the famous ikat cloth on hand looms, a cloth of many motifs, the yarn is wrapped and dyed prior to weaving, a strategic operation requiring much skill in order to come up with a clean precise pattern. Everywhere curious children find us just as intriguing as we find them irresistible. We are at the mercy of the people to feed us and provide shelter as tourists are as yet an unknown species.

Besides the theatricals played out in glowing technicolor, this trip has also given me time to get to know these players in the field, even Jogya John having recovered from his drunken orgy under the cover of the Sumbanese night, now recognizes me as a potential human. We had walked together while the rest of the crew slept off the funereal aspects of our trip, on foot to villages where people still stuck in the stone age welcomed us into their life, falling for John's ribald renditions of the Indonesian tongue. He confides in me, as we stroll of his involvement with a Dutch Indonesian woman, I only too happy to be a confident rather than a target.

Daeng's star is rising, arriving in Bali armed with a stash of art and just the clothes on his back, he is now surfacing as a bona fide aficionado, gaining respect from his peers and all who are lucky enough to sample his aura. He has bought land and is in the process of erecting a temple to tribal art, to house his family and growing position. He is a comrade, a man who would cover your back in a tight situation. He's interested in my reaction when face to face with a piece, I find myself wanting to believe his word, but I already know this to be dangerous territory with any dealer, personal knowledge is the key.

An, a Chinese Indonesian, a clove cigarette constantly hovering between his lips, reveals a former existence as an automobile mechanic, that he went against Chinese practice by marrying a Balinese, who he now keeps with his three children in his family compound in Denpasar. She is still allowed to practice Hinduism, the religion of Bali, a way of life he readily embraces, as well it seems, any other variations that cross his path. He is entirely comfortable amid the swirl of differing values and is only too happy to engage in all the differences, much to the despair of this secluded spouse. The Javanese pair quietly enjoy their time together, not wishing verbally to join in.

Landing back at Polos, which in Indonesian means plain, implying the opposite to reality in this instance, just to confuse, as is often the case on this territory, cold beer emerges from the kitchen and numerous plates of spicy Sumatran dinner are piled high on the long table.

An, afflicted like many dealers, wanders through his gallery adjusting, repositioning pieces, always trying to improve the presentation, he has a feminine grace and sensibility. He suggests driving up country to bathe in the public fountains of Singapadu, to join the people in their nightly ablutions or he adds, just to watch, which sounds more appealing to my ears, I'm not quite ready to abandon my sarong in the company of this crew of banditos. We race past rice paddies, the moon gleaming off their submerged beauty, the cool night air gliding over bronzed skin, washing away any lingering thoughts of the carnage recently witnessed.

The next day I visit Darweiko. He mentions he is heading up to the northern edge of Bali to Singaraja, a historic port city once crawling with traders from the East, on a brief expedition to track down fresh material, would I like to come along? Relishing all the contacts he must have in an area I had not yet explored, I jump at the chance.

After a less than impressive arrival, former glory nowhere in sight, we consume a nondescript meal in less than pristine circumstances before checking out the art scene. Darweiko snaps up a few items which I consider not up to my standards, having learnt that only the best examples with style, age and imbued with a feeling that lets you know they were made by a passionate skilled hand are worth hauling eighteen thousand miles back home.

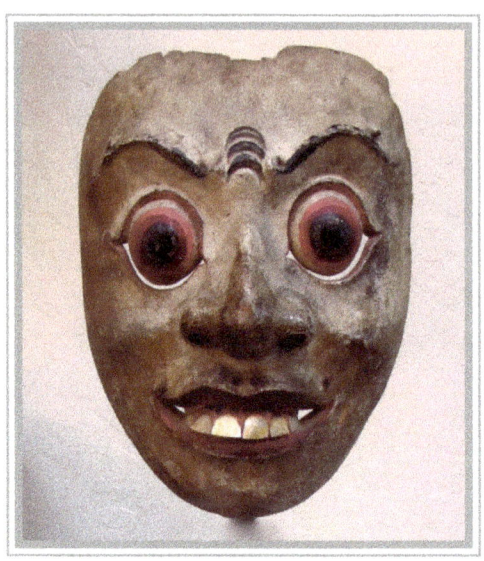

*Mask Bali Jauk Manis depicting a demon
in destructive mode 19th/early 20th century*

Arriving at the hotel of his choice, I find that only one room has been reserved. Thoughts of ulterior motives on his part had flitted through my mind-but he's old, married with five daughters! I ask him "what would you think if one of your daughters, was propositioned in a similar way?"

Entrenched in my own quarters, that I had demanded and paid for, before bedding down thankfully alone, I find a man at my door clutching a wood mask used for dancing. The lips smile and leer at the same time, curling up at the sides to expose a set of mother of pearl teeth, round eyeballs sizzle in their sockets piercing the night air. Part human, part demon, the piece almost jumps out of the shy hands pushing it in my direction, as if alive. The original paint is dirty, the moustache and eyebrows are missing, it's a little frayed around the edges and the back shows signs of much sweat from the men who had danced it, a nineteenth century piece. The owner, bent

The Most Important Part of Life is Death

with age seems thrilled to receive fifty dollars in exchange. It's a prize I do not intend to show my less than stellar companion.

The following morning after a night spent happily apart, we motor down south, Darweiko stopping off to buy grapes and apples for his wife, crops that flourish in the mountain air, with no word of the clash of the night before. Relieved to say goodbye, I have no plans to rush back to see him soon.

Deciding not to just sit around and let moss grow between my toes, I take to the air, destination Java is within reach, I'm on track to overdose on a bowl of golf ball size rubbery mystery meatballs floating in noodles, with a jug of jackfruit stewed in a caldron of coconut milk doused in sugar on the side and also to visit Yamin who has relocated to Yogyakarta. As usual he has been busy, has bought land, constructed a mansion, married a girl from Acheh and is diving full hog into expanding his empire from furniture to designer handbags, fathering one son with another in the oven and hoping to produce even more, maybe enough for a soccer team, on his time off.

Never one to hang around without a motive he loads me into a jeep and we set off into the countryside. Arriving unannounced as is the custom, new and old cronies are delighted to find him adorning their doorstep. We are ushered in with fanfare. Of course we need sustenance to sustain us on each and every visit and are plied with the mandatory cups and plates of goodies as we listen to elders recall news of their village. We wait until the time is ripe to be introduced to their stash.

Roaming and rooting through dusty crumbling interiors we interrupt spiders actively spinning webs. Heads of wooden carved deer stare down, gazing at us with wild eyes, maybe of this world as well as another, no doubt in touch with past lives, relaying our actions to the ancestors as they follow every footstep, taking in every move, racks of original antlers sprout from their heads. Architectural rendering from old Javanese houses, intricately carved, rich with patina lie in stacks, waiting to be reused in a new setting.

After accumulating the sweat and dirt offered by any Indonesian day and bursting from the all the mandatory delicacies offered at every stop along the way, we head back, the jeep jammed to the rafters with old wood. Yamin's faithful retinue are waiting, ready with the evening meal. His wife does not sit with us at the table, no doubt heeding Islamic culture, a pity. I have been introduced to this woman, elegantly attractive in a dark Persian way and would have liked to get to know her. I fly back to Bali with boxes of deer heads as my luggage.

The rainy season is about to arrive, a time when streets can be taken over by several feet of water, when the sight of mattresses on roofs hoping to dry out is a familiar sight and washed clothes never really dry, retaining an odor of rotten water. A time when the magic mushroom springs out of cow pies overnight and discreet hole in the wall eating establishments serve up the spoken menu offering omelets, tea and soup laced with the potent fungi and when some deluded souls under the influence of such are known to lie on the tarmac at the airport under the stars as the planes take off and land.

After so much time on the circuit searching for loot, I decide to drop in for a spot of afternoon tea with a fellow entrepreneur, also camping out at Three Bros. We try the omelet as well before heading to the beach to secure a now much in demand patch of sand, planting our towels as a display of temporary ownership. Entertainment is all around, the peanut man plying his trade, steaming peanuts, transferring the wet nuts with a slotted scoop into a newspaper cone, this afternoon takes on a vaudeville flavor, the nuts self launching into the air, he springing into a frenzy trying to capture them and confine them to the newsprint. We drift off only to wake to find that we are part of a performance, surrounded by Balinese in ceremonial gear, fringed umbrellas swirling above as the gamelan group musically seeks connection with spirits beyond the grave. A woman vendor is pushing pineapple in our faces. With one swipe, like that of a French guillotine in the days of Louis XVI, the top rolls in the sand, the outer husk discarded and the body sliced into circular offerings. Girls in thongs and wearing a tan writhe like snakes in a pit. Glittering white sand sticking between our toes, puffs up into clouds and floats off. The palm trees wearing feathered crowns weep and wail at the human squalor that has taken over paradise. Toxins coursing through our bodies, hamper our dreams and remind us that we are still human.

Tonight the Balinese lifeguards, who save many a tourist being swept away in the strong sea current, look more handsome than ever.

During times of little rain the fungi merchants spike their dishes with alternative potions. News of foreign bodies found floating in the stagnant waters of the Denpasar river circulate. Falling out of favor, like anything else here in Shangri-la with the powers that be, the mushroom parlours disappear.

The island of Lombok is half an hour away by a small prop jet, the sort of craft that seems to be made of plywood and held together with duct tape. The airport is a strip, the perimeter a jungle, stairs are rolled out for disembarkation. Cakranegara the main town offers a choice of two losmen. Choosing the less threatening, I'm ushered into a ten by eight foot expanse of peeling walls and a single cot, lacking even a top sheet. The facilities out back are a triumph of basic plumbing, a hole in the ground, a tub of cold water and a plastic bucket. But I'm not here to lounge in luxury. In the marketplace, chickens flap and squawk, the usual army of rats run among the stench and produce. I'm here to find baskets, tobacco containers, tightly woven, some so exquisite, the fibers have melded together with loving wear, developing a rich glossy patina. "Please visit my house", one vendor suggests after I buy everything he has.

He lives with many wives and children. Lunch is served, a mountain of rice and a sprinkling of Taliwang chicken, the jewel of Lombok cuisine. I've already heard much about this bird, word of it's delicious attributes having even spread to Bali. I'm not terribly awestruck, but after a few days realize there's not much else to eat on this patch of soil. Everything is washed down with tea-forget about having a cold beer on an Islamic island.

Runners are lined up at my squalid sanctuary on my return and I'm spirited away on a motorbike over a dirt road through ravishing greenery. A seat is waiting for me and sitting like a white raja, villagers present pieces created for their personal use, some so beautiful they translate into art when viewed by a western eye. Baskets, weavings, betel nut paraphernalia, clippers with gold and silver handles, cases to hold cock fighting knives and candle holders. Small but elegant artifacts. They are thrilled to get ugly money for their ancestral wealth.

That night before hunkering down on the hard cot, I try the restaurant across the street. Sitting alone at a plastic table, the Taliwang chicken is brought forth, the only thing on the menu besides rice. I notice the Lombok mosquitos are bigger, hairier and more aggressive than their Balinese cousins. Back in the bed I pull my sarong over my head for protection.

Breakfast is served, a steaming container of tea and one cold hard boiled egg. Happy to escape, I glance down as the craft gains altitude at unspoiled beaches, no human baggage in sight.

CHAPTER THIRTEEN

Bifurcation

Starting each month with no guaranteed paycheck can be challenging when balancing three mortgages and two sets of tenants. Traversing the state I check where, what and who might be a suitable target to ambush with my silver jewelry collections. Being more of an introvert than an extrovert this is grueling stuff, but my voracity knows no limits. Dressing for the part, promoting my stuff, I arrive cold without notice, after introducing myself to the mover and shaker in charge, I seem to be able to parley my way into a deal most of the time, I find people are happy to have a distraction arrive on their doorstep. Maybe it's the British accent or "exotic" presence as many have described my appearance (hard to believe, not a term readily applied to the English).

In the middle of this flurry of activity, no longer up in the air, slaving away inside an aluminum tube I notice cracks erupting and developing into craters on the marital front. Everything appears to be disintegrating and spiraling headlong into a vat of uncompromising incompatibility. This has probably been underway for some time but it's always easier to cover up the truth than confront it. The reality that my once wedded bliss is scattered with scars and fraught with deception now stares me straight in the face. The fabric of my relationship is, in fact, threadbare, in shreds. I find that flightless, my feet now planted firmly on terra firma, crumbs previously swept under the carpet before I arrived back from a trip are now blatantly vying for my attention. They have been there for a long time.

The husband and I had sprung from the green, pleasant land of England, had grown up in the then tightly knit structure of the waning British Empire, eating fish and chips out of newspaper and singing God Save the Queen, an island people, an indestructible force when faced by an alien breed. Being British we considered ourselves a team, a team now blasted apart, which no amount of Spotty Dick or Toad in the Hole can fix. Our bond has evaporated after twenty-six years.

My trust had been implicit and except for a few infractions (we all slip up occasionally), life carried on. I now realize that we are strangers. Our paths have parted, that the palpable magnetism that had drawn us together, the envy of many, has withered and crashed into a big dark void. Humorous repartee has been replaced by snide sarcasm. That equity taken out of our real estate empire for maintenance and building projects has evaporated into thin air.

Letters are arriving from the Internal Revenue Service demanding unpaid taxes followed by knocks on the front door that might be debt collectors, all adding to the drama of the continual parade of the tenants from hell. I'm fifty percent of the deal but my opinions are discarded, thrown under a passing truck by the guy presiding as the landlord. I'm becoming aware that, in fact, I'm the joists that keep the joint from collapsing, the mortar in between the bricks, the breadwinner nonpareil disguised as a worker bee, trying to hold up a crumbling façade.

Another incident provides more fuel to my growing anxiety. On returning home from a business trip to Indonesia, I discover my faithful Honda incapacitated, stuck on the carport. The engine burnt out, thanks no doubt to the maintenance and driving skills of my spouse and that it's sinking under a quagmire of parking tickets that now need to be paid with interest. Who knows what ports of call it had made, nights spent on foreign soil and alien parking decks?

Straining to retain my sense of humor, I purchase a pair of size fourteen black and white wing tipped men's shoes from Goodwill and place them neatly in the clothes closet. When returning home after a night of working overtime—who knows what the project might be—the spouse finds these alien boots on his turf. Instead of getting the joke, he considers this prank a complete violation of his domain, which of course does not add any joy to our already fragmented relationship. But where is the sense of humor I so admire? We are reaching a new low in our unraveling relationship.

I wonder what it would be like if we lost gravity? That's how I feel, as if everything is dropping off the surface of the planet, buildings shooting off into space, sheep floating into the atmosphere, grannies disappearing into black holes. My world is shattering into shards.

A man, an art dealer has shown interest in me for several years, he now wants to become my confidant. He's a pushy individual, but I feel on the verge of exploding keeping my dilemma locked up inside. I need to talk with another human and he is available and willing, breaking my rule of not discussing my personal life, I bare my soul.

But divorce? No one in my family has ever entertained such a solution. Both of my grandmothers had been unhappily wed, that era being a time of male dominance, when women knew their place and that was not in a divorce court! During their lifespan women didn't expect to be happy in marriage but didn't complain. One put up with the inconvenience.

My spouse's father, having attained the age of eighty-eight years, one British morning while riding his bike is thrown from his steed into the air by a passing truck. The tough old bird recovers, but is never quite as mean as before, and after a few years it results in his departure from his earthbound routine. Peter leaves for the motherland for a week and the funeral. I figure this to be a great opportunity to mend the deck I had fallen through and reconstitute the mailbox that's lying sadly on the soil, not realizing that I'm trespassing on my husband's engineering territory by hiring a contractor to repair these gaping structural deficiencies. This is to prove a step too far.

Three weeks later when Peter returns, having found the time to fit a tour of England into his curriculum after attending the burial, instead of showing his pleasure at my accomplishments, he throws a tantrum. The custard pie he has hand carried from the British Isles hits the wall. This is the last straw, necessitating a pair of friendly California cops to pass by to resolve the fracas.

I file for divorce. My former mate cannot understand why? He doesn't want a divorce and will never agree to one. A mutual friend attempts to mediate a truce and settlement, but to no avail. I call my parents to break the news, my mother answers. Not a woman to mince words she replies to what I consider an earth shattering decision "I never liked him anyway" and that was that. I hire a lawyer and the fireworks begin.

My attorney is a rather rumpled round figure, a man I immediately feel comfortable with. His first question is whether my hopefully soon to be ex spouse possesses a firearm. Apparently car parks

Bifurcation

outside of courthouses before an individual is screened for the purified air of the actual courtroom are prime locations for an angry party to seek instant revenge.

My father dies, I have to go to England for the funeral. I ask my soon to be ex if he can look after our son for a week. The dear man tries to use my plight as a bargaining chip - I book two seats to London. On a bleak, blustery, typical English spring day, the day of the cremation, my mother finally realizes that she has lost her best friend. In the church as the coffin moves from sight to behind a curtain on a movable turntable reminiscent of a baggage belt at an airport arrival lounge, mother springs forward out of the pew wanting a last glimpse of her departing spouse. She lifts the curtain, behind which the casket has disappeared, in disbelief!

Back in the courthouse, Judge Dufficy presides over our divorce. He seems to sleep throughout much of the litigation, only opening his eyes to advise us to return in two weeks, to prolong the torture. Of course, the attorneys are only too happy to oblige, to stretch, to string out the agony is to their monetary advantage. It appears to be an unwritten law, to spite the unwitting plebeian innocently seeking justice, who instead is toyed with, used as a bate, the victim of injustice.

I will later find out that neither of the attorneys heading off in our case are members of Dufficy's incestuous squad of law men and women lured to his country manor house for bacchanalian sprees and to further their mutual causes, lining their pockets in the process. Knowing there will be no extraneous cash reward feature in our proceedings, Dufficy shows no interest.

The epic divorce tale teeters forward at a tortoise-like pace. Bifurcation of our wedded blight arrives one year later after twenty-six years of ever diluting happiness. The now non-existent bond is sliced in two!

After such abuse in the courtroom I often seek solace in the company of my good friend, Brent West, dropping in chez lui to sip tea out of 19th century bone china, accompanied by a slice of freshly baked carrot cake or some other miracle that has freshly emerged from his kitchen, to soften the carnage of the courtroom!

We spill the beans about our ongoing life sagas, laugh at the absurdities. Brent always finds the time to bend an ear. He's a man who knows how to set a table, the napkins are always cloth and ironed. At Halloween mice and witches cavort alongside the pumpkin pie. At Chinese New Year, the appropriate beast is beatified, the rabbit, the dragon, whatever the anointed animal of the year. It's Mr. West who after inspecting my meager kitchen guides me in the pure basics of culinary essentials, the necessity of a workable area to produce food in a professional way, to be able to present and preside over a successful dinner party. These are details my mother had overlooked, not considered important. She had found cooking a bore and eating a necessity.

Splitting up the remains of the union plods along requiring years of court hearings, piles of paperwork and the added surprise feature of people bearing subpoenas jumping out from behind trees. My ex seems to want to continue any sort of contact even in a court of law, he just can't seem to let go. Accidentally colliding with him in other surroundings, having the misfortune not to have spotted his presence at a distance, he blasts me with his agenda as bystanders fall back in horror.

After my father's exit, my mother the formerly avid painter is never again to pick up a paintbrush. Diminished, her will to carry on wilts and after a couple of drab years my brother calls "Mum's in hospital – come over quick."

I buy a bunch of anemones, her favorite flower. I hold her hand.

Bifurcation

I'm happy that she recognizes me even though she's flying high on medication and too weak to speak. I know she's relieved, I've arrived to be with her. Even though she was often in my thoughts and I sent her gifts from wherever I went, she never really seemed to grasp or be interested in my life, never asking questions and I had always avoided giving details knowing they would meet with dismissal or disapproval. She had never expressed a desire to visit America even when I offered the tickets, in fact she never left the British Isles. She had always wanted me to come back home to be within her confines where she ruled the roost, dominated her world. Perhaps a trip on alien turf might cause a loss of control? We would write letters back and forth and towards the end when these evaporated I would dutifully telephone every week. I watch as her life slowly ebbs away, as she drifts into oblivion. I hadn't expected her to die! I order a pile of red roses to be placed on her casket, losing this woman who had always been in my life or at least in my thoughts is devastating. A woman who had given me so much, had set me on a footpath to adventure but had not wanted to set me free, she always wanting to be the center of attraction.

A divorce settlement is finally reached in the corridors of law between the lawyers, not in the courtroom by the presiding Judge Michael Dufficy. Years later, I read in the local rag that this same man, the judge who had presided over my divorce, a man who had been awarded the privilege of donning the courtly robes after assisting a politician acquire the job of thirty-fifth governor of California, is fighting to retain his position. He has been charged with judicial favoritism!

I'm awarded the original house my now ex spouse and I had purchased with a down payment from the sale of the primrose yellow 'E' type Jaguar. It's now a trashed shack on a hill cowering on the fringes of the Golden Gate Recreation Area. An orange box, bleached by the sun, whipped by winds and in distress from lack of attention. It's not my choice but the pure ownership without the impediment of my former liaison trumps any doubts. Maybe now I can get on with life!

With the help of the local cops I shoehorn my ex out of the basement before setting about decontaminating the interior and reconstructing the exterior, a project that will keep me out of the meat market for years. As my funds dictate, I have to be part of the renovation putting my painting, plumbing and electrical skills to good use. Luckily, the guys down at the local hardware store are always ready to let me access their vast knowledge if I encounter a problem. The bliss of being free of the rancid court system, dragged down by opposing forces, is balm to my frazzled brain.

Alex is starring in the local soccer team "The Magic." They are on track to compete for the Northern California Cup, another feature of my now brimming agenda. Weekend trips are made to far flung soccer fields; practices are daily. I roar and cheer with the other doting parents doing their duty, as our team slays the opposition and wins the trophy. We dine on fast food, the only recognizable sustenance in these outposts of civilization.

In the midst of all this cacophony, my former confidant ratchets up his interest. After the battle scenes of bifurcation and the ensuing clashes over the chattel, being wined and dined is somewhat of a reprieve. The idea that maybe I'm still desirable is intriguing, a viewpoint I have not enjoyed of late and is definitely tempting.

He's an art dealer, a man I had met at the Tribal Art Shows, maybe an interesting study of how such an entity functions, an insight as to the workings of such a quantity could be helpful to my own aspirations. I find out that a lot of business is carried out

Bifurcation

horizontally in bed while watching television, an entirely different approach to my own.

With this new consort sometimes at my side, I have acquired a man more than ready to vocally diminish ex-husbands and tribal art studs who dare to challenge my stuff, which is increasingly the case, coinciding with my gradual rise in the tribal field.

When competing with the boys in the marketplace, conflict tends to rear its hideous head, I just want to be equal with no feminine frills attached. O.K. guys, I understand that you need to define women as something that can be conquered and purloined but can you just get over the fact that we, your female counterparts, are as adequately equal on the playing field of acquiring and recognizing good art and are just as capable of purveying the material as astutely as the best of you? It's not a God given agenda and has no correlation to what you have between your legs. It's not a male affliction to recognize and source art; any sex is capable of such a transaction.

One of my clients with ulterior motives is also subject to this new admirer's lethal opinion. A client intent on purchasing a collection of material, who seems to want to coerce a little action on the side. Although he has adequate funds to complete the deal he insists on dragging his feet, doling out the dues in a meagerly fashion, making appointments to rendezvous at his house. Turning up to collect the check, soft lights and music greet me, a scenario inferring more than just handing over the required dough. My new weapon destroys this maneuvering dilettante, dismembering him slowly, diminishing his collection of African art piece by piece with faint praise. He plays with the pride of this client with covert ambitions like a tiger pawing a rat, reducing his tribal investments to a heap of bogus acquisitions and making it clear his dallying with me is dishonest and disrespectful. An ability he wields like a whip but a whip that can change direction and can be aimed at a new target, even a woman interested in a man declaring himself to be available. He is a wildcard who like so many men who have been let loose, thrust back on the merry go round after marriages, children, other life styles, sometimes abused sometimes the abuser, it's for the next interested party to discover.

It's with this beau, who's always on course to study art of any dimension that I embark on a trip up country to investigate American Indian material. On this foray I have my first encounter with a man of great insight and expertise, an entrepreneur I will have the good fortune to know better at a later date. Gary Spratt shows us his collection of Navajo jewelry, my first brush with the best silver and turquoise examples to be found of this genre. He's as generous in his presentation as he is with his knowledge, His daughter is just surfacing as a teenager. The wife toils in the kitchen, not wishing to mingle as the boys jostle to impress me with tales of the tribal underworld.

It's show-time in L.A. and my booth is just starting to take shape when an emerging dealer in the Indonesian market with a less than stellar reputation, shows great interest in my set up, peppering me with questions but with no obvious intent of whipping out his checkbook. But on the last day of the show, two men who give the impression they would be more suited to perusing the pages of Hustler Magazine than the aisles of a Tribal Art Show, want to know about an antique tooth necklace from Irian Jaya and tortoiseshell combs from Sumba. Pinned in my booth by a barrage of questions I'm unaware that word is quickly spreading through the show that the Department of Fish and Wildlife are on the prowl, that merchandise is being stealthily whisked from displays to the safety of anonymity beneath draped tables. The dogtooth necklace is transposed

Bifurcation

by the duo into dolphin teeth, and the tortoiseshell combs, in spite of being antique and over one hundred years old, are all seized with the parting words, "We will be in contact with you."

Rattled, steaming back up Highway One on my way home, thoughts coursing through my mind about whether the dealer who had harangued me during setting up had been instrumental in the appearance of Fish and Wildlife in my booth, I'm jolted back to reality by a light aircraft flying directly over my getaway path. Having always wondered about those signs stating "patrolled by aircraft," I now realize it to be true. Sirens wail and the King City Police pull me over and hand me a $358 dollar speeding ticket. They had clocked me in at ninety miles an hour although in actuality I had been careening along in my Honda Civic crammed to the gills at about 120 m.p.h.

A notice from the Department of Fish & Wildlife arrives two months later, I'm guilty of attempting to sell material which contravenes the guidelines of the Endangered Species Act. There's a long inventory of offenders, I'm listed after Hermes, the luggage guys not the Olympian god. Hermes has been charged with using crocodile skins in some of their products. At least I'm in good company. Hermes has been doing business since 1837 and are at the top of their game. As with any event, good or bad, in the news, one's reputation soars, maybe dives but everyone knows who you are and along the way many forget the context.

I delve into libraries and find photos depicting so called primitive types wearing the dogtooth necklace. I dig up evidence that firmly acknowledges the teeth on this piece to be from a dog and nothing to do with anything formerly attached to a dolphin. I unearth laws that state that tribal art imported prior to 1975, instead of having to be over one hundred years old is exempt from the Endangered

Species Act, all the while keeping religiously in contact by phone and mail with my persecutors.

After two years and a mountain of paper, Fish and Wildlife decide to return the dog tooth necklace but keep the rest of the stuff. How can I refuse their proposal, knowing that the deep pockets at their disposal could sink my ship? I also know that F & W will, after settling the case, auction the remaining pieces off to the highest bidder.

I just hope they make money in their efforts to crush a minor player in the field of small business. I believe Hermes survived too!

CHAPTER FOURTEEN

Under the Surface of Serenity

The aircraft wheels have deployed, the runway is in sight, a myriad of palm trees wave, welcoming me back, I need to man up and dive in, the money god is bristling at my back.

In the taxi to Three Brothers I notice a concrete jungle is spreading farther out of town, a mosque has sprung up along the route, a rare sight in Hindu Bali. Each side of the road, long bamboo poles tower above, drooping gracefully, dripping with woven decorations that flutter above the fumes. Offering boxes have been placed half way up to feed any hungry god passing by.

On reaching the Inn, I ask what all the fuss is about. Oh no - the important religious celebration of Galungan and Kuningan is about to transpire. A festival when gods and ancestors return to earth and it lasts for ten whole days, the only work carried out relating to the ceremonies. I might as well join in the fray, nothing else is happening. A trip to the cultural enclave of Ubud is the only choice, where such events take on a more glamorous hue.

Alex is at my side, luckily he has the same passion for traveling. We stay in a family compound catering to a few guests on a budget. Alex helps the young men of the family make breakfast and to deliver it to the guests, and they teach him how to wrap and wear a sarong, how to tie the mandatory sash, to be worn when entering a place of worship. In the streets Balinese women wind their way to the temple. Exquisite in batik sarongs, over which hand worked lacy kebayas float. Offering trays piled high with food for the visiting spirits perch on coils of their thick black glossy hair.

The good pig, the Barong Bangkal has been removed from the temple and is dancing in the road, jerking now and then to avoid the evil spirits as he bestows the protection of the gods all around.

It's a good time to take in some theater, a chance to see the masks I love actively danced. Arriving early, we sit cross legged right next to the stage. We watch a man scale the temple walls and place candles to illuminate the spectacle as the gamelan troupe attired in matching jackets and batik turbans, a flower placed behind an ear, tune up the instruments. Alex as a kid is allowed behind the scenes to see the dancers wrapped and clad in gold painted costumes. To watch the makeup applied to the women and masks presented to the men, as they ready themselves to deliver a centuries old tradition, to this day still practiced as in the past. Now the audience waits for the chance to be transported into the spirit world. Of course there is always the ugly tourist who plants himself and camera bang in front, blocking the view, taking that all important photo, that nobody back home wants to see.

Luckily a few eating parlors are open to service the swelling ranks of pilgrims from afar. Checking one out we bump into an

Under the Surface of Serenity

The Barong Bangkal being danced in Ubud at the time of Galungan & Kuningan

The Jauk Dance, Bali

Englishman sitting at the bar, who appears to relish the opportunity to speak English in the true sense of the vernacular. He has been living here for years but his appearance leaves no doubt as to his roots, he is the quintessential Brit complete with glowing white skin and a mouthful of bad teeth. He has bravely bared his feet, revealing toes that have done time in tight "startright "shoes during their early years, the toes pointing to the left and right seem not sure where to go. In true British style he hasn't picked up a word of the native tongue, wisely keeping away from the inner sanctum of the Balinese mind, a fellow Englishman, away from home and delighted that he is. He is now thrilled to use his cutting wit on a person traveling on the same wavelength, in fact we grew up about thirty miles apart.

He introduces us to Ibu Murni who owns the cafe and also it turns out an art gallery. Yes-we can take a look at the stuff even though the doors are firmly shut for the ongoing rites. She has to be diligent and discreet, since her rise out of poverty she has evolved into a leading light in Ubud, having acquired enough money to gain respect in her society. But -there always being a dark cloud hovering over any silver lining, she is now obliged to finance and attend the many ceremonies that constantly erupt on the fabric of life. To be available when villagers show up on her porch with family woes and financial fiascos, seeking her help. She is owned by the village and the gods, is under constant pressure to uphold her reputation, every movement and action recorded. She has to take long trips abroad to keep her sanity intact.

Ibu Murni is a direct link to life in Bali, born and bred in the rice paddies here in Ubud. To date, most of the Indonesian minds I have had the pleasure of infiltrating, have been from other parts of the archipelago. As we sit in her gallery amid the wayang kulit puppets and gold and silver jewels, we listen as she includes us in her life. The jealousies that rumble beneath the serene surface that the visitor delights in, which she portrays as a mere facade to keep life played out in close quarters, palatable. A Balinese has already let me know that "we like foreigners to stay no longer than two weeks, to drop money and go." Staying a little longer, cracks appear in the superficial coating of society and envy can be seen spewing out.

Happy to be with us, away from the constant demands, Ibu Murni can relax, speak her mind, she knows that having arrived at the pinnacle of the money tree, here in the sacred republic of Ubud if she does not submit to demands levied on her purse and person, a bout of bad karma could arrive as revenge. She is careful not to ruffle local feathers. She invites us to her up country retreat, a trip we will make on another day. I have to gird my loins and jump into the hustle, the seamy side of life erupting by the sand down south.

Alex in Bali

Daeng Iskandar the Raja of tribal art & Ibu his wife

Back on track, chasing the elusive masterpiece, Alex and I decide to visit Daeng. As a man steeped in Islam he will probably be open for business behind closed doors. Jumping in the ramshackle jeep, we find streets still clogged with processions, we wait as religion takes preference over business. Daeng has purchased a plot and constructed his temple far from the circus of downtown politics, way past the Kreboken Jail, home to many a tourist caught doing or smuggling drugs by the vigilant police and left to molder in a rancid cell if lucky. Do drugs and die is the motto here!

Ibu, Daeng's wife is there in the outside kitchen producing succulent miracles, conjured up from scratch with produce she buys fresh and frequently still alive at market. She's Javanese, one of the best female variations to be found in these islands, I'm told, by many an Indonesian male.

Daeng's man Friday is also here and he welcomes us. In this sanctuary of all things tribal, I immediately spot what I want, an ancestor figure from Timor, immaculately eroded by the elements, standing in ethereal splendor, rising up above the stacks of other stuff, it radiates an aura of being between this world and the next.

Daeng is nowhere to be seen. The news is that he is off on one of his wild sprees, this time to Singapore, a local wench of television fame the object of his attention. As yet Daeng has kept this other persona under wraps when I'm around, so this is news to me. His wife still smiling, is a woman who will always stand by her man, she knows this is just a feral fling which will run out of steam in a few days, apparently it's happened before and she will stoically be there when he returns. She is a woman I admire who does not just flutter in the background. She is astute and knowledgeable in the art field but studiously accepts her role in life, letting her man strut and hold court. Besides she has a son Rusti, her great joy and is thrilled to see him and Alex get together, making paper airplanes that they launch in the air as business takes place in the shop. She's fascinated by western ways, which she tries to understand, divorce, independent women challenging men, unthinkable events in her world.

I have registered my interest in the piece of eroded wood and just hope it will be waiting for me when I return, knowing it's impossible to whisk it away, out of the spotlight, without Raja Daeng around to seal the deal. I figure I will be lucky to ever set eyes on the splendid object again.

As Alex and I take our leave, Alex happy to have had the chance to sample some of the inspired morsels emerging from the vast bubbling pots in Ibu's kitchen, Yamin strolls in through the tall gates. He is back in Bali doing deals and revisiting old friends. The former lanky frame is now concealed under a new

ESCAPE FROM ENGLAND

Ceremonial shoulder cloth Palembang, Sumatra 19th century

rotund exterior, the afro has dwindled to a sparse finial but a smile still hovers on his face. He puts on a good show, is pleased to see familiar faces, talks of hitting the bright disco lights but his inner spirit seems to have lost its sparkle, I am unaware that his time with the living is limited.

On our return to the Inn, two runners are lining up for attention. One has heard that I am looking for the Lawon textile, a shoulder cloth worn by women in south Sumatra, a large rectangle of a single color surrounding an inner rectangle of another. A textile not particularly admired by Indonesians, but having bought a few that resulted in rapid sales, I'm ready to find more. The Lawon is a silk cloth now hailed by the western eye as Rothkoesque, akin to the paintings of Rothko as displayed in many a museum. Rothko is considered a master of his trade and the Lawon textile is now in demand by western decorators and when mounted to fully show it's splendor can bring good money. The women of south Sumatra have made and used this cloth for centuries, way before Rothko discovered the concept of painting rectangular forms in few colors that float on canvases, way before he was hailed as a leader in the Abstract Expressionism movement in New York. Heri promises to return the following morning to show me what he has.

The other, a slight boyish figure, introduces himself as Irjan. He shyly lets me know he has ancient beads and invites me to his place to see. He lives in a small room, which he shares with a large color T.V. and his cousin, who it seems he has taken for a wife. A fragile individual, he caresses his beads with delicate, tapering fingers, a look of reverent tenderness flitting across his face.

Sitting outside his room on a broken white plastic chair his wife brings forth the hot tea as Irjan lays eleventh century glass beads on the concrete at my feet. A kid of about nine from next door is sitting a few feet away getting ready for school. He pulls the socks, an intricate web of holes over his feet. I notice that luckily the still intact tops are the only part to be seen after his tired shoes are in place, giving a mirage of respectability.

Some of the beads are similar to millefiori or mosaic beads, dating from Phoenician times. I've picked up enough Indonesian to be able to converse, a necessity, as many of these runners do not speak English. Irjan in gentle tones tells me of their age and history. Even though I sense he is telling the truth, I still have to make sure for myself. I pick some up and run my fingers over the surface, some have been interred so long in acrid soil they have a slightly rough exterior. The holes are nicely worn and uneven. The colors have ripened with age, having lost their original bright intensity. They glow neatly arranged on the concrete. The neighbors peer from the adjoining cubicles, all ears, wanting to get in on the act.

After picking my choice, Irjan and I retreat into the tiny place behind to agree on a price. He is fair, which confirms my reason to feel good about him. I want to be his first port of call in future, when the good stuff arrives in his hands. He has no use for dollar bills, so a trip to the money changer is in order and after making sure I get the right amount of rupiah, the local currency, which always has to be avidly checked, I arrive back with a large bundle of bills.

Walking home over the crumbling excuse for a pavement, a woman in rags approaches, with a baby slung in a sling around her neck, orally attached to one naked breast. As she sticks a hand in front of my path a cluster of small children surround me, on course to unzip the fanny pack around my waist. I try batting them away like flies but they persist. Releasing a blast of unsavoury Indonesian seems more effective and sends them scuttling. Families working the pavements are a familiar sight for a while before disappearing, no doubt taken en masse to a remote spot never to return. After all, the tourist is becoming an indispensable source of income on this piece of paradise and needs protecting.

Three Brothers has installed a swimming pool just in time for Alex's pleasure and he is busy with an Australian friend and family. Why not revisit Darweiko to see if he is still kicking and has anything to offer? It has been a few years, enough distance to take care of any previous predatory indiscretions.

Under the Surface of Serenity

I find him sitting in his shop waiting for some action to arrive, his wife as always hovering in the background doing his bidding while stoically putting up with his endless roster of bad behavior. After a tour of his latest finds, he invites me to stay for lunch.

A real Balinese feast featuring roasted cow's nose as the 'dish de resistance' arrives surrounded by a panorama of indistinguishable companions, all purchased at the local market.

Authentic Balinese food is a culinary treat not readily offered to those unfamiliar with such delicacies, the gourmet qualities being difficult for the western palate to comprehend. That I find includes me, I'm in for a disgusting brush with slime and sludge, hard to imagine as enticing to any human. Memories of my former struggle with the turtle dish come to mind.

Mentally holding my nose, while attempting not to show I'm mortified by the tableau before me, I gingerly pick at the gross morsels staring defiantly up from their Styrofoam boxes, as Darweiko munches hungrily. I guess revenge is served in a take out lunch! He probably had a good laugh after my hasty retreat, I having cracked a tooth on a sliver of boney bovine nostril.

At eight the next morning I sit outside my room waiting for Heri, the man with the Lawon, to show up. At last I have time to inhale the vibrant garden that surrounds me. Since arriving, I've been racing around non stop trying to restock the shop, as they say "you can't sell from an empty cart".

Heri finally puts in an appearance, perspiring like a leaky hose, but he has a stack of the Lawon textile. I check out each piece for age and damage, both deciding factors as to worth. Four pieces meet the criteria, with brilliant color and good condition. We dicker back and forth about the price, he seems to have all the time in the world and appears to be an excellent target to practice my Indonesian with.

Chinese and Indonesian blood course through his veins along with, I notice, an overdose of alcohol, which I attribute for his late arrival. Recognizing that his uncontrollable love affair with beer is impeding his life, he plans to visit a Chinese herbalist, a man with a reputation for converting an addiction into repulsion. A plan I fully endorse and encourage Lawon Heri to embrace. Go for it. Clean up your act. I let him know that the more Lawon he comes up with the merrier and to run them by me first.

I need to develop a relationship with this man which I suspect could bode well monetarily for both of us.

After being embedded in the bamboo chair on my patio for several hours I develop a formidable itch, a possible invasion of my backside by the bamboo beetle, a species known to reduce its' habitat to dust and inflict relentless agony on a piece of human flesh. Before I rip the skin off my rump I need to visit the apothecary, handily just up the road, manned by a local medical whiz who knows all about the indigenous maladies and hands out potent remedies.

Having a quick bite at the restaurant along with a blast of fumes from the traffic now polluting the rear end of Three Bros., I notice a shop front behind a hedge of parked bikes. This must be the bunker where the infamous Hadj Samsudin presides, a character known for his dubious dealings when capturing and flogging his merchandise. Samsudin a man who dispatches runners on dangerous missions to obtain sensitive pieces. Missions that sometimes result in the runners' demise if they are caught stealing or in possession of ancestral art that was obtained without the knowledge of the tribal chief.

Hadj Samsudin sits cross legged on the floor, his sarong hoisted to accommodate his stance. He glances up as I stroll in, revealing a treacherous minefield of facial flesh spotted with deep dark pock marks. He sits puffed up like an adder under his black velvet hat.

Under the Surface of Serenity

I tread lightly on this turf to avoid the pitfalls waiting to swallow up a feckless art dealer. Gems can be found amid the fakery, to be weeded out with a knowledgeable eye. Samsudin plays an elevated game of spot the real piece.

He greets me with an effusive smile and sends his man out for the mandatory refreshments. Rising from the floor he ushers me towards a table and chairs. This is a man who is well practiced in ingratiating himself with his prey. He introduces me to what he describes as exquisite pieces that have just arrived, fresh from the field, as yet unsoiled by an alien eyeball, hoping to lure me into a sale.

I find it fascinating to study tactics and charm, the vocal weapons of an art dealer, even a superbly slimy one such as Samsudin, as long as there is an exit nearby. Jogya John arrives, for once I'm glad to see the competition and hope that his appearance will defray the undivided attention I have been awarded by this latest admirer of my wallet. Bowing to protocol I return the barrage of flattery that is charging the room while planning my imminent escape, of course promising to return soon.

Daeng I hear is back in town, I need to race up and pay my respects. Alex and I jump into the jeep. As we make an entrance, runners are lining up, art in hand, for a chance to be granted a show and tell moment with the Grand Mufti of the Tribal art scene. Foreign dealers sprawl on the patio slurping black coffee, chomping on kretek cigarettes, scented smoke hangs in air thick with gossip.

Daeng is back without a whiff of his recent waltz on the wild side, low key and charismatic as before. Relieved I see the statue I coveted still floating above the action taking place on the ground. Blown away that it has not yet been spirited away by another hand, man Friday says he saved it for me, that's it now mine to purchase. Honored by this show of sincerity, I can hardly believe my luck!

Ibu hands me a coffee and tells me she is leaving for Java to hand pick a future bride for the only scion of the house of Iskandar, her son Rusti. An arranged marriage is in the works to a young lady from a similar background. A girl from a family who pray to the same god and are of like social standing, the tried and true formula for a perfect match. The fated female will come and live in Daeng's house and be at her mother in law's disposal and produce sons.

Alex absorbs the news as if it were everyday stuff. He's into rising late, eating his way through a heap of honey banana pancakes and riding a surfboard while rapidly becoming aware that partying and driving are available to any who can pay the price.

Time on planet Bali expiring, I need to see Heri to cement our previous conversation and drop in for a visit. He sits drinking tea, his new beverage of choice. After the visit to the medicine man, now even the smell of alcohol makes him vomit. His wife is by his side, a Balinese babe forced to ditch her colorful sarong, she is now swathed in black, her curves wrapped under the cover of Islam. The room is hot and stuffy, we sit and sweat like pigs with prior knowledge that a barbecue spit is looming on the horizon. Heri agrees to send any Lawon he finds. I have tried to seal a deal but I know that loyalty is not a word frequently used or maybe not even really understood in this milieu. Sad to say, but I can't help but notice, that Lawon Heri has replaced his love affair with alcohol for an obsession with Islam, trading one addiction for another and in the process is losing his sense of humor.

Down on the beach decompressing from the recent fervor of activity it is unusually calm. Where are the hordes, the acres of flesh exposing their bulk to the elements, the barrage of Balinese stalking their quarry? Where is the surge of traffic, racing toward death on the new stretch of macadam behind the strip of grit.

Under the Surface of Serenity

On the horizon, a fleet of Balinese testosterone in ceremonial attire is striding into view, walking abreast, keris, the ceremonial dagger firmly entrenched in the backs of their ceremonial sashes.

Now I recall murmurings of the prescient demise of the demigod for life, the current usurper of power, until now president of this corrupt nation. Whispers have been circulating that he, Suharto, is finally on his final path to ejection. The crowds have fled, warned by their embassies of the danger that might ensue in the wake of his removal.

1998 marking the year this amazing feat is underway, the removal of a political tyrant with 31 years of bad behavior under his belt, a wife, nicknamed Madame ten percent, her cut of every unsavory deal and the thugs, the offspring of the duplicitous duo, who are always on the wrong side of the right side, they are all now on their way to the other side. In spite of the democratic image bestowed upon them by the western world that has supported their nefarious rule with unseemly amounts of viable currencies while salivating at the abundance of natural resources backing such a tawdry ruler and his clan.

Alex is catching some waves while I vegetate in the shade of a thatched roof bar along with a plastic bottle of water. The native flotilla are now striding onto the sand and heading in my direction. I have never had this many men bearing down on me before, is this the popularity I had never sought?

On reaching my perch they throw the bar stools and booze crashing to the floor. Grasping that I am not the attention of their raging hormones, visions of my bloody corpse making the cover of Paris Match or at least a copy of Time magazine now surge through my mind. But I am nothing but a bystander, there to witness the hate they have in their hearts for their neighbors.

"No thongs or topless ladies please on our sacred sand" had been a sign erected by the Balinese elders, in order to protect their pristine point of view, surprising considering their history of semi naked women. But the local lads gave up the fight to preserve their prudish ways, realizing that educating an ever changing group of barbarians was not in their financial interest. But now when Javanese business men start to sell booze under a thatch roof on their beach the natives are not amused. Now under the cover of the impending doom of a vilified president this latest incursion into their lives needs to be addressed.

It's the start of a time of unrest, when people will stay home and Chinese residents will pick up their ever ready passports and flee, they always being the scapegoats in troubled waters. They will bolt as they have before, hopefully still with the hair on their heads, to Singapore and Hongkong where they have socked away fortunes. Those that stay risk the prospect of their property being burned and their head placed on a spike. Stories abound of people being forced out of taxis on their way to the airport, of being robbed and killed.

Like any other, these times will pass, the tourist will return, the episode all but forgotten.

CHAPTER FIFTEEN

The Real Thing

Tiring of my ongoing long-distance romance with my Southern California art dealer admirer and verbal lethal weapon of mass destruction who has defended me from the ex husband and many other voracious males and in spite of the fact that distance sometimes is a benefit, I decide to turn down the heat, to promote a gradual waning of interest, not that I have another moving target in sight. I know this will be a difficult task, somewhat similar to removing gum from the pavement. A gradual let down will be best. I've avoided the matrimonial plans offered by this suitor and excluded him from accompanying me on trips to Asia, well aware of this gent's incapacity to take a back seat. Realizing that his loud, pushy personality would raise eyebrows and hackles in Indonesia where the low-key subtle approach keeps harmony flowing. Why kick myself in the rear by taking a fellow competitor along for the ride and undermine my own chances at raiding the store?

After endless displays of disinterest on my part, to my delight, the man in question informs me that he has decided to take another girlfriend closer to home but intends to retain me as his Northern California destination, thereby divvying up the spoils. I have no interest in participating in a trio but I'm thrilled to be off the hook, euphoric that another casualty has encumbered her life, sacrificed her soul to set me free. He has acquired a fresh victim to verbally build up before inflicting a vicious swipe, aimed at shattering any confidence, a lethal blow to the ego. This is a man who writes off previous partners as demented disasters probably just to cover up his own inadequacies. A man who always has to be right, changing his position if the wind blows in a different direction.

A few months into the miraculous end to this bygone tussle, the phone calls from my former assailant resume. The incessant need to know where I am, what I'm doing has returned, a performance somewhat reminiscent of a tsetse fly having an orgasm. I enjoy informing him that I'm already on to fresh material. The good news is that he, the former contestant, will not be present at the forthcoming Tribal Art Show, having unfortunately slipped on the stairs of his Hollywood house and is now nursing broken ribs.

The woman who graciously took over the task of filling my boots will, at a later date wander into my booth after she has been caste off, wanting to share past experiences. A former bubbly blonde dwindled to a sad reflection of her former self, she buys a silver bracelet from Timor to seal our mutual bond.

At future events Superglue tries to interject his annoying presence into my life, a performance somewhat akin to a rhinoceros diving into a bathtub, the motor mouth functioning at full speed. He's frightening away the clientele. I have to ask him to leave, but being unable to tear himself away, he plants his bulk just outside, on the perimeter, taking photos, conversing with passersby, delivering a polished performance as an undesirable nuisance, a part he is so adept at playing.

There are a few more contenders for my affections, or at least my body, after his departure. The first is a Jewish art dealer. I'm shopping at Office Depot and notice him hovering close by, circling to get a closer look before he finally invites me to dinner at Chez Panisse, one of if not the best restaurant in the Bay Area. It's the season to be jolly so I've already made plans for Christmas and New Year, much to his regret. This is the time when singles get depressed and suicidal, but tough luck. I secretly hope that he will just disappear into the bucket seats of his Porsche and drive off, so I won't have to deal with the dilemma of should-I-put-myself-in-that-position-again so soon after the last debacle?

Two weeks later he calls, the dinner at Chez Panisse is still in the offing. At least the food will be good. He wants to invite me over to meet his dog. I take this in stride. I've known and liked many a four footed furry friend in my life. His expensive chunk of real estate in a tony neighborhood is furnished with a bed, a sofa and a television set, framed photos of his past canines are everywhere, I'm introduced to each and every one. His other passion is basketball; no match is left unseen. His idea of cuisine, apart from Chez Panisse is take out to be eaten straight out of the box chez lui.

In retaliation, I invite him over for dinner, my son views him from afar and judges him not to be up to scratch. One of the great joys of having a teenage son is that they are often a major deterrent to prospective men in your life. They have, at least in concept, sprayed their scent over their terrain not wanting any other male hormones littering the joint, interfering with their life or their mother.

I drag the new candidate to a tribal art party in Sonoma and notice how inadequate he appears in a social setting. There are many choices cluttering the highway of the middle aged, newly single woman, most of which should be avoided at all cost, and I'm starting to realize that this latest proposition is just another train wreck to be avoided.

On the way home we see a stray dog wandering down the road, a sight so distressing to my borderline boyfriend that he jumps out of the car to rescue the poor lost soul, leaving me sitting in the middle of the road in the dark! How many more red flags do I need waved in my face before realizing that I might be on the wrong track?

A hound found on the Oakland freeway is temporarily living with my new male object of diluting interest. My maternal dog instinct says "yes." Oscar can stay for three weeks to recuperate from his past grief. Oscar a mongrel tries to fit in but is restless and wild, with a killer instinct if a caller crosses our doorstep. He adores Alex waiting endlessly for him to return, ignoring my advances. This dog has an endless infatuation with balls. He decimates Alex's backpack, gnawing through multiple plastic layers to rescue the tennis ball hiding therein. As I'm strolling in the Republic of Berkeley with Oscar on a tight leash, a child tries to pet him, Oscar's not happy but luckily I restrain his indignation.

I love this beast but, like many of the men I have encountered, he's not fit to successfully tread this planet. I return him back to the boyfriend who later delivers the news that Oscar's been euthanized. I hang up. We're both dog people but not for each other.

Having cleared the decks of any romantic scenarios, and with that, time previously allotted to endless long distance telephone calls, physical and mental skirmishes and the worship of the canine species, I now have the space and energy to evolve.

The Real Thing

My tribal art coffers are bulging with beads and jewelry demanding attention. Many jewelry designers have already creamed off the cheaper end, leaving me with the high-end expensive elements. Always ready to take aim at any possibility in the name of financing my destiny I decide that it's my turn to resurrect these gems, to re-invent them for monetary gain. To take pieces and parts and weld them into radically different wearable conclusions. The array of colors, the elegant shapes, the allure of these handpicked jewels is exciting stuff and I discover therapeutic. Having a natural flair for improvisation, I coerce these baubles into new formations, as time slips by unnoticed, the combination of their beauty and my eye giving them new life.

Shuffling through my rolodex I know that somewhere I have the name of a woman who can string my designs into the wearable format I need. Yes, here is the phone number. She comes with excellent credentials, having a gilded history of party girl, pole dancer and bartender at one of the more juicy striptease destinations in town. Longing for a quieter more sedentary lifestyle she stumbled across the chance to learn the craft of knotting cord. She has the strongest hands, a prime requisite for this task. Her skin is translucent, blue veins flow under the diaphanous surface and due to Teutonic ancestry, she is blessed with an ample pair of breasts, which will later prove to be one of the banes of her life. She came of age in the nineteen seventies in Louisiana and nothing makes her happier than New Orleans style cooking. She has never met a drug she didn't like and considers work a necessary evil.

Rising at eleven of a morning my bead stringer can be relied upon to never return a call in a timely fashion. Rapid is not her style. Deadlines, what a bizarre concept! Her inability to stay on track is without question and she has an amazing ability to attract trouble, especially the male variety. Trying to help with advice, I eventually realize that none of it will be taken and not to waste my time. And in spite of the fact that she can be found still lounging around in a bathrobe in the afternoon bereft of any effort to improve her appearance, her attention when actually overcoming her instincts is precise. Every bead has its place, and she makes sure it stays that way. My work combined with her skill results in a piece that's beautiful on sight but even better when worn.

What joy to be totally in charge after the ravages of a bifurcated marriage and the subsequent quagmires. During the waning years of wedlock I'd been mentally alone, caught and throttled by insidious layers of wire netting while trying to carry on a so-called normal life. It's easy to forget, to fail to remember what "normal" actually is, bogged down in a morass of craziness, built up like plaque, with an intimate enemy, but when the millstone is removed, the dragon vanquished, hope returns.

Unattached I'm viewed by many happily married couples as a threat, a blight on society. A single woman, somewhat attractive but unencumbered, is not an entity invited to a respectable soiree. It's assumed I'm on the loose, probably desperate to attach myself to anything male. I view with sympathy couples cloistered in an unhappy situation for dread of change, the fear of the unknown, chained to a partner because they already have twenty, thirty years of connubial rights under their belts. How could they throw that away? Who cares if one is dying inside from day after day of pure dreariness! Although my marriage could never have been mistaken for an uninspired charade, divorce for me had been do or die! So what if I don't get invited to attend couples-only parties to be bored to death. What a miniscule price to pay.

A few brave spirits are not deterred, people secure in their souls.

My gay friends are always there, especially during the seasons to be jolly, inviting Alex and me over for a feast with all the special touches. Beautiful table displays, scrumptious grub and what is that I see at the top of the Christmas tree? Golly, it looks like a naked guy with a rather large gift!

Being a member of a gym gives me mental and physical strength during my marathon divorce proceedings, easing the stress, as well as an opportunity to wade through my ongoing dramas while raising the dumb bells, a way to fight gravity and the perfect place to spot scantily dressed men flexing their muscles. As an art dealer I'm always ready to rest my eyes on something well formed, coordinated and handsome and there right in my field of vision is a smooth, tanned specimen, beautifully proportioned, a prolific crop of black hair cascading over a set of photo perfect features. I fantasize about his background – maybe Tibetan? – there's something of Asia about him.

I now realize that even the most attractive men are flattered when a woman shows interest, and that a conversation might ensue! He's Chinese. I tease that with such stellar looks he must be a movie star, but no, he's masquerading as a male model but on course to reach the silver screen.

He's the product of a family that strictly adheres to the traditions of where they came from rather than adopt the ways of their new life. Because of his heritage and the differences he has endured growing up in that discipline, he now tries desperately to be a full-blooded American. He wants nothing to do with Kung Fu or any other Asian exploits, which I think might be a selling point in his career. He drives an enormous Ram truck that needs a running board to gain access to the seats and sports a baseball cap.

Being tall dark and handsome can be fun, but not at the expense of developing that space between the ears. Relying on good looks is a pathway to disaster in later years.

I go for the fun and target this boy toy. At least during this brief encounter I'm able to report to a tribal art stud inquiring about my availability that I'm currently involved with a younger guy whose bodily parts all still function, and I have the pleasure of seeing his jaw flop to the floor. Poor boy, he doesn't have to take it so personally!

Enough of that I have a son to mold into a man, money to make. That's enough of a challenge.

Brent West can be spotted most Sundays at the Sausalito Flea strolling through the aisles with his partner and dog, Wallace. His boyfriend is the special events director at Saks Fifth Avenue in San Francisco and best friends with the manager of the designer jewelry department, a coincidence that seems like a tremendous stroke of luck, something I'm not used to. I'm granted an appointment to show my creations.

Another role to play. Taking the tradesman's entrance into the bowels of Saks, clad in my designs, I waft past the Jimmy Choo shoes while discreetly enjoying the fact that I, too, am a designer, at least for the moment. I take in the antics of the lipstick ladies preening behind the glass cases of their beauty products, the embodiment of all that plastic surgery has to offer. The air is heavy with the latest perfumes and thick with gossip as these makeup mavens hold court regaling each other with tales of their latest fashionista exploits, while waiting for a client to be sucked into and enthralled by the mythical powers of their potted potions.

The necklaces, are met with approval by the reigning elite of designer jewelry. "But where are the bracelets, earrings, pins and rings, to complete the collection?" I have a stash of bracelets; that's not a problem, and having learned the art of improvisation, growing

The Real Thing

up in the frugal years after WW11, I can put a pair of tribal earrings together—no sweat. Then there's Marija, a Yugoslavian beauty, a former marine engineer, who fled the strife in her homeland and rearranged her life in Indonesia. Together we solve the remaining challenges, reworking artifacts into a modern concept.

With my new ammunition I'm welcomed into the designer stable at Saks and awarded my own showcase by Brenda Stowers, the designer jewelry savant, who orchestrates the dazzling displays. A gorgeous black woman, always exquisitely dressed, she can carry off any look effortlessly and sweeps through life with grace, admiration following in her path.

There's Gloria presiding over the Designer Jewelry Department, elegant, immaculate, the personification of sophistication, a woman who lives and loves jewelry. Resplendent Gloria, the designer jewelry chief sales lady, is always impressively turned out, splendid in her daily array of dazzling hardware, the epitome of how to successfully wear and promote tribal wealth. She's a killer commodity on the sales circuit; her sincerity and charm are legendary. Jewelry is necessary equipment to define and enhance and Gloria is the sales person to make your shopping expedition a rewarding experience, always radiant, shining, positioned right up front. The jewelry displays are the first attraction when arriving for an escape from reality through the doors of Saks Fifth Avenue, away from the weariness of the outside world.

I am gathering speed on the jewelry terrain. As when success arrives in any field, barbs and jealousies arrive simultaneously as a consequence. It can be seen as a challenge to competitors with inflated egos, who irrationally believe their exclusive domain is being invaded. I'm happy to note that this is an equal opportunity arena and that I'm receiving enemy fire from both male and female strongholds.

After seven glorious years of Saks promoting my jewels, Brenda, the reigning queen of designer jewelry, the stunning black woman with green eyes and amazing grace disappears and apparently not on her yearly pilgrimage to the deserts of Egypt.

A year later I'm invited to attend a memorial service at the Buddhist Temple in Japan Town, Brenda has died at only fifty-eight. Details of the cause are shrouded, death is not a topic to take up air in the vaunted heights of an exclusive enclave like Saks where reality is a rude word, it might ruin a sale or tarnish the atmosphere. Brent informs me under his breath that it was a cancer that extinguished her flame.

Against a backdrop of a stunning gilded Buddhist shrine the High Priest in flowing gowns informs us that there is no word for memorial service in the Buddhist way of life. For Buddhists when they leave this world they pass on to the next stage, that this is a cause for joy, not sorrow, and those left behind can celebrate the completion of a successful life. I have lived these thoughts, deep in the tropics of Indonesia, the cycle of life completed being cause to celebrate.

The High Priest reminds us that those left behind should examine our lives to make sure that we are on the right path, that we are here for but for a moment in time and to make the most of it.

The Designer Jewelry Department flounders on under the auspices of different buyers who attempt to fill the void. Designers are disappearing, the ranks are thinning out. The jewelry department is now located farther to the rear having lost first and frontal exposure to designer handbags. The boat is without a pilot but Gloria and Christian the two senior sales people persevere. I now have five cases, heady stuff, especially as most of the competition has been snuffed out by the powers that be.

The Real Thing

The head office in New York, full of bright young executives decides that individual designers are not the way to go, that every Saks store has to carry the same brands, making it impossible for small, one-of-a-kind designers to compete. They ignore the San Francisco sales people who insist that they are a one-of-a-kind destination, catering to a discriminating clientele.

Fired up with passion having put together a new collection, I'm kept waiting in the wings. Eventually one Saturday afternoon I receive a phone call from a Saks' customer wanting to know where she can find my designs as I am no longer available at Saks. This is the first I hear of my imminent departure.

The latest manager, a performing marionette totally under the influence of the New York cabal, sheepishly informs me, when I demand to know what's happening, of the new world order. Gloria and Christian, having personally lobbied for my continued presence, now apologize profusely for the company's indiscretions. Having massaged and infused their clientele with enthusiasm on my behalf for years, they are demoralized to see so much hard work evaporate and they still have to man the stage and explain that the designers they have promoted for so long are no longer available but replaced by designs that can be bought at any store almost anywhere in America. Rich as hell socialites who flew in just to shop at the designer jewelry department, haven't been spotted since.

A troop of San Francisco self described experts in the field of tribal art decide to get together to combine their respective client lists and promote small shows, to discuss the joys and tribulations of their livelihood in a non competitive way. Once a month we meet and mingle, munching on takeout, quaffing wine before getting down to the grittier stuff. Gary Spratt, a man I had previously admired and had incendiary thoughts about is one of the gang.

We organize a show to coincide with the re-opening of the De Young Museum, a time when many "important people" will be in town. The friendly rapport quickly gets flushed down the toilet as squabbling erupts over space sizes and locations. Members less than enthusiastic about participating are targeted as obstructionists. Bickering and ankle biting ensue, as dealers strain to hear transactions transpiring in more active booths. Some, thinking they are more equal than others, try to grab the lead, to dictate policy, to subjugate those with other ideas to the back benches.

I find one dealer in my booth conversing with a museum curator, attempting to kill a piece with faint praise. Against all protocol he has taken the piece in question from the stand and is now striving to detract from its obvious authenticity and beauty. He fumbles, dropping the piece to the floor, making himself look like the charlatan he aspires not to be. A shadow of a blush almost colors his grey facial flesh as I diminish his presence by mentioning that with Irish ancestry and such ability to deceive, he would have made an excellent Catholic priest. Maybe he had missed his calling!

Gary Spratt invites me to lunch. He is putting on a show at the Charlie Campbell Art Gallery. Would I like to participate? I invite him to dinner, along with my two best gay friends. They are aghast that I would invite a still married male to dine!

Gary, a wild beast from Idaho, somewhat tamed, having left the freezing temperatures at a tender age and discovered San Francisco, is on the line calling from Santa Barbara to wish me a Happy New Year and requesting my company for dinner. He has parted ways with the wife and is seeking finalization of the fact. Luckily I'm sitting down, I feel my life change, intuitively knowing that it will never be the same.

Now with a tall, dark, handsome to say the least, elegant, epicurean, wine worthy, witty specimen of a virile male vying for my attention, I try to be cool and calculating. I'm ready for the challenge and available in this instance for a victorious conclusion. I've met my match and both of us know it.

Attending a party at the De Young Museum for tribal art dealers, this magnificent man takes me on a tour of the tribal galleries. While the rest of the dealers stuff their faces with free food and cheap wine in the lobby, their eyes follow our egress to the upper level. We float up the stairs to be alone at last with a magnificent collection of Papua New Guinean ancestors, now the only eyes upon us.

On February 14th I invite the Idahoan over for hors d'oeuvres and wine. He arrives bearing a bunch of shell pink tulips and a gift of sixteenth century Italian love songs. Luckily, I always have a supply of new toothbrushes on hand.

I tiptoe warily into what might be the real thing, testing the turf but still flying my flag, while furiously but subtly declaring to be single forever, a real warrior, having survived many a battlefield.

We have many friends and acquaintances in common but when our mutual attraction becomes apparent, amazement and curiosity is quickly followed by waves of gossip, suspicion and advice. Gary is cast as the good guy, the worthy husband ensnared by a calculating hussy! It makes the married women nervous and the single jealous. Change throws a wrench in the wheel of life and makes the stallions restless. "How could he leave a woman he has been married to for over twenty years, a good Catholic woman at that?"

I'm portrayed as a home breaker, a man hater and trouble. Several of my new beau's so called cronies are so appalled they refuse to meet me and have to be discarded along the roadside of incompatibility. Warnings from women I know land on my deaf ears, "Miranda, how could you, he's already been married three times!" I receive one phone call congratulating me on my state of happiness.

We try to keep it under wraps but, Gary being much more popular than I, is inundated by friends worried about his welfare, his state of mind. Our pursuits entail being in the public eye, it's difficult to conceal obvious desire but we somehow navigate all of these human reactions. Why not? Nothing else matters. We're just happy to have found each other!

Interestingly, many men who have been toying for years with the idea of asking me out now seem to be upset that they have missed the boat. Even men I have never even conversed with suddenly become intrigued, ready to challenge the successful stag. I momentarily become a magnet for male attention.

Gary Spratt

CHAPTER SIXTEEN

The End of an Epoch

*"Where the spirit does not work with the hand
there is no art"*
—LEONARDO DA VINCI 1452-1519

The major ingredients in the making of an art dealer apart from being obsessive and compulsive are curiosity and passion— you have to love the stuff! A dealer needs to be aware and able to recognize a piece made from the heart by a skilled hand and accomplished by an artist with no ulterior motive. Some dealers possess a natural eye, a God given asset, others need to spend much time viewing and handling material. Not all succeed! It's a skill that has to be constantly honed and practiced. Living with or visiting great art keeps the eye exercised. In the constant company of lesser examples the eye can lose the cutting edge.

A masterpiece has a life of its own, is imbued with a magic that differentiates it from an anemic imposter or the work of an ordinary man.

If curiosity and passion are lost or overtaken by the driving force of monetary gain, critical appreciation can deteriorate. Greed and deception can rear their duel dirty heads. Even a dealer with an excellent eye can fall foul to this dragon.

Showing in a gallery is the softest landing strip for selling art, letting gallery owners and employees do the fatiguing footwork.

The alternative is the show circuit, a much more grueling concept, the springboard for success or doom. There is tentative joy in unpacking the latest acquisitions on which the dealer's livelihood rests, positioning each piece to maximum advantage, to catch the eye of a passerby. After eight hours of defining and redefining, however, one is either ready to carouse or drag the tired body back to the cave.

I miss the old days of slapping stuff on tables, when flimsy curtains divided the booths. Now, with hard walls separating the competition providing a more sophisticated approach, booth displays are planned and perfected.

The display is the visual projection of the dealer, the offerings a direct line to his soul, if he has one. A dealer is what he has in his booth. Many puffed up individuals fall for the deception that every piece presiding in their hallowed sanctuary, approved by their eye, must be a masterpiece. The same piece might have previously languished in another's hands, but when acquired by a superior eye, it becomes a work of art. The gorgeous shape, the form, even the spaces in between become immortalized. The fact that tribal art was originally created as a prerequisite to sustain existence in some far off fetid jungle gets lost in the action. Tribal art was not conceived to enthrall the western taste, as an object of interest or beauty, but as a necessary part of maintaining life. Now it has been transformed into an art form by the dealer. It is a creation of the dealer's imagination, the real creator forgotten in a fog of magnificent superlatives.

There are many techniques used to sell. Some dealers drown any show of interest with knowledge, ranting about the glories of their acquisitions. The softer style, the more gentle approach, is where a person can linger and appreciate the offerings without being bombarded by attention. There are many interesting paths on this tortuous highway, even taunting clients who hesitate with, "If you don't recognize this superb art form, you don't deserve to own it." On the other end of the spectrum, a dealer I once set up near spent the whole show immersed in a book, appearing to be annoyed when interrupted.

A vetted show is a fine idea if democratically carried out, but is often flawed by jealousy, incompetence and ego, especially if those performing the task are selling in the same show. It seems just plain old boring common sense to select knowledgeable individuals not doing the show or swayed by filthy lucre to weed out the fakes, forgeries and material not up to scratch.

Having previously received the dubious honor of being selected to be party to this procedure, I find these bands are often comprised of those who either want to wreak havoc in the competition's space or have something to hide in their own. As the decision to oust offending offerings has to be unanimous, the most verbally aggressive individuals are prone to override the rest of the troop. Sometimes nothing is achieved. Material that should have been removed is left to loiter untouched, lowering the overall quality of the show and demeaning those who strive to maintain standards.

Opening night arrives, hopes are high. The food is edible, the drinks flow, and the music plays. The local elite are out in force,

At the San Francisco Tribal Show

strutting their finery. Art connoisseurs parade through the aisles. Prospective clients, on their way to forage the night's culinary offerings, wanting to get the price of the entrance fee out of the food court, may spend so much time pursuing and satisfying the needs of their bellies, it takes away from time spent ogling art. To do well on opening night is a shot in the arm, a bright beginning, a prelude to success.

A regular performer at one of these events evolves into an intrinsic part of the show. Attendees get acclimatized to seeing the same dealer perched in the same booth year after year, and the dealer becomes an essential factor of what they perceive as a delightful excursion. For the dealer these people are often just a blur from some bygone transaction. Some stick in the mind, past brushes with them indelibly stamped on the conscience to be either embraced wholeheartedly or avoided at all cost. This is the price one entertains to do business.

The End of an Epoch

The clients who know what they like, listen to what the dealer has to say, can make decisions and are thrilled to make a purchase are rare and beautiful experiences. Those possessing humor and taste are pure joy to encounter.

These gatherings, of course, attract other less than viable entities, people who have traveled in their previous lives and need to relive their moments of past glory and hope maybe something in the display jogs their memories. While the dealer is interested in each and every potential client, she is not in residence to provide a platform for a complete historical rendition of youth spent in some far-flung place. Although this might be entertaining if uttered from a brilliant mind when one has time to spare, a dealer is there to put crusts on the table, not to be the recipient of a personal biography. The dealer has parted with a wad of money for this temporary expanse of real estate, for the thrill of being in the mix and hopes that the investment will pay off.

The individual who is there to gain or impart knowledge takes up much time garnering information or professing to know more than the dealer. He might take it upon himself to critique the offerings in the dealer's space to potential clients, often attempting to take over, intruding with his perceived perceptions but with no intention of making an acquisition. He's just there to promote his own personal glory. A dealer has to cast off, dismiss the fluff and concentrate on the real, live, aspiring transactions that actually might be consummated in order to survive on this circuit and not let these human obstacles prevent authentic action.

An earth dweller approaches and is excited about a piece in the showcase. He has something similar to what you are offering. He wants to know what is the current value for such a specimen. Of course, his example was purchased twenty years ago for a tenth of the price and he now glows with the knowledge that he made a sound investment.

Let us not forget the people who arrive clutching a treasure, wanting a free appraisal or posing the question, "What is it?" This is not *The Antiques Road Show*. The types who are present not to buy but to sell, who wander into your zone pulling objects out of a backpack forgetting that this is not show and tell and not an appropriate time to take over the dealer's cubicle with their agenda.

Some just need therapy. The entrance price to a show is cheaper than a visit to a psychiatrist. They want attention, which they attempt to gain by appearing interested in something in the booth. Jewelry is a real draw for this type, so much to try on. Sequestered in the confines of the space, the dealer is often traumatized by tales of torment, the ongoing tragedy of their divorce, the death of their cat. It's a good idea to get the conversation back on track and focus on the material poised in the balance, but all this type really requires is your ear. Their desire is to entangle your soul in a one sided conversation, to drag you into their dialogue of personal disasters.

One of the more frustrating forays is into the mysterious mind of the potential client who takes great pains when looking at an object, which he claims to love and would buy if only it was different. He points to everything that he perceives as wrong or doesn't like.

He carefully, deliberately delineates why he should not buy it. It is almost perfect but not quite right. If only!

I often wonder how these people get through life. It must be a dreary, uninspired existence. Nothing is exactly what they want, never perfect.

Then there are the girls who just want to have fun! Which means trying on the jewelry, preening in front of the mirror. They arrive in twos and threes, goading each other on as if participating in a

The End of an Epoch

game. It's like playing dress up, pure entertainment, getting their fill before they flee to invade another unfortunate's booth to be further distracted.

I am fascinated by the way women try stuff on, gazing into the glass. Some are so enamored by what they see, they pout and pose, enthralled by their reflection, almost falling for the image in the mirror. Some really look at the jewelry and how it interacts with who they are. Does it enhance or detract? I'm there to match the piece with the person, to help the clientele look their best, to make the world a more beautiful place. Buying should be pure pleasure.

One must not forget the saga of *Mr. and Mrs. Beback*. They peruse the booth, absolutely adore that piece, almost making a purchase but they have only just arrived. They must visit the rest of the show first, only to be overwhelmed by the multitude of other offerings. Some do return but it's an uncommon occurrence.

Let us not neglect to mention the individual who requests that a piece be put aside, withdrawn from public view. She will return with her checkbook later. A fine idea, but a timeframe has to be established, as some fail to reappear with even an apology, obviously forgetting decency amid so many distractions.

Who is that lovely older lady studying my photos of Indonesia? She rewards my interest with a tale of growing up with her Dutch family in Batavia, now known as Jakarta, the capital of Indonesia, during World War Two. When she was fourteen the Japanese invaded, taking over possession of this territory from the Dutch colonial masters. She became separated from her family, thrown into a concentration camp and forced to perform hard labor. These are now distant but still pungent memories revived by my photographic renditions of life as it had been during her childhood before the horrors that engulfed her.

Here come the boys and girls sporting labrets and tattoos, seeking a new pair of Dayak earrings, heavy brass ear weights with which to further extend their already drooling earlobes. There's Mimi Miloradavich, a local interior designer once wed to a dashing Russian cavalry officer, who always wore white gloves especially when picking up babies. I've enjoyed and profited from many a lunch at her Atherton table, enthralled by her legendary exploits. Basil Jenkins a previous curator and director of the Fowler Museum at UCLA is approaching brimming no doubt with tales of his courtly Russian heritage.

One never knows who might turn up to entertain or dismay. Movie stars often grace the halls. I refrain from acknowledging, even if I recognize such entities. They're on their time off! But my son is impressed when he notices a check made out to me from a well-known heavy metal band member. (All I remember is that this particular guy made me eat the tax!)

Do I want to accept a check from a guy with pink hair who looks as if he slept last night in the gutter? But look who he is with. Don't you recognize that celebrity on his arm?

My own personal adversary has dispatched her minions, draped in her designs, to strut back and forth in front of my space. They pop in to see how my show is going or to cast an evil eye in my direction. I guess that being a thorn in some one's side is in itself an achievement or an overdose of flattery.

The long pigs are always out there snuffling for truffles, looking for opportunities to distract other dealer's clients, attempting to drag them off to their quarters, trying to kill their competitor's deals, trying to find any which way to piss on a rival's material. They circle like carrion, tugging at any flesh they can find, stealing eggs from other's nests. They hover near booths, ears swiveling, attempting to hone in on conversations, striving to disrupt the balance, to haul the client back to their den.

Non-exhibiting dealers who pay the entrance fee but are not performing in an expensive booth are stealthily patrolling the aisles, ready to swoop on any worthwhile collector who strolls by. They stalk down known entities or fresh meat, jostling to make contact. They are ready, equipment primed, if they get a spark of interest, to present slideshows of what they have to offer. Maybe they have placed material in another dealer's showcase, they linger tentatively to see if a fish bites the lure and swallows the bait.

I'm delighted when dealers do well at a show, that the money is out there and someone is benefiting! It promotes an aura of possibility. For some the show is perpetually great no matter what. "Best show I've ever had!" They seem to have forgotten how to give a straight answer. Lies come more naturally. Well, there's no harm in having a positive attitude. How else are they going to unload that crock of inventory they have amassed?

Sometimes the answer is, "I've sold enough to pay for my expenses." Which literally translates as inventory has actually been given away in order to pay for the booth and the overhead. Some are content with having encountered possible sales in the distant future. "After show sales look likely to occur." Pre-show sales are often cited by those idling unbothered in their space. Then there is, "I bought my way out of the show," meaning the show sucked but by acquiring well, future sales are imminent. Some dealers actually tell the truth, shocking as that might seem!

The stunning Kikuyu bride of one of the African art dealers dazed by the never satiated appetites of the American public remarks, "All you really need is a roof over your head and food in your stomach."

With the rise of the internet and the fall of the economy the show circuit takes a big hit, unraveling and imploding, almost vanishing into thin air overnight. Without a surge of younger buyers beating on the door (technology having taken over their minds and imagination, as they find themselves living in small and smaller apartments where they only have enough room to turn on their latest tech toy) the outlook is bleak.

The era of hauling viable stuff home from distant lands is almost a faded memory. These fabled former destinations are already plundered, no longer a source of future inventory, although a ready supply of reconstructed monstrosities and imposters has flourished and is now being actively promoted by some misguided dealers as authentic. A prime example of fouling one's own nest, all adding to a demise of interest in this field. The more astute dealers have forsaken this over trodden trail and instead are combing the homeland for artifacts already in collections, purchased long ago and now ready to come back on the market. The paucity of material, the high price to pay for anything worthwhile, the demise of good dealers, and the rise of lesser models makes for uneasy, choppy years ahead.

There are, of course, the upper crust, the wealthy, who pursue the acquisition of art as an investment through an art investment advisor. They are only interested in where to place their overflowing funds and choose only high end art, usually paintings by known artists which their advisor has deemed will appreciate monetarily, the subject matter not being of importance or even understood.

The emergence of auction houses as the main and most popular purveyor of material has squashed many individual traders into the dirt, but most are still attempting to dust themselves off, wondering what hit them, readying themselves for yet another lackluster show, not realizing that this is the end of an epoch. Timing

The End of an Epoch

is everything, to be aware, alert and on the ball, to have gathered and accomplished within this realm was a great lifestyle while it lasted. To recognize its annihilation is in itself a supreme acknowledgment of the art market today.

A few shrewd tribal art dealers who bought well in solid fields now often have more luck putting their material up for auction, attracting a worldwide audience, rather than participating in an art show with a limited exposure, but this is not an option for purveyors of secondary or lesser known material who would lose their pants in this pursuit. Not an engaging prospect considering this aging part of the population!

It's time to reinvent myself once again, to find another role to play, a different part to be performed. Perhaps I will even write a book of good times achieved at the right time.

"Feminine virtue is nothing but a convenient masculine invention"

—NINON DE L'ENCLOS FRENCH AUTHOR,
COURTESAN & PATRON OF THE ARTS 1620-1705

"If I were a cassowary on the plains of timbuctoo I would eat a missionary cassock, bands and hymn-book too"

—SAMUEL WILBERFORCE, ENGLISH BISHOP
IN THE CHURCH OF ENGLAND, 1805-1873

www.ingramcontent.com/pod-product-compliance
Lightning Source LLC
Chambersburg PA
CBHW062021290426
44108CB00024B/2730